Urban Landscape

Reviews of *The Historic Urban Landscape: Managing Heritage in an Urban Century*

. . . the crux of the book's message: 'transition from the classical paradigm of conservation to the one of managing change' and addressing acceptable levels of change . . . This is an important book, destined one hopes to be essential reading for those involved in urban conservation globally: scholars, practitioners, managers, students.

Ken Taylor
Journal of Landscape Research, 2012

Heritage has become a recognized economic driver, and the authors are proponents of the integration of urban conservation into urban development. The Historic Urban Landscape methodology, therefore, becomes a tool for the management of change. . . . (This book) is well written, straightforward and easy to understand. Its concepts are an evolution of current practices in a rapidly changing world impacted by urban migration and globalization. *The Historic Urban Landscape* will change in a major way accepted notions of historic cities' preservation.

Pamela Jerome
Association of Preservation Technology Bulletin, 2012

. . . with this volume, Francesco Bandarin and Ron van Oers manage to make a most valuable contribution to this body of literature with a thoughtful and practical approach . . . I would recommend the book to scholars of urban planning, but also as a must read for any policy-maker and officers of local authority working in the field of heritage conservation and heritage site management.

Laura Pierantoni
SPANDREL, 7 (2013)

The Historic Urban Landscape

Managing Heritage in an Urban Century

by

Francesco Bandarin

and

Ron van Oers

WILEY Blackwell

This edition first published 2012
© Francesco Bandarin and Ron van Oers

Registered office
John Wiley & Sons, Ltd, The Atrium, Southern Gate, Chichester, West Sussex, PO19 8SQ, United Kingdom.

Editorial offices:
9600 Garsington Road, Oxford, OX4 2DQ, United Kingdom.
The Atrium, Southern Gate, Chichester, West Sussex, PO19 8SQ, United Kingdom.

For details of our global editorial offices, for customer services and for information about how to apply for permission to reuse the copyright material in this book please see our website at www.wiley.com/wiley-blackwell.

Library of Congress Cataloging-in-Publication Data

Bandarin, Francesco.
  The historic urban landscape : managing heritage in an urban century / by Francesco Bandarin and Ron van Oers.
       p. cm
  Includes bibliographical references and index.
  ISBN 978-0-470-65574-0 (hard cover : alk. paper) 1. World Heritage areas Conservation and restoration. 2. Historic districts—Conservation and restoration. 3. Historic sites—Conservation and restoration. 4. Historic buildings—Conservation and restoration. 5. Architecture—Conservation and restoration. 6. Urban landscape architecture—Conservation and restoration. 7. City planning. 8. Cultural policy. 9. Urban policy. 10. Cities and towns—Growth—Social aspects.
  I. Oers, Ron van, 1965– II. Title.
  CC135.B353 2012
  363.6′9—dc23
                          2011034249

ISBN: 9780470655740 (hardback)
ISBN: 9781118932728 (paperback)

A catalogue record for this book is available from the British Library.

Wiley also publishes its books in a variety of electronic formats. Some content that appears in print may not be available in electronic books.

Set in 10/12.5 pt Avenir by Toppan Best-set Premedia Limited
Printed and bound in Malaysia by Vivar Printing Sdn Bhd

1   2014

For Patrizia – For Cristina
For the motivation and support, at home and away.

Also by the Authors

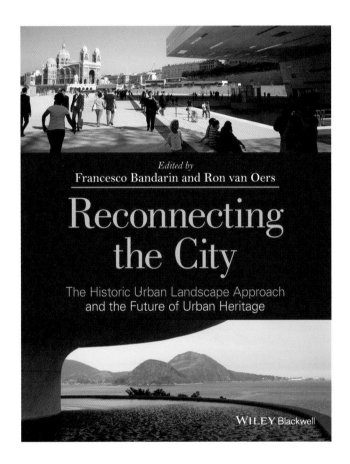

Reconnecting the City:

The Historic Urban Landscape Approach and the Future of Urban Heritage

Francesco Bandarin and Ron van Oers

978-1-1183-8398-8

Contents

Preface

A new approach to urban conservation

Urban Conservation: a Modern Utopia?

The twentieth century has seen the rise of many urban utopias. At a pace unprecedented in the previous two centuries, social thinkers, architects and urbanists – a new profession dedicated to addressing urban problems – have tried to define and build 'the perfect city'.

Theodor Fritsch's 'Future City', Ebenezer Howard's 'Garden City' and Tony Garnier's 'Industrial City' are just the most well-known of the many proposals aimed at countering the 'evil' of the nineteenth-century industrial city, and at proposing rational, efficient and liveable urban models.

Urban utopian thinking has been at the core of the Modern Movement, epitomised by Le Corbusier's 'Radiant City' or by its American counter-point, Wright's 'Broadacre City'. This direction has predominated through-out the second half of the century: from Yona Friedman's 'Spatial City' to the 'Megastructure' proposals of Archizoom, Superstudio or Koolhaas, architects have constantly played with utopian ideas. One could also argue that even the New Urbanism proposals, or contemporary attempts to define the 'Sustainable City', also fall into the category of utopian thinking.

Among the utopias generated by modernity, there is also urban con-servation. Strictly speaking, urban conservation is not a utopia, but rather a policy and planning practice that is present in many countries of the world.

And yet, urban conservation is steeped in legend, rooted in the public's fascination for past built environments: the representation of history, personal and collective memory values, spirit of place. These legends reflect the values of the historic city, and are at the same time at the centre of the concerns of urban conservators, confronted by

Çatalhöyük, Turkey (the first map of a city ever found)

The 2010 Shanghai EXPO

Cities have been man's most elaborate creation since the beginning of human society. During ten millennia, they have been the places of power, culture, technology and conflict. In the twenty-first century more than half of humanity lives in cities. This is, and will be, the most significant environment for the human species. Managing it with care and guiding its development, with attention to its past and its cultural meaning, will be the major challenge for the urban century.

the gradual erosion of the physical and social structures that support these values.

Cities are dynamic organisms. There is not a single 'historic' city in the world that has retained its 'original' character: the concept is a moving target, destined to change with society itself. And this is natural: social structures and needs evolve, the physical fabric adapts constantly.

As a consequence, important conservation objectives such as the safeguarding of the authenticity or integrity of the physical and social fabric of an urban complex are doomed to remain a myth or, at best, an approximation. The goal of conserving traditional structures in the historic city remains an aspiration that is subject to continuous compromise and adaptation.

Does this mean that urban conservation is a chimerical dream, a collective illusion?

Certainly not.

At least not as long as the historic city continues to express values that societies strive to preserve because these values are guardians of collective identity and memory, helping to maintain a sense of continuity and tradition, for aesthetic pleasure and entertainment.

If utopias are thought of as collective representations of communities or societies, idealised conditions expressing shared value systems and common goals, then defining urban conservation as a utopia becomes a positive and constructive approach.

In the past century, urban conservation has attracted enormous attention, and this has generated a plethora of principles, theories, practical experiences, technical and normative tools; an entire professional world is associated today with the policy processes and tasks of urban conservation.

The narrative developed around this mighty task provides many stories of successes and failures, of intellectual breakthroughs and polemics, of political endorsement and rejection. In a way, it is a story that has accompanied urban planning and urban development for the last century, and one that will continue to influence the discussion on our urban future as well.

The management of the urban environment has always played a major role in representations of society. Although mass urbanisation is a relatively recent phenomenon, cities have always been the centre of power and social identity. In the experience of the majority of modern humans, cities represent the context of daily life and activity, the place of social and economic exchanges, the ambiance of experience and feelings.

The emergence of global processes has created palpable tension in the world of urban conservation. On one hand, criteria and principles largely based on the Western experience have had to confront the variety of traditions, value systems and practices existing in the world, and undergo adjustment and reassessment. On the other hand, processes of change have been accelerated by social transformations linked to

Cape Town

Dubrovnik

Mexico City

Sydney

The urban landscape is a defining feature of every city, a value to be understood, preserved and enhanced through attentive policies and public participation. Historic fabric and new development can interact and mutually reinforce their role and meaning.

economic and political changes. The rise of gentrification, tourism uses and real-estate pressures in and around the historic cities has posed significant threats to the idealised image of the historic city as one of the modern utopias.

Conservation of the built environment has therefore a plurality of meanings: the preservation of memory, the conservation of artistic and architectural achievements, the valuing of places of significance and collective meaning.

Conservation addresses the past and the future at the same time. It is an intellectual process of mediation between different forces, searching for an equilibrium centred on the interpretation of the value systems of a social formation.

This book is an account of the evolution of this utopia in modern times, and an examination of its value for the contemporary discussion of the future of the city.

It is also an account of the contemporary attempts to revise the classical paradigms, and to integrate – or, to be more precise, re-integrate – urban conservation principles and practices into urban development.

The Historic Urban Landscape Approach: Conservation in the Urban Development Process

Although the idea of urban conservation can be traced back to the time of the French Revolution and the emergence of a new social order in Europe during the nineteenth century, it was almost a century later before a formal theory of urban conservation was developed in Europe. It took even longer to define and put into practice the necessary legal and institutional measures. During the nineteenth and twentieth centuries urban historic areas underwent massive transformation mostly linked to the vast urban sanitation and development programmes of the time, while the international spread of the principles of the Modern Movement, radically opposed to urban conservation, gave additional impetus to many urban removal and renewal programmes worldwide.

In the past fifty years, a thorough revision at the international level of the architectural and urban planning paradigms defined by the Modern Movement has taken place, and a strong institutional and professional system has been established to support heritage conservation. This has fostered the development of preservation of the historic city as a recognised heritage type and the internationalisation of the concept of urban conservation. As a result, and in spite of a situation which is far from ideal, cities nowadays are, in most parts of the world, under some form of protection aimed at preserving, in whole or in part, their historical character.

Today this process has reached a peak: historic cities have acquired high status in modern life, based on the quality of their physical spaces, the persistence of their sense of place, the concentration of cultural and artistic events that support local identity, and an increasingly important economic market, as historic cities have become icons of global cultural tourism. But in spite of these advances and achievements, there is a growing awareness of the challenges urban conservation faces in the coming decades, as new processes and forces of change gather momentum.

Historic urban conservation has become a specialised field of practice, focusing on a sector of the city. While this has allowed theoretical and operational approaches to advance, it has also isolated the world of conservation from the management of urban processes. After more than half a century, there is a growing understanding among practitioners that this approach needs to be revised to make way for a truly integrated view of urban management, one that harmonises preservation of what is defined as 'historic' and management of urban development and regeneration processes.

This is why in this book the term 'urban conservation' is preferred to 'historic urban conservation' when looking at the new attitude towards the urban environment.

Urban conservators today have at their disposal a rich and diversified toolkit: a system of internationally accepted principles of conservation is in place, which is reflected in important international legal instruments such as the 1972 World Heritage Convention. Furthermore, elaborate planning frameworks are available, as well as the accumulation of an extensive body of experience over a century in different contexts.

However, the system often proves to be weak and powerless in the face of the types of change that characterise our contemporary world and its urban scene. These are linked to urbanisation and environmental change, and to the shift of decision-making power from national to local governments, as well as from local to international actors in areas such as tourism, real estate or business. These forces are all pulling in different directions, leaving the conservation discipline often confused and in disarray, unable to take advantage of important opportunities.

More than a decade of regular and systematic monitoring by UNESCO has revealed that many of the most important historic urban areas existing in Europe, Asia, Latin America and the Islamic World have lost their traditional functions and are in the process of transformation that threatens to undermine their integrity and historic, social and artistic values.

Urban conservators are increasingly aware of the gap between the ideal world of conservation principles and the practical reality, especially in emerging societies, and are calling for new approaches and tools to tackle the new challenges.

In October 2005 UNESCO's General Assembly of States Parties to the World Heritage Convention adopted a Resolution that called for the elaboration of a new international standard-setting instrument designed to

Esphahan

Florence

Kathmandu

Quebec

Historic cities' heritage is a major value for all societies. It is an important dimension of civic identity and memory and a cultural resource for social and economic development.

recognise and guide investment in, and development of, historic cities, while at the same time honouring the inherited values embedded in their spatial and social structures.

Following the 2005 Resolution, an international framework for the development of a new UNESCO Recommendation, a non-binding 'soft law', has been outlined in cooperation with a large group of international experts from all regions of the world. The adoption of the Recommendation on the Historic Urban Landscape by the General Conference of UNESCO in November 2011 represents the culmination of this process.

This book examines the background and rationale for this approach, and it seeks to clarify its conceptualisation, as well as its potential.

In looking at the origins of the Historic Urban Landscape approach, one aspect will certainly stand out: until recently (meaning the last 30 to 40 years), discussion of heritage conservation, and in particular urban conservation, was predominantly influenced by Western thinking and value systems.

In recent times, however, international practitioners have paid more attention to existing cultural contexts in order to identify models adapted to the value systems of different traditions. In particular the 1994 Nara Document on Authenticity has cautiously opened the way to a culture-based appreciation of conservation values. This has resulted in important adaptations to operational approaches, and the recognition that an understanding of the diversity of cultures is the solution to ensure an effective and sustainable link between a society and its heritage – a key message also incorporated into the Historic Urban Landscape approach.

The debate on the future of urban conservation, which developed around the Historic Urban Landscape approach, has proved that the international conservation community has a keen interest in reassessing practices adopted over the past half-century in the field of urban conservation.

The need for this stems from several converging factors: the acknowledgment of how cultural diversity affects values and approaches to conservation; the awareness of the link between natural and cultural factors in the conservation of the built environment; the new challenges brought about by rapid social and economic changes; the increasing role and status of the historic city as the centre of the arts and creative industries; and the need to ensure a sustainable future for heritage conservation.

The Historic Urban Landscape approach is indeed a new way to include all these aspects of conservation in an integrated framework. As with all normative tools of its type, it is an outgrowth of modern needs and thinking, but also rooted in the history of urban conservation.

The Historic Urban Landscape approach is not designed to replace existing doctrines or conservation approaches, but rather is envisaged as a tool to integrate policies and practices of conservation of the built environment. In this sense, the Historic Urban Landscape approach comprises the layering and diversity of visions and methodologies that have been handed down from a century-long tradition.

The Historic Urban Landscape approach has indeed this objective: to define operational principles able to ensure urban conservation models that respect the values, traditions and environments of different cultural contexts, as well as to help redefine urban heritage as the centre of the spatial development process – in other words, to recognise and position the historic city as a resource for the future.

The Structure of this Book

This book provides a comprehensive overview of the intellectual developments in urban conservation, of its modern interpretations and critique, and of the way in which the classical approach has been challenged by the evolution of the conceptual and operational context of urban management.

Chapter 1 takes a look at the origin of modern urban conservation paradigms, largely based on European models and conceptual approaches developed from the end of the nineteenth century onward. While thinkers and planners at the turn of the nineteenth and twentieth centuries tended to deal with the challenge of urban conservation within a broader approach to urban development, a radical break accompanied the emergence of Modernism, which rejected conservation and defined the historic city as an area separated from the main path of urban development.

The chapter traces the ways in which post-war architects and planners responded to the failures of Modernism and created the intellectual and operational framework for the international expansion of urban conservation principles and practice. The historical review unveils the contradictions and complexities inherent in the contemporary vision of urban conservation, and in particular the gaps existing between the 'ideal' world of the planners and the realities of the market, as well as of the processes of social and economic transformation.

The emergence and expansion of urban conservation is examined in Chapter 2, through an analysis of the process of development of the main international Conventions, Charters and Organisations for heritage conservation in the post-war period, a process that has allowed the establishment of internationally recognised principles and practices of great significance for the contemporary world.

The contradictions of urban conservation and the need to integrate it into a broader urban development framework are at the origin of several attempts to update and revise the international conservation principles, both through regional charters and through the discussion initiated by UNESCO on the concept of Historic Urban Landscape. This process of revision concerns several aspects of the conservation paradigm that need to be examined by the international conservation community.

Chapter 3 outlines the global processes that underlie the need to revise the conservation paradigm. Those that are directly related to the future of the historic city include the global urbanisation drive; the need to promote urban sustainability; the impact of climate change; the changing role of

Cusco

Delhi

Sana'a

Djenné

Local communities are the custodians of the tangible and intangible heritage of historic cities. Inhabitants and visitors alike share a responsibility for the preservation of the sense of place.

cities in the global economy; the rise of tourism as a main new urban economic sector; and, finally, the changing perception of heritage values of the historic city and the greater role played today by the intangible dimensions of heritage.

All these processes reinforce the need to pay more heed to the impact of contemporary transformations, and indeed to define conservation as the management of change. Chapter 4 looks at the innovative approaches that have emerged at the international level in the field of urban planning and urban conservation in recent decades, as a response to these challenges. These approaches have been brought in by the major development organisations, such as the specialised agencies and programmes of the United Nations (UNESCO, UNDP, UNEP or UN-Habitat), as well as other important actors (World Bank, European Union, OECD), to promote the reform of urban governance and finance, and to pursue their primary goal of poverty reduction.

Within this context, cultural heritage – and, in particular, the historic city – has assumed an important role, both as a factor of identity and social stability, and as an economic sector, connected to tourism and creative industries. The emergence of issues related to sustainability, resilience and adaptation to climate change have strengthened the international dimension of urban policies.

Not unexpectedly, the new policies have generated an array of innovative tools, aimed at addressing specific issues in the areas of regulation, community engagement, technical analysis and financial support, as examined in Chapter 5. A number of these tools aim to provide a higher degree of coherence to the planning and management of urban processes, and are therefore based on spatial and social integration and on community involvement and collaboration. The use of tools generated from different disciplinary fields has proven fertile and has led to innovative proposals.

The last and concluding part of the book, Chapter 6, presents the Historic Urban Landscape approach as an attempt to address many of the issues raised: the need to address challenges to urban conservation unleashed by the forces of change associated with globalisation; the need to integrate conservation and urban planning and development into a unitary process; and the need to revisit the classic conservation paradigms in order to recognise cultural diversity and the dynamic nature of urban heritage.

Finally, a word on the targeted audience of this book. The issues addressed are clearly those of the professional community working on urban conservation issues. However, the book is also relevant to a broader range of professionals such as architects, planners and landscape designers, as well as policy-makers involved in planning the future of the city and learning about innovative models and new ideas. As these issues are also aligned with the core interests of academics and students, the book has been enriched with notes and extracts taken from different sources (including web-based, such as Wikipedia) that will facilitate an understanding of the theoretical and practical processes that are discussed.

Francesco Bandarin & Ron van Oers

Acknowledgements

The idea for this book developed during several years, as the authors were engaged in a policy process aimed at drafting a new international standard-setting instrument for urban conservation within UNESCO. The book has therefore benefitted from the work and the advice of many colleagues and experts from various parts of the world. First of all, we would like to thank our colleagues at the UNESCO World Heritage Centre, and in particular the Cities Team, for their contribution to the overall reflection on the issue. Sachiko Haraguchi has provided substantial research assistance, while Paloma Guzmán has developed the case material. Denise Young edited the final version of the text. We would like to acknowledge the support of the Getty Conservation Institute in Los Angeles, in particular of Tim Whalen, Jeanne-Marie Teutonico and Susan Macdonald in the research phase. Initial versions of the book have been reviewed by colleagues, who provided comments and views that have helped to shape ideas and to limit oversights. In particular, we are grateful to Alain Bertaud, Jukka Jokilehto, Shahid Yusuf, Francesco Siravo, Jyoti Hosagrahar and Michael Turner. Naturally, the views as well as the errors remain the sole responsibility of the authors.

Francesco Bandarin and Ron van Oers
Paris, 2011

Abbreviations and Acronyms

AFD (*Agence française de développement*)
AKTC (Aga Khan Trust for Culture)

CABE (Commission for Architecture and the Built Environment)
CBD (Central Business District)
CDS (City Development Strategy)
CECI (Centre for Advanced Studies in Integrated Conservation)
CIAM (*Congrès internationaux d'architecture moderne*)
CIVVIH (ICOMOS Scientific Committee on Historic Towns and Villages)
CTBUH (Council of Tall Buildings and Urban Habitat)

DOCOMOMO (International Committee for Documentation and Conservation of the Buildings, Sites and Neighbourhoods of the Modern Movement)

ECTP (European Council of Town Planners)
EIA (Environmental Impact Assessment)
ERDF (European Regional Development Fund)
EU (European Union)

GDP (Gross Domestic Product)
GIZ (*Deutsche Gesellschaft für Internationale Zusammenarbeit*)
GTZ (*Deutsche Gesellschaft für Technische Zusammenarbeit*)

HIA (Heritage Impact Assessment)
HUL (Historic Urban Landscape)

IAIA (International Association of Impact Assessment)
IBRD (The International Bank for Reconstruction and Development – The World Bank)
ICCROM (International Centre for the Study of Preservation and Restoration of Cultural Property)
I.C.L.E.I. (Local Governments for Sustainability)
ICOM (International Council of Museums)
ICOMOS (International Council on Monuments and Sites)
ICT (Information and Communications Technologies)

IDB (Inter-American Development Bank)
IDP (Integrated Development Planning)
IFC (International Finance Corporation)
IFHP (International Federation of Housing and Planning)
IFLA (International Federation of Landscape Architects)
IIED (International Institute for Environment and Development)
IMEMS (Integrated Metropolitan Environment Management Strategy)
IMEP (Integrated Metropolitan Environment Policy)
IPCC (Intergovernmental Panel on Climate Change)
ISoCaRP (International Society of City and Regional Planners)
IUCN (International Union for the Conservation of Nature)

JCIC (Japan Consortium for International Cooperation)

KCCC (Kyoto Center for Community Collaboration)

LEED (Local Economic and Employment Development Programme)

MAB (Man and the Biosphere Programme)
MDG (Millennium Development Goals)
MOST (Management of Social Transformations Programme)

NGO (Non-Governmental Organistaion)

OECD (Organisation for Economic Cooperation and Development)
OMA (Office for Metropolitan Architecture)
OWHC (Organisation of World Heritage Cities)

PUF (*Presses universitaires de France*)

RGPP (*Réforme générale des politiques publiques*)
RPAA (Regional Planning Association of America)

SACH (State Administration of Cultural Heritage of China)
SAM (Stakeholder Analysis and Mapping)
SEA (Strategic Environmental Assessment)
Sida (Swedish International Development Co-operation Agency)
SIDS (Small Island Developing States)
SPD (Supplementary Planning Document)
SUD-Net (Sustainable Urban Development Network)
SWOT (Strengths, Weaknesses, Opportunities and Threats)

UCLG (United Cities and Local Governments)
UIA (International Union of Architects)
UNCHS (United Nations Centre for Human Settlements)
UNCTAD (United Nations Conference on Trade and Development)
UNDAF (United Nations Development Assistance Framework)
UNDP (United Nations Development Programme)

UNECE (United Nations Economic Commission for Europe)
UNEP (United Nations Environment Programme)
UNESCO (United Nations Educational, Scientific and Cultural Organisation)
UNFCCC (United Nations Framework Convention on Climate Change)
UN-Habitat (United Nations Human Settlements Programme)
UNWTO (United Nations World Tourism Organisation)
USGBC (United States Green Building Council)

WUC (World Urban Campaign)
WWF (World Wide Fund for Nature)

1. Urban Conservation: Short History of a Modern Idea

Of this I am quite sure, that if we open a quarrel between the past and the present, we shall find we have lost the future.

Sir Winston Churchill

The Origins of Urban Conservation: Between Engineering and Romanticism

Urban conservation is an idea of modern times. While the sense of community, identity and pride linked to civic tradition and beauty is as old as urban civilisation and certainly belongs to all cultural contexts, the idea of urban conservation was developed in the aftermath of the French Revolution, when a new social and economic order in Europe was emerging in the nineteenth century. The basis of the modern vision of cultural heritage was developed in recognition of the value of the historic monument, as shown by Françoise Choay (1992).

The emergence of the notion of 'heritage' is linked to the establishment of modern nation states and the need to define their own traditions and identities.

In the drive to forge national identities, which characterised the nineteenth and twentieth centuries, the 'historic monument' became a way to celebrate national epics and to create traditions (Hobsbawm, 1983).

Institutions such as the *Commission des Monuments Historiques* created in France in 1837, extensive inventories of monuments such as the one developed by Prosper Mérimée[1] in the mid-nineteenth century, and the

---

[1] Prosper Mérimée (1803–1870), writer and conservator, was the key figure in the development of French Institutions for the documentation, conservation and restoration of monuments. In 1834 he was appointed Inspecteur Général des Monuments Historiques and conducted extensive campaigns to build up the heritage inventories of France.

The Historic Urban Landscape: Managing Heritage in an Urban Century, First Edition. Francesco Bandarin, Ron van Oers.

Athens

Beijing

The safeguarding of 'historic monuments' has been at the centre of the theory and practice of conservation over the last century. This influenced the approach to historic cities that focused primarily on monuments and less on the urban fabric and public spaces.

Society for the Protection of Ancient Buildings created by William Morris[2] in Great Britain in 1877, demonstrate the growing importance of heritage and monuments in the development of modern society in Europe, supported by the greatest intellectual figures of the time, such as Victor Hugo.[3]

This important movement, however, did not concern the historic city, but was rather focused on individual monuments of the past. Throughout the nineteenth century, and for a large part of the twentieth century, public policies concerning the city were aimed mainly at addressing the representation of the powers of the state, the modernisation of transport systems, the improvement of public spaces, the residential needs of the emerging upper and middle classes and the improvement of housing conditions of the working classes.

The Industrial Revolution had brought the rural masses to cities that already lacked basic hygiene. For most of the century, and until a new awareness of its heritage value was created, the historic city was viewed essentially as a place of physical and moral decay. The denunciation of these conditions by Engels[4] about England (1845) and Considérant[5] about France (1848), to mention some famous examples, gave rise to a wave of innovative and utopian experiments led by social thinkers, philanthropists and politicians.

The *Phalanstère* of Fourier[6] and the New Lanark of Robert Owen[7] were utopian responses to the crisis, which inspired important social reforms and

---

[2]William Morris (1834–1896) was an English artist and writer associated with the English Arts and Crafts Movement. The Manifesto of the Society for the Protection of Ancient Buildings, published in 1877, was the first attempt at advocacy for conservation and establishment of conservation principles.

[3]Victor Hugo (1802–1885), among the most important French writers of the nineteenth century, was a leading and influential advocate of monuments' preservation. In the 1831, in the Preface of his work, *Notre-Dame de Paris*, he writes: '. . . *en attendant les monuments nouveaux, conservons les monuments anciens. Inspirons, s'il est possible, à la nation l'amour de l'architecture nationale.*'. Two years later he published his *Lettre sur le vandalisme en France*.

[4]Friedrich Engels (1820–1895), a German philosopher, was a socialist and friend and companion of Karl Marx, and shared with him most of his life and political battles. He is the author of several basic texts on Marxism.

[5]Prosper Victor Considérant (1808–1893), a French philosopher, economist and social reformer, was a follower of the ideas of Fourier. Throughout his life he conducted campaigns for the rights of workers and women, and for the advancement of democracy. During a period of exile he created a Phalanstère in Texas, which was an unsuccessful experiment.

[6]François Marie Charles Fourier (1772–1837), a French philosopher, developed a theory of universal harmony. The *Phalanstère* was a utopian community building hosting around 2,000 people and dedicated to agricultural production. The *Phalanstère* was conceived as the organisational basis of a new state.

[7]Robert Owen (1771–1858) was a social reformer and one of the founders of socialism and the cooperative movement. His reform proposals of the industrial manufacturing process were implemented in the cotton mill factory of New Lanark, which he partly owned. This experiment became a model for the improvement of the social conditions of the working classes. In 1821 Robert Owen published his 'Report to the County of Lanark of a Plan for relieving Public Distress'.

Paris

Cairo

Demolition in the name of health and security has been an established practice since the nineteenth century in Europe and in many other regions of the world and it is still continuing today. The loss of fabric and the change of uses often impact on the meaning of places.

represented a key contribution to the definition of modern urban planning principles.

They did not, however, create a force of change for the historic city as powerful as that of the 'urban engineers' movement that intended to remedy the unsanitary conditions of the working classes (Calabi, 1979; Zucconi, 1989). The main concern of the engineers was to demolish large parts of the historic city to create better housing, open spaces and sanitation infrastructure: these policies had an extensive impact on urban planning for over a century and are in place in many cities in the emerging world even today (among others in China).

Every industrialising country, in Europe, America, and even in Meiji Japan, developed regulations and plans to clear the decayed parts of the city: many historic cities witnessed renewal processes ranging from the demolition of the inner city walls to the opening of new squares and avenues.

Even places of great civic tradition such as Florence in Italy were not spared, when in 1865 the old *Piazza del Mercato Vecchio* was replaced by the present *Piazza della Repubblica*, wiping out the medieval quarters and the old ghetto. This *risanamento* (sanitisation) subsequently served as a model for many other cities, both in Italy and elsewhere.

Certainly, however, no renewal plan equalled and became so influential in the world as the *grands travaux* launched by Baron Haussmann[8] in Paris between 1850 and 1870.

Haussmann's plans were not aimed at local situations; rather, they sought to redesign the entire city to respond to the demands of modern life (traffic in particular), to develop new residential and commercial spaces for the high-income and middle-income classes, and to facilitate tighter military control of the city after the 1848 uprising (Pinon, 2002).

The extent of the changes brought about by Haussmann was only surpassed by reconstructions of entire cities destroyed by disaster or war, such as London in the seventeenth century, Lisbon in the eighteenth century and Berlin in the twentieth century.

Moreover, the 'Haussmannian model' was applied in many other capitals and historic cities, both in Europe and elsewhere; the historic centre of Rome, after it became the capital of Italy in 1870, was the subject of a similar plan. Cairo, Teheran, Sofia and Istanbul, as well as many colonial capitals in the Mediterranean, were also inspired by the successes of the Baron in their grand plans.

As the urban historian Spiro Kostof[9] has shown, 'Haussmannian' methods have never really disappeared: we can find their traces in the work of Robert Moses in New York in the 1950s, as well as in many 'urban renewal' projects that have been undertaken in Europe, America and other parts of the world in the post-Second-World-War period, not to mention processes currently under way in many Asian cities.

---

[8]Georges-Eugène Haussmann (1809–1891) was a French civil servant and planner chosen by Emperor Napoleon III to direct the renovation work for Paris. His work, from 1852 to 1870, changed the face of the French capital.
[9]Kostof, 1992: 266–279.

Throughout the nineteenth century, the historic city was not recognised as a heritage system. What mattered were the monuments that were symbols of its tradition: the cathedrals, the palaces, the gardens, and the statuary.

The historic city as a heritage category in the modern sense was defined much later, towards the end of the nineteenth century and in the first half of the twentieth century. And only in the second half of the twentieth century did the conservation of historic cities become a subject for planners and architects, first in Europe, and later in other regions.

The 'institutionalisation' of heritage that followed the French Revolution, with the creation of specialised bodies of conservators, was society's response to the emergence of this concept and testimony of its value in the public domain. This was matched by an important intellectual debate around heritage that shaped modern conservation methodologies and practices.

Most of the modern concepts of heritage were developed 100 to 150 years ago by a group of theoreticians and administrators, who viewed the preservation of monuments of the past as a pillar of social and cultural development. John Ruskin[10] – and later William Morris – saw in the pre-industrial city one of the most important legacies of history and he struggled for its preservation.

This 'romantic' approach was essentially a form of opposition to the ongoing modernisation and destruction brought about by the Industrial Revolution. While it did not generate a theory of urban conservation, it certainly contributed to the development of a vision of the historic city as 'common' heritage, beyond national borders.

This important period witnessed contradictions and even clashes between different conceptions of heritage, the most remarkable being the clash between the romantic vision of Ruskin in England and the militant interventionism professed and practised by Eugène-Emmanuel Viollet-Le-Duc[11] in France.

In his famous book, *The Seven Lamps of Architecture*, Ruskin says: '*Neither by the public, nor by those who have the care of public monuments, is the true meaning of the word restoration understood. It means the most total destruction which a building can suffer: a destruction out of which no remnants can be gathered: a destruction accompanied with false description of the thing destroyed. Do not let us deceive ourselves in this important matter; it is impossible, as impossible as to raise the dead, to restore anything that has ever been great or beautiful in architecture.*'[12]

---

[10]John Ruskin (1819–1900) was an English art critic, social thinker and artist. He was extremely influential in the Victorian and Edwardian eras. Ruskin rejected Classical tradition in his book *The Stones of Venice* – one of the nineteenth century's most influential books (Ruskin, 1960; first published from 1851 to 1853).

[11]Viollet-Le-Duc (1814–1879) was a French architect, whose public fame was linked to the restoration of medieval monuments throughout France. He was also an important theoretician, and his writings, characterised by rationalism, provided inspiration to several masters of the Modern Movement.

[12]Ruskin, 1989: 194.

For Viollet-Le-Duc, restoration of a building was the reconstitution of a 'complete' and 'ideal' state of the monument, one that perhaps never existed. As he observed in the *Dictionnaire Raisonné*, restoration of a building is not to maintain it, repair or rebuild it, but to re-establish it in a complete state that may never have existed at a particular moment. And this approach applied not only to individual monuments, such as Notre Dame in Paris, but also to urban complexes, as shown by his restoration and reconstruction of the city of Carcassonne.

However, Viollet-Le-Duc does not reject the past. His thinking is resolutely forward-looking, as shown in his *Entretiens sur l'architecture* published between 1863 and 1872, a fundamental book for understanding how the social and technological changes of the nineteenth century transformed the role of architecture and the city (Viollet-Le-Duc, 1977).

In looking at ancient buildings, Viollet-Le-Duc sought to find a method to identify the continuities of architectural development, in order to establish the basis of a practice that would allow modern society to find its own language, beyond the many revivals of the time. In a way, Viollet-Le-Duc opened the way to a modern interpretation of architectural and urban heritage, which was later developed by the Austrian architect Camillo Sitte.[13] While other positions on the issue of restoration emerged in other parts of Europe,[14] the polarisation between the *nostalgic* and *interventionist* approaches, just described, remained alive for a long time, and may not have completely vanished yet.

Thanks to the contributions of these visionary thinkers and practitioners, the scene was set, at the turn of the twentieth century, for the appearance of modern ideas on conservation.

The key theoretical development came from the great Viennese art historian Alois Riegl,[15] whose ideas defined the role of heritage in contemporary society and still form the basis of our theories of heritage conservation.

In his seminal book, *The Modern Cult of Monuments* (*Der Moderne Denkmalkultus*), he identifies two categories of value of heritage (Riegl, 1903).

The first category is the value of 'memory' (*Erinnerungswerte*) and refers to the 'antiquity' of heritage as a factor of importance. Appreciating the 'value of antiquity' does not require a special education, and, on the contrary, is a concept which is easily accessible to the public (the 'masses').

---

[13] Camillo Sitte (1843–1903) was an Austrian architect and architectural theoretician. He greatly renewed the vision of the city, by proposing urban planning and management principles based on the observation of the aesthetics and function of the existing public spaces and on the integration of history into urban planning.

[14] Important is, for instance, the position of Camillo Boito (1836–1914) in Italy, who was in favour of respect for the authenticity of the monuments, but also in favour of an active restoration practice (Boito, 1893).

[15] Alois Riegl (1858–1905) was an Austrian art historian and critic. He was Conservator at the *Österreichischen Museum für Kunst und Industrie* in Vienna, from 1886 to 1897, and then Professor at the University of Vienna. When he wrote 'The Modern Cult of Monuments', he was also President of the Historical Monuments Commission.

Ankara

Axum

Washington

London

Urban monuments have taken a prominent role in the creation of national identities in all parts of the world. They celebrate the founding fathers of a nation (Kemal Atatürk or George Washington), mark the institutions of government, (for example, Westminster), or are re-appropriated to become symbols of national pride, like the Axum Stele.

The second category of value has to do with the 'contemporary' (*Gegen-wartswerte*) and the 'use value' of monuments, a character that allows them to be differentiated from archaeology and ruins. The use value has an 'art value' and a 'newness' value (*Neuheitswert*). The first refers to the artistic qualities of the ancient monument that we are still able to perceive, while the second refers to the 'untouched' appearance of the work of art, which confers on the monument a higher value in the eyes of the masses.

Riegl brings about a fundamental conceptual innovation, one that has influenced thinking on heritage up to today: interpreting the conservation of monuments through a theory of values.

Furthermore, he looks at the way in which 'conflict' between different values of heritage (for instance, between the historic values and the use values) can be resolved. This book therefore provides a critical guide to administrators and practitioners as to how to deal with heritage. But its intellectual ambition goes beyond this, as it deals with an element that has become critical in today's conservation policies: the growing interest of the general public in the values of antiquity, and the development of a major industry around it, that of cultural tourism. With the work of Riegl, heritage is finally associated with modernity (Choay, 1992).

While these early developments did not specifically focus on the historic city per se, they certainly provided the foundation of the modern approach to urban heritage conservation. Some of the concepts that we find in modern charters and that are also reflected in the Historic Urban Landscape approach were developed in this phase: the memory value of heritage, the right to its aesthetic enjoyment, and the collective responsibility for its conservation.

The Historic City as Heritage

This delay in the definition of the historic city as heritage can be explained by the complexity of the urban organism with its dual nature of place, containing monuments of great symbolic and artistic value, as well as a fabric of 'minor' architecture, the vernacular, which is much more exposed to transition and substitution. The lack of interest in, and knowledge of, this fabric, of cadastres and technical documentation, was a factor in this significant lag.

It was only at the end of the nineteenth century that an 'operational' concept of the historic city was devised, in parallel to the development of a new discipline, city planning. The foremost urban thinker of the time, Camillo Sitte, gave voice to the idea that the historic city carried with it an 'aesthetic' value, superior to that of the modern city.

In his 1889 book, *City Planning according to Artistic Principles* (Sitte, 1965), which marked a turning point in architectural theory and lies at the origin of city planning (Collins and Crasemann Collins, 1986), Sitte looks at the city for the first time as an historical continuum that must be fully understood in its morphological and typological development, in order to derive rules and models for the development of the modern city.

For modern principles of urban conservation, Sitte's theory is important for two reasons: it establishes the historic city as an aesthetic model, a source of inspiration for modern design; and it paves the way for the development of urban conservation practice.

His idea of continuity in urban development is also an important corollary for the future development of a conservation policy. The work of Sitte was criticised by advocates of Modernism, and in particular by Le Corbusier and the CIAM, who saw in his theory a reactionary approach, contrary to the ideals of modern urbanism. However, his innovative ideas inspired urban conservation projects in Europe and in the colonial world, and provided the basis for the development of new approaches to architecture and planning, for the first time dealing with urban conservation from an operational viewpoint.

One can indeed trace back to this period the origins both of modern town planning and urban conservation. The works of Sitte and some of his followers, such as Werner Hegemann[16] in Germany (Crasemann Collins, 2005), Raymond Unwin[17] in England (Unwin, 1909), Gustavo Giovannoni[18] in Italy (Giovannoni, 1931), Marcel Poëte[19] in France (Poëte, 2000) and Charles Buls[20] in Belgium (Smets, 1995), to mention only some of the most significant representatives, show a capacity to project the modern metropolis into the future, while at the same time interpreting and valuing history and continuity.

Urban monuments and the historic urban fabric are seen as concrete anchorage for modern design. The city is not conceived as a static object, but, on the contrary, as one in a state of constant transformation. This concept represents a radical departure from the approach of the urban

[16] Werner Hegemann (1881–1936) was a German urban planner and architectural critic. In 1910 he was the secretary of the first international urban planning exhibition. He travelled and worked in America and then settled in Germany in 1921, until he left the country in 1933 due to Nazi persecution. He was a Professor at the New School for Social Research at Columbia University in New York City.

[17] Raymond Unwin (1863–1940) was one of the most influential English architects and town planners of the first half of the twentieth century. His particular interest was the improvement of working-class housing. He was the author of several innovative urban plans in England. From 1919 to 1928 he was appointed Chief Technical Officer for Housing and Town Planning. Unwin was President of the Royal Institute of British Architects (RIBA) from 1931 to 1933, and served as consultant for President Roosevelt's New Deal in 1933.

[18] Gustavo Giovannoni (1873–1947) was an Italian architect and engineer, and a follower of Camillo Boito. He was a practitioner and a teacher, with interests ranging from architectural and art history to urban planning and architecture. From 1927 to 1935 he directed the School of Architecture of the University of Rome, where he taught Restoration of Monuments.

[19] Marcel Poëte (1866–1950) was a French historian and urban planner who specialised in the history of Paris. He was a co-founder of the *Institut d'Urbanisme de Paris*, and contributed to the development of the discipline and practice of urban planning in France in the first half of the twentieth century.

[20] Charles Buls (1837–1914) was a Belgian politician, urban planner and educator. He was the Mayor of Brussels from 1881 to 1899. His main action as Mayor was the conservation of the arts and heritage of the city, and notably of the *Grande Place*. His essays were extremely influential in Europe. He worked extensively as an educator, and in 1866 he contributed to the opening of the *École des Arts décoratifs*, annexed to the *Académie royale des beaux-arts* of Brussels.

'hygienists' and defines the main goal of the planner and the architect as the art of marrying functional need and beauty, a programme and analytical method termed in different parts of Europe as 'Art Public' or 'Civic Art' or 'Art Urbain' and as the 'City Beautiful Movement' in America (Bohl and Lejeune, 2009).

In this rich period of intellectual ferment, perhaps the most innovative thinkers and practitioners were the German architect and critic Werner Hegemann and the Scottish urbanist and biologist Patrick Geddes.[21]

Werner Hegemann based his work on the proposals of Sitte and was able to transform them into a complete and innovative methodology of planning (Crasemann Collins, 2005). He was also the first planner who bridged the architectural discourse between Europe and America, as shown by the production of one of the most extraordinary architectural manuals of modern times: *The American Vitruvius* (Hegemann and Peets, 1988). In this work, published in 1922, significantly subtitled *Handbook of Civic Art*, he uses the analytical method inaugurated by Sitte to demonstrate, through examples taken from different times and places, the universality of the principles of urban creation.[22]

The relationships between mass and void constitute, according to Hegemann, the elements of continuity of a city, in a harmonious process of development. He sees the city as a continuous and incremental *collage*, where all the parts, while maintaining their identity, interact to create a new spatial meaning. From this derives the importance of the historic city as the physical outcome of the long-term process and the 'manifesto' for its development.

Patrick Geddes, certainly one of the most innovative urban planners of his time (Welter, 2002), looked at the city from another angle compared with the approach of Sitte and his followers, mostly based on visual and aesthetic appreciation. He sees the city as an organism in evolution, where physical and social components interact in a complex web of change and tradition.

This 'organic' concept – typical of a naturalist – finds its concrete manifestation in the medieval city, already celebrated by Ruskin and Morris, and reinterpreted by Geddes as a continuously evolving context, where every generation brings its own contribution to the physical space, by changing and adding structures and functions. In his 1915 book, *Cities in Evolution*, he sees the historic city as a model to be studied to understand its functioning and design principles and to identify management practices for the care of collective spaces. He sees for

---

[21] Patrick Geddes (1854–1932) was a Scottish biologist and town planner. He was one of the most influential modern thinkers in the field of urban planning. A follower of John Ruskin's belief that spatial forms influence social processes, he had the opportunity to demonstrate his ideas in the course of a long professional career during which he authored several urban plans in the UK (Edinburgh), India and the Middle East (Jerusalem, Tel Aviv).
[22] Calabi, Donatella. 'Handbooks of Civic Art from Sitte to Hegemann'. Bohl, Charles C., Lejeune, Jean-François, 2009: 161–174.

the first time the importance for city planning of understanding the spirit of place, the *genius loci*. The traces, memories and collective associations of values to space are key determinants of urban transformation (Geddes, 2010).

Geddes looks at the city in a truly comprehensive manner: from a morphological, as well as from a social, point of view. He looks at its history as the basis of civic education and cooperation. He looks at the relationships between the city and its geographic and natural context. For him, the whole city should be considered for conservation, not merely a limited district or section. To promote urban conservation, he coined the term 'conservative surgery', a practice aimed at minimising the destruction of historic buildings and urban spaces to adapt them to modern requirements, which he implemented in Edinburgh and Dublin, as well as in India, in Balrampur, Lahore and other cities.

The importance of these visions of the city in inspiring new urban design models in different parts of the world in the first half of the twentieth century cannot be overstated. They represented an attempt to integrate into the new design the values (aesthetic, functional and symbolic) embodied in the city as a result of its historic transformation, while at the same time attempting to define the city design process as a continuation of the past.

The ideas of Geddes were influential in Europe and played a role in the creation in the early 1920s of an important movement in the USA, the Regional Planning Association of America (RPPA), under the initiative of a group of architects led by Clarence Stein[23] and supported by the intellectual input of the historian and critic Lewis Mumford.[24] The RPAA, in spite of its small size,[25] became the most influential advocacy group in urban and regional planning in America, promoting the respect of local cultural values and their harmonious integration into urban

---

[23] Clarence Samuel Stein (1882–1975) was an American urban planner, architect and writer, a major proponent of the 'Garden City' movement in the United States. In 1923 Stein co-founded the Regional Planning Association of America to address large-scale planning issues such as affordable housing, the impact of sprawl, and wilderness preservation. His projects include the design of Sunnyside Gardens (1923), a neighbourhood of the New York City borough of Queens, and the plan for Radburn in Fair Lawn, New Jersey (1929). In the 1930s Stein and the other members of the RPAA saw their social-housing cause adopted by the government.

[24] Lewis Mumford (1895–1990) was an American historian, philosopher and literary critic. He was a polymath and wrote influential books in the fields of history of technology. He was especially recognised as an influential thinker in the field of urban history and planning. He was critical of the process of urban sprawl and linked the social problems of Western societies to the structure of their cities. He is considered a pioneer of the environmental movement and ecological planning.

[25] The RPAA was essentially a loose circle of friends, mainly from the New York City area, with never more than twenty-five members. It was created in 1923 and included, besides Stein and Mumford, the American Institute of Architecture *Journal* editor Charles Whitaker, Forester Benton MacKaye, economist Stuart Chase, architects Henry Wright, Russell Van Nest Black, Fred Ackerman, Robert D. Kohn and Fred Bigger, social scientist Robert Bruere, and housers Edith Elmer Wood and Catherine Bauer. The group worked together until 1933 and influenced all the New Deal urban and regional policies.

development, and opposing land speculation in favour of socially oriented planning.

The importance of these perspectives would be acknowledged in the second half of the twentieth century, as a reaction against the anti-historicist and functionalist approach of Modernism. Among architects, planners and social thinkers of the time, perhaps the one who best understood the role of the historic city in modern society, and defined the tools for urban conservation, was the Italian architect and urban planner Gustavo Giovannoni (Zucconi, 1997). In fact, he defined a technical approach to urban conservation that constitutes to this day the basis of the urban conservation practice (Choay, 1992): it was he who coined the term 'urban heritage'.

The new thinking inspired by Giovannoni arose – as in Sitte – from the needs of modern urban planning. The historic city was not considered adequate for an era of machines and mass communication, which required wider spaces, urban expansion and planning at the territorial scale.

If the time of the compact, dense city was over, the historic city could still play an important role, not linked to production and communication, but rather to living and social exchange. The historic city, in this innovative concept, is seen as part of a network of urban functions, not just as a model for the creation of new urban centres, as in Sitte's view, but as an area where new functions compatible with traditional urban morphology can be absorbed. The aesthetic function, the beauty of the historic city, is an element that further strengthens this role and establishes a hierarchy and dialogue between old and modern urban forms.

The modernity of Giovannoni's approach is remarkable: both the romantic, memorial function of Ruskin[26] and the rational, model approach of Sitte are recomposed in a unitary vision, which is able to integrate the range of societal needs into one comprehensive view. In a sense, this approach is the opposite of theories expressed by Modernism and symbolised by Le Corbusier's *Plan Voisin*, a proposal that was de facto wiping out the historic city to replace it with a fully rational, functionalist modern grid.

The contribution of Giovannoni is not limited to this theoretical framework. As he was a militant practitioner, he also developed a complete

---

[26]In his 1849 seminal book, *The Seven Lamps of Architecture*, one of the first modern architectural treaties, Ruskin defined the functions of architecture in modern society, with terms that are still present today in the discussion on the city, architecture and conservation. The 'Seven Lamps' are:

1. *Sacrifice* – the meaning of architecture in relation to values (spiritual, social etc.).
2. *Truth* – the honest display of materials and structure.
3. *Power* – the expression of the human effort and achievement.
4. *Beauty* – the search for harmony and nature.
5. *Life* – the creativity in the design and in the building process.
6. *Memory* – the respect of the culture of the place.
7. *Obedience* – the rejection of extravaganzas and the adherence to cultural and social values.

methodology for the management and conservation of the historic city, which remains today as the basis of the disciplinary approach. An integrative planning system is seen as the key management tool for the historic city in modern urban development. This is necessary to establish and guide the choice of its functions, to properly connect it with the new urban fabric and with the communication systems, and to preserve the social structure of the population.

A very important principle established by Giovannoni was the need to conserve the built 'environment' of historic monuments, the urban fabric that represents the layers of time, a clear position against the 'dismemberment' of buildings that was – and still remains in many parts of the world – an 'easy' practice.

Urban environments require an approach to conservation similar to those adopted for individual monuments. Within these basic principles, and respecting the urban morphologies and building typologies, it is admissible to develop a strategy of reintegration of missing parts, and de-densification (*diradamento*) of additions that prevent an adequate functionality of the urban fabric.

Giovannoni was strongly opposed to the museum-like freezing of historic centres, a common practice at the time in Italy and other countries, consisting of the isolation of the historic fabric from contemporary life, and the creation of a specialised district used for tourism purposes. Considering the complexity of his approach, we can consider him the precursor of the conservation policies that were developed internationally, largely under his influence or the influence of his followers, in the second half of the twentieth century.

The development of urban planning as an independent discipline in the first part of the twentieth century provided the foundation of the modern approach to urban conservation. In a way, it even provided approaches that were theoretically more comprehensive than the ones that emerged in the second half of the century on urban conservation. In fact, the founding fathers of urban planning saw the city as an historical continuum and an environment connected to its wider territory. Even the anti-urbanism utopias that materialised as a reaction to the poor living conditions in the city were based on historical models (Fishman, 1977).

These concepts are of great importance in the development of the modern approach to urban conservation, and are reflected in many contemporary documents and charters; indeed, the need to link urban conservation to a wider context and to the natural environment is at the heart of contemporary thinking on urban conservation.

Fracture: the Modern Movement versus the Historic City

It would be impossible to understand the present challenges of urban conservation without a reference to the big break in the vision and practice of architecture and urban planning which came about as a result of the Modern Movement.

Box 1.1 Imperial Palaces of the Ming and Qing Dynasties in Beijing and Shenyang (China)

The property was originally inscribed onto the World Heritage List in 1987 as the Forbidden City with its landscaped gardens and main building complexes. In 2004 it was extended to include the Imperial Palace of the Qing Dynasty in Shenyang with its 114 buildings. The Forbidden City, the largest palace in the world, has been subject to pressures from tourism and air pollution while its surroundings have developed rapidly in the last two decades. Beijing's successful bid for the 2008 Olympic Games included the planned development of urban projects in the vicinity of the World Heritage listed property in 2003, which drew the attention of the World Heritage Committee. An urban development project along the traditional streets of Nanchizi neighbourhood caused special concern, as it aimed to renew the historic district within the limits of the buffer zone of the property. In response to the World Heritage Committee's concern, the Beijing Municipality cancelled the project, thereby preventing another of Beijing's traditional neighbourhoods being razed to the ground to make way for a massive real estate development project. In addition, the Municipality developed a Plan for the Protection of the Imperial City, which strengthens the protection of the buffer zone of the World Heritage designated property. With these actions, the property's extension was approved under criteria (i), (ii), (iii) and (iv), with specific recommendations on land use and tourism control within the buffer zone.

Sources: World Heritage Committee State of Conservation Reports 27 COM 7B.43 and 28 COM 15B.54

This intellectual movement did in fact redefine the role and principles of architecture and planning in modern society, and developed a vision aimed at managing the needs of mass society, while it renewed design aesthetics in a way that has marked most of the twentieth century.

The Modern Movement shifted the attention of urban planners away from the idea of harmonious development, promoted by the movements of the late-nineteenth and early-twentieth centuries, to the idea of functional urban development.

In those years, movements such as the *Arts and Crafts Movement*[27] in Great Britain and America, the German *Deutscher Werkbund*[28] and the *Wiener Werkstätte*[29] in Vienna had renewed the language of architecture

---

[27] The Arts and Crafts Movement was an international design movement that originated in England and flourished between 1880 and 1910, continuing its influence up to the 1930s. Instigated by the artist and writer William Morris in the 1860s and inspired by the writings of John Ruskin, it had its earliest and fullest development in the British Isles but spread to Europe and North America as a reaction against the impoverished state of the decorative arts and the conditions under which they were produced. See: Kaplan and Crawford, 2005.

[28] The *Deutscher Werkbund* (German Work Federation) was a German association of artists, architects, designers and industrialists. The *Werkbund* was to become an important actor in the development of modern architecture and industrial design, particularly in the later creation of the Bauhaus school of design. The *Werkbund* was founded in 1907 in Munich, existed through 1934, and was then re-established after the Second World War in 1950. See: Schwartz, 1996.

[29] The *Wiener Werkstätte* (Vienna Workshop) was a visual artists' production group that originated in 1897 out of the *Sezessionsstil* (Vienna Secession). This workshop gathered

and urban design to cope with the needs of a new industrial society (Pevsner, 2005). Other innovative proposals aimed at coping with the needs of the modern industrial city were conducted in parallel, sometimes in the great tradition of urban utopias, such as the *Cité industrielle* of Tony Garnier[30] (Garnier, 1917).

Many of the great architects of the Modern Movement, like Le Corbusier and Mies van der Rohe, either took part in, or were inspired by, these movements, but the collapse of the old order in Europe with the First World War, the Russian Revolution and the development of mass industrial societies created the conditions for the intellectual revolution that was Modernism.[31]

The intellectual life of the post-war period – indeed in all areas of artistic expression – found its expression in the development of avant-garde schools like the Bauhaus[32] in Germany or Vkhoutemas[33] in Russia, as well as in movements like De Stijl in Holland. In 1923, with the publication of his *Vers une Architecture*, Le Corbusier redefined the paradigm of architecture and urban planning (Le Corbusier, 1977), urging architects not to remain attached to models and styles of the past, which were detached from the needs and realities of the present.

The doctrine of the Modern Movement, developed in the 1920s and 1930s at the international level through the CIAM (*Congrès internationaux d'architecture moderne*), made a radical departure from the approach to the historic city espoused by the most advanced thinkers of the previous generation (Mumford, 2000). The CIAM approach favoured the destruction of the traditional city and the creation of a new modern urban complex,

---

architects, artists and designers interested in the production of everyday objects of great aesthetic quality, bringing together crafts and the major arts. The *Wiener Werkstätte* ceased its activities in 1932. See: Fahr-Becker, 2008.

[30] Tony Garnier (1869–1948) was a French architect and urban planner, and author of an urban utopia based on modernist principles of separation of urban functions and industrial activities. His 'Cité Industrielle' was very influential in the post-First-World-War period, especially in the Soviet Union. He worked mostly in his home town, Lyon, where he authored several important architectural projects.

[31] It is interesting to note that during Le Corbusier's formative years, Sitte's book was his main inspiration: years afterward he viewed it as a symbol of reactionary and obscurantist thinking, a nostalgic attempt to deny the progress of technique and society.

[32] The Bauhaus was an arts and crafts institute created in 1919 in Weimar by the architect Walter Gropius, and it became extremely influential in the fields of architecture and design, as well as in photography, costume design and dance. Some of the most important artists and architects of the European avant-garde taught courses there. In 1925 the Bauhaus moved to Dessau where Gropius designed its new offices. After Gropius left in 1928, the Bauhaus was directed by Hannes Meyer and Ludwig Mies van der Rohe. The school was closed by the Nazis in 1933.

[33] The *Vkhoutemas* (Higher Art and Technical Studios) was a Russian school created in 1920 in Moscow by Lenin, with the aim of providing artists with the high qualifications needed for industrial production. The school had about 100 teachers and 2,500 students. The school was the centre of some important movements in art and architecture like constructivism, rationalism and suprematism. The school that was linked to the Bauhaus was closed in 1930.

based on high-density public housing, with functional and innovative housing typologies and elaborate transport infrastructure.

The Plan of Amsterdam of Cornelis van Eesteren,[34] himself a leading figure of the CIAM, was the first concrete demonstration of modern principles, based on the separation of functions, layers of traffic circulation, flexibility and modularity of spaces and social cooperation.

The social experiments of the 1920s and 1930s in Vienna, Berlin and Russia, as well as the work of great masters like Le Corbusier, Walter Gropius,[35] Ludwig Mies van der Rohe[36] and Hannes Mayer,[37] to name but a few, established models that influenced housing and urban development throughout the twentieth century.

Le Corbusier[38] was undoubtedly the greatest theoretician of the new vision, who proposed provocative projects, such as the *Plan Voisin* to replace the centre of Paris with a modern grid of high-rise architecture, or the plans for Algiers (*Plan Obus*) or Rio de Janeiro, where the old city was essentially ignored or replaced by mega-structures (Le Corbusier, 1935). He also led the way to the drafting by CIAM of its most important manifesto: the *Athens Charter*, which was discussed and negotiated during its fourth Congress[39] in 1933, but published only in 1943 by himself (Le Corbusier, 1957).

---

[34] Cornelis van Eesteren (1897–1988) established, with Theo van Doesburg, the architectural principles of Neo-Plasticism. He was responsible for the General Extension plan for Amsterdam (1936), where he was Chief Architect of the Town Planning Department for nearly half a century. He was president of CIAM (1930–47).

[35] Walter Gropius (1883–1969) was a German-born, and later naturalised American, architect. He was one of the most important representatives of twentieth-century Modernism. In 1919, he succeeded Henry van de Velde as Director of the School of Arts and Crafts of Weimar, which he transformed into the Bauhaus, the most influential school of modern architecture and arts of the time, which he directed until 1928.

[36] Ludwig Mies van der Rohe (1886–1969) was a German-born, and later naturalised American, architect, widely considered as one of the masters of modern architecture. From 1930 to 1933 he directed the Bauhaus, as successor to Walter Gropius. He left Nazi Germany in 1937 for the USA, to become the Head of the School of Architecture of the Illinois Institute of Technology in Chicago.

[37] Hannes Mayer (1889–1954) was a Swiss architect and Second Director of the Bauhaus in Dessau from 1928 to 1930. After being dismissed as Director of the School, he moved to Moscow, forming a group called the Left Column, which worked on architectural and urban planning projects inspired by socialist ideals. After this experience, he moved to Mexico to work for the Mexican government as the Director of the *Instituto del Urbanismo y Planification*.

[38] Le Corbusier, pseudonym of Charles-Édouard Jeanneret-Gris (1887–1965), was a Swiss-born, and later naturalised French architect. He was one of the most important architects of the Modern Movement. As designer, urban planner and prolific writer, Le Corbusier was a dominant figure in world architecture throughout his life. He was the main inspiration for the CIAM, and author of masterpieces of modern architecture in all fields. In the 1950s, he and his cousin Pierre Jeanneret were the designers of the new capital of Indian Punjab, Chandigarh.

[39] The CIAM 4 Congress took place in 1933 aboard the cruise ship SS Patris II in the Mediterranean and in Athens. During this Congress, the principles of the Functional City were established. Following Le Corbusier's principles, expressed in the same year in his book *La Ville Radieuse*, the main 'Resolutions in Principle' of the Congress defined modern urbanism. See: Mumford, 2000: 84.

Santiago

Edinburgh

The fracture created by Modernism has had significant impacts on the conservation of the historic city, with long-reaching effects until today. The way in which architects should deal with historic contexts is at the core of the contemporary debate.

In this text, the historic city is a negative model, characterised by excessive density, lack of light, ventilation and sun exposure, where services are distant from the residential areas. The solutions proposed are simple and straightforward: demolition of the unhealthy neighbourhoods and their replacement with green spaces and modern housing units. A specific section of the document deals with urban heritage, seen essentially as a set of monuments, to be respected in the name of their historic and 'sentimental' value, surrounded by 'slums' that could be demolished, with the exception of some 'samples' that could be preserved for their documentary value.

The inevitable shortcomings of the vision of the Modern Movement, which first emerged – not insignificantly – in the motherland of the revolution, the Soviet Union, did not prevent the Movement from influencing in a significant way most of the twentieth-century urban planning (Curtis, 1996).

With qualities varying from place to place, zoning has been for most of the century the main tool of urban development; block social housing has dominated the new urban landscape and has largely affected the historic city; infrastructure for individual transport has guided the choices of urban design (Relph, 1987).

In a few cases, like Chandigarh and Brasilia, the Modernist dream became reality and an entire city was built according to unified principles. Overall, this model has dominated, both in the developed, and in the developing, world, for a good half century, albeit with results distant from the original utopia.

Box 1.2 Historic Centre of the City of Graz (Austria)

The historic centre of Graz was listed as a World Heritage site in 1999 as a fine example of a Central European urban complex with a harmonious blend of architectural styles and artistic movements that had succeeded each other since the Middle Ages. During the first years of this new century the inscribed property saw a series of contemporary architectural interventions, which touched upon a decades-long debate in architectural and conservation circles concerning building in historic context. A 2005 mission reported three cases where new architectural interventions, often severely contrasting with the historic context, had replaced historic buildings, among which the construction of the *Thalia Centre* that had resulted in the demolition of the protected building of the 'Kommod-House'. These new and contrasting architectural creations in the World Heritage site raised the question of the integrity of the property and the priority imposed on urban development projects which did not harmonise with the existing historic urban fabric, thereby threatening the site's Outstanding Universal Value. In order to prevent further fragmentation of the historic ensemble, a Management Plan was developed and put in place in 2007. Moreover, the World Heritage property was extended to include *Schloss Eggenberg*, so as to preserve the historical link that existed between the city and the castle and thereby strengthening the integrity of the property. The extension resulted in a new, enlarged buffer zone.

Sources: World Heritage Committee State of Conservation Reports 29 COM 7B.63 and 30 COM 7B.76

Certainly the radical rejection of the historic city has prevented modern architects from appreciating the 'layering' process as the basis for the quality of urban spaces and the role of established social networks in shaping development patterns. Given its ideological origins, it was impossible for Modernism to tune in to the important discussion about heritage conservation and the urban form that was ongoing during the same period.

It is an irony of history that the first important modern document on conservation, which is today commonly referred to as the *Athens Charter* (although it was never issued under this name), was produced almost at the same time as the CIAM manifesto (Iamandi, 1997).

Inspired by an international group of architects, archaeologists and conservators, including Gustavo Giovannoni and the Belgian architect Victor Horta,[40] the Conference represented the outcome of more than a century of discussion and theoretical developments concerning the conservation of ancient monuments and sites.

In a way, this is the point of departure of modern conservation, and the founding of an international (albeit at the time predominantly European) movement for heritage conservation, which opened the way to the modern Charters, the creation of many international organisations for conservation and the adoption of international Conventions such as the 1972 World Heritage Convention. The 1931 Athens Conference offered for the first time an opportunity to compare different national approaches to conservation and legislation, and to establish exchanges between different disciplines.

While its main drive remained an 'aesthetic' vision of heritage, typical of the traditional European approach, the Conference opened up new ways of dealing with issues such as the education of the public and the use of science for conservation. Finally, the Conference pioneered the concept of urban heritage, supported the integration of built heritage into urban planning, the conservation of the uses of historic fabric and respect for the setting of the monuments, especially when new buildings are planned.

Although the conclusions of the Conference were already acknowledged by the League of Nations in 1932, its importance became evident only after the Second World War, with the adoption of the 1964 Venice Charter and the growth of an international conservation movement under the aegis of UNESCO.

The practice of urban planning in the first half of the twentieth century is one of great diversity of principles and practices, and that diversity is still a part of contemporary debate. However, other dominant themes have been the growing role of urban conservation and the establishment of an international movement able to influence policies not only in the Western context, but also, for the first time, in other regions of the world.

---

[40]Victor Horta (1861–1947) was a Belgian architect and among the greatest interpreters of the Art Nouveau style. He was a prolific architect and teacher, and became highly influential in his time, anticipating modernist language and style.

Modern policies on urban conservation are based on the recognition of the historic value of the urban fabric, on the understanding of its structure and form, as well as on an understanding of the complex layering process that has supported them. This is the intellectual capital that we will retrace in all modern theories and charters, which is also present in contemporary thinking on urban conservation.

Out of Modernism: New Approaches to Urban Conservation

The fracture created by Modernism between the rationale for heritage conservation and that of new development has had a severe impact on the conservation of the historic city. While the principles of conservation of monuments, at least in the European context, were already enshrined in several national legislations in the nineteenth and early-twentieth centuries, and specialised conservation institutions created, most of the historic urban areas were not protected as 'heritage', a situation that enabled the 'planned' removal of many historic districts, both before, and after, the Second World War.

Modern building types and technologies seemed fit to cope with the urgent and extensive needs of post-war reconstruction and economic expansion, and policy-makers showed little interest in conservation during the first two decades after the war. However, two important processes took shape in those years.

The first process was the reaction against Modernism that sparked a rich debate among architects, planners and public officials on policies and methodologies for new design and city management. This debate is critical to understanding the evolution of urban conservation in the post-war period, as it is in this period that many of its social, physical and cultural objectives were established and new operational tools developed.

The second process was the growth of an international conservation movement that was able to establish its own national and international institutions and to define principles and operational practices. In the 1960s, it became evident that the standardised application of modern planning and architectural principles was responsible for poor housing quality, monotonous and repetitive urban spaces and social marginality.

The poor quality of modern urban spaces exposed the contrast between the new developments and the historic city, where, in spite of poor housing conditions, urban spaces were far more enjoyable. The crisis of the Modern Movement became evident even in its own circles: in 1959 the CIAM held its last meeting,[41] its members acknowledging the end of the movement and branching off in different directions. And even before the professionals had developed their new approaches, a backlash came from the grass

[41] The last meeting of CIAM was held in Otterlo, The Netherlands, in 1959. At this meeting, the opposition to the post-war CIAM structure, expressed by the younger-generation architects of Team 10, put an end to the experience.

roots, exemplified by the cogent critique of Jane Jacobs[42] in America (Jacobs, 1993).

The time had come for the architects and planners to find new ways to manage development, respecting historical patterns, the meaning of space and social links.[43] However, the principles of Modernism have continued to operate for many decades in different regions of the world, often with local adaptation, such as can be found in the Indian or Latin American context, but the main thrust of the movement had ended.

The intellectual season opened by the end of Modernism was extremely rich in contributions that have oriented the contemporary approach to urban conservation and helped shape its operational tools. The different currents of thought, which emerged from the crisis, can certainly be traced back to the intellectual debates at the turn of the nineteenth century, while at the same time reflecting the spirit of a modern, democratic society.

As urban conservation paradigms were defined later than those of monuments, and have remained quite open to changes and interpretation, the variety of approaches of the post-war period provides a very diverse range of urban conservation models.

The interest in social planning that was at the root of the Modern Movement continued in the work of younger members of CIAM, such as that of the Dutch architects Aldo van Eyck[44] and Jacob Bakema,[45] the British Alison and Peter Smithson,[46] the Greek George Candilis[47] and the Italian Giancarlo De Carlo,[48] to name only some of the founding members of the Team 10 group, a secession from CIAM. The work of these authors was extremely

---

[42] Jane Jacobs (1916–2006), writer and activist, played a fundamental role in fostering a revision of planning practices in America, re-empowering the communities ahead of private interests. Her interests spanned from urban issues to labour economics and social philosophy.

[43] Jacobs' work was very influential in spreading participatory planning approaches in different countries, and inspired planners such as Paul Davidoff, the founder of 'advocacy planning' in the USA.

[44] Aldo Van Eyck (1918–1999), was a Dutch architect and professor at the Amsterdam Academy of Architecture (1954–1959) and at the Delft University of Technology (1966–1984). He was editor of the architecture magazine *Forum* from 1959 to 1963 and also in 1967. Aldo van Eyck was a member of CIAM and then in 1954 a co-founder of Team 10.

[45] Jakob Bakema (1914–1981) was a Dutch architect, a protagonist of the reconstruction of Rotterdam after the Second World War. In 1946 he began attending meetings of the CIAM and became its Secretary in 1955, and he was a core member of its offshoot, Team 10.

[46] Alison Smithson (1928–1993) and Peter Smithson (1923–2003) were British architects, who formed an architectural partnership, and were throughout their careers active critics of modernist principles. At the 10th and final CIAM Congress in 1956, the Smithsons broke with CIAM as part of Team 10.

[47] George Candilis (1913–1995) was a Greek architect who became after the Second World War one of the main collaborators of Le Corbusier. He was in charge of the construction of the Unité d'Habitation of Marseille. He developed a successful professional career especially in the area of high-density housing. He was a founding member of Team 10 and remained a member throughout the life of the group until its last meeting in 1977.

[48] Giancarlo De Carlo (1919–2005), was an Italian architect and professor at the Institute of Architecture of Venice. He was the youngest member of CIAM, and among the founders of

influential in establishing a new approach to urban design and urban conservation, as well as in turning the issue of human habitat into one of international concern, a drive that eventually led to the creation of the UN Habitat Agency in 1978.[49]

Of this group, the Italian architect Giancarlo De Carlo was the one who broke new ground on the management of historic urban areas. He criticised the technocratic model typical of the age of Modernism, and favoured citizen participation and consensus as a tool of planning and architectural design (De Carlo, 1972).

Consequently, his architecture sought to reflect the nature of the context, with its cultural, physical and historical components. Through this methodology, he was able to address the issue of contemporary design in the historic city in ways adapted to the realities of modern democratic societies.

While establishing as a primary goal the conservation of the values of the past, he was able to convincingly articulate a new design language compatible with the historic fabric. His most significant contribution in this field remains the Master Plan for the Italian Renaissance town of Urbino, where he was able to harmoniously integrate his new university buildings into the urban landscape (Guccione and Vittorini, 2005).

In reality, even before these experiments, the participatory and 'bottom-up' approach to design and planning had found an important practical and theoretical basis in the work of the Egyptian architect Hassan Fathi,[50] who,

---

Team 10. Alongside his professional carrier, he directed the international journal *Spazio e Società – Space & Society*, and created the International Laboratory of Architecture and Urban Design (ILAUD).

[49] The UN-Habitat Agency was created on the occasion of the first United Nations Conference on Human Settlements (Habitat I), held in Vancouver, Canada, in 1976. Among the many Recommendations issued by the Conference, the following concern the existing urban fabric:

'Recommendation B.8 Improving existing settlements:
(a) Settlement planning cannot merely focus on new urban development for many settlements already exist. The improvement, renewal and rehabilitation of these settlements should therefore be continuous. They thus present a major challenge in improvement of quality of life, and of the existing fabric of settlements. When ill-conceived it may result in the destruction of the economic and social fabric of entire neighbourhoods.
(b) Settlements must be continuously improved. Renewal and rehabilitation of existing settlements must be oriented to improving living conditions, functional structures and environmental qualities. The process must respect the rights and aspirations of inhabitants, especially the least advantaged, and preserve the cultural and social values embodied in the existing fabric.
(c) Special attention should be paid to:
  (i) Upgrading and preserving the existing stock through the development and use of low-cost techniques, and the direct involvement of the present inhabitants;
  (ii) Undertaking major clearance operations only when conservation and rehabilitation are not feasible and relocation measures are made;
  (iii) Providing for the welfare of the affected inhabitants especially with respect to employment opportunities and basic infrastructure;
  (iv) Preserving the area's social and cultural fabric which may be the only de facto source of social services including care of children and the aged, maternity care, apprenticeship, employment information and security'.

[50] Hassan Fathi (1900–1989) was an Egyptian architect and professor who studied and adapted the traditional construction techniques of rural areas, in order to provide cheaper and self-built housing for the poor. He is the author of numerous projects, the most well-known being the Village of New Gourna in Luxor. UNESCO has launched in 2010 a project for the restoration of the village of New Gourna, currently under way (2011).

New Gourna

Rio de Janeiro

The growth of informal settlements on a global scale has pushed architects and planners to rethink the way in which governments should address the needs of the poor, and to recognise the value of traditional knowledge and techniques.

as early as 1945, had started working with the vernacular architecture of southern Egypt, reusing the millenary construction techniques of the local peasants.

This innovative exercise, albeit largely ignored at that time, became universally known with the publication of his influential work in 1973, *Architecture for the Poor* (Fathi, 1973). Hassan Fathi has been recognised as a precursor of the urban management ideals that took shape at the end of Modernism (Aga Khan Trust for Culture, 1989), and his work demonstrated to a generation of architects and planners the possible alternative views for the conservation of historic cities in many parts of the developed, and developing, world.

Continuing in this tradition, and inspired by the teachings of De Carlo, was the British architect John Turner.[51] Drawing on many years of field experience in Latin America, he developed a set of important planning and architectural principles of self-help and 'self-building' (Turner, 1976) that opened the way to a generation of architects and planners interested in rediscovering local traditions as a tool to preserve the social and physical integrity of places, while providing affordable shelter.[52]

Turner supported the view that housing, both new and old, is best managed by the inhabitants rather than by external planners. Assisted self-management proved to be the most effective way to achieve sustainability and to preserve the social links that form part of the city. Turner's view was that the developed world has much to learn from the developing context and that the 'freedom to build' was the way to value local experience over the technocratic approach of traditional planning.

While the application of these principles was not as widespread as imagined by the social reformers, it certainly played an important role in reinforcing the view that urban conservation must be participatory, and in establishing the preservation of the social fabric of the historic city as one of the most important goals of planning.

Another important current of thought that emerged from Modernism focused on the physical structure of the city as the outcome of an historical layering process. This approach, which had its roots in the field of geography (Whitehand, 1992), was developed by the urban geographer Conzen[53] in Great Britain and was then applied to different regions of the world.

---

[51] John Turner (1927–) is a British architect and professor who has written extensively on housing and community organisation. Turner's central thesis argued that housing is best provided and managed by those who are to dwell in it rather than being centrally administered by the state.

[52] In particular, in this field significant contributions have come from architects such as Walter Segal (1907–1985), Cedric Price (1934–2003) and John Habraken (1928–).

[53] M.R.G. Conzen (1907–2000) was a British (German-born) geographer and a pioneer of the field of urban morphology. After coming to England in 1933, he began working in the Geography Department of what would become the University of Newcastle-upon-Tyne. Conzen produced a series of ground-breaking studies, perhaps the most important of which was Alnwick, Northumberland, which was published in 1960.

The object of this analytical approach is the dynamics of urban space, a study of the marks left on the landscape by every phase of society, and of the forms that reflect the needs of its day (Conzen, 2004). The 'townscape' is characterised by its historicity. Conzen notes that, up until the twentieth century in most of the world, the relationship between townscape and 'occupant' society did not witness any tensions that were able to threaten the physiognomy of the towns.

This allowed the townscape to become 'historic', i.e. to accumulate through time a variety of historical forms and meanings. This long historic process generates a cultural identification of the inhabitants with the physical structure of the town that needs to be included in the planning and management process. Recognising the need to manage the townscape as a 'palimpsest' requires the development of adequate analytical tools, based on the understanding of the complex morphological processes (including building fabric, building types, plot patterns, blocks and street patterns).

While the approach promoted by Conzen and later developed by White-hand[54] allowed the development of an interesting analytical framework for the description and explanation of urban historic development processes, its practical application has been very limited.

Box 1.3 Ancient City of Aleppo (Syria)

---

[54]Whitehand, Jeremy W.R.. *Morphology and Historic Urban Landcapes.* Van Oers (ed.), 2010: 35–44.

The project of the rehabilitation of the Ancient City of Aleppo required close to 15 years of cooperation between the city authorities and the German Development Agency, or GTZ (now GIZ). The GTZ primarily provided technical assistance to build capacity (not to implement projects) and Aleppo provided the essential human capital and institutional infrastructure to implement the project. Based on extensive analyses executed in the period of 1993 to 1997, a Development Plan was elaborated in 1999 and approved by the authorities in 2000. Under this Plan complete areas, including public spaces, are being upgraded, such as Bab Quinniserin and Jdeideh, while the Farafra area around the Citadel was recently finished. The rehabilitation project involved a renewal of the water supply (98% implemented) and sewer networks (80% implemented), environmental improvements including paving and traffic management (reduced around the Citadel), the provision of financial and technical support for the rehabilitation of private houses (through the establishment of a Housing Fund), and the design of a special Building Code for the Old City (as the Antiquities Law of Syria doesn't allow re-use and development of monumental structures to accommodate new functions). A Toolkit for Urban Conservation and Development was elaborated, which explains in detail the integrated approach taken with a focus on Arab historic cities in particular – and most of these with the active participation of the resident population, who have seen their living conditions improve significantly while heritage values have been retained. All this has provided a strong impetus for private-sector investments, which are noticeable in a number of high-end boutique hotels currently under development in large monumental palaces in the Old City.

Source: http://www.gtz.de/en/praxis/8234.htm

The Italian school of architectural typological and morphological analysis developed in the 1950s and 1960s under the stewardship of Saverio Muratori[55] has had a greater impact on the development of planning methods, conservation legislation and management practices.

---

[55]Saverio Muratori (1910–1973) was Professor of Architecture at the University of Rome and Venice. Besides being the author of architecture and urban design projects, he pioneered the field of urban morphology with his ground-breaking studies on Venice and Rome.

The critique of Modernism formulated by Giovannoni in the first half of the twentieth century was the starting point for this creative thinker and architect, who defined a new method, the typo-morphological analysis, to understand the evolution of urban forms. The method developed by Muratori hinges on the analysis of the building types, based on the use of cadastral cartography, as the basis for understanding the evolution of the structure of urban areas. This approach is aimed not only at analytical results, but also seeks to be 'operational' (Muratori, 1960), prescriptive, and to develop a theory of city design.

Subsequent developments were overseen by the Italian architect Gianfranco Caniggia,[56] who was able to clarify the 'evolutionary' process of typological transformation. Caniggia tried to relate every building type to a limited number of basic spatial configurations, called *Basic Elements*. Through this method, the structure of the urban form could be explained in a unitary model that included both the physical and the man-made elements (Caniggia and Maffei, 2001).

The concrete application of these principles gave rise in 1979 to important results under the leadership of architects and planners such as Leonardo Benevolo,[57] epitomised in the conservation plans for Bologna[58] and many other historic cities. The typo-morphological approach proved extremely effective in guiding decisions on the conservation and renewal processes of the historic fabric, and is largely used as a basis for planning and management of the building transformation process. Although the British and Italian schools of morphological analysis originated independently and with different backgrounds and aims, their dialogue has given birth to an interdisciplinary field and allowed the principles of typo-morphological analysis to spread to different contexts.[59]

The reaction to Modernism inspired many architects and planners of the post-war generation to update their analytical tools, with the contributions

---

[56] Gianfranco Caniggia (1933–1987) was an Italian architect and Professor at the University of Rome. His main theoretical contribution was the analysis of the historical development of building types. He was a follower of Saverio Muratori and developed his insights, clarifying the basic principle according to which typological transformations occur differently over space and time. His approach is linked to the principles of Structuralism.

[57] Leonardo Benevolo (1923–) is an Italian architect and architectural historian. He has taught at the Universities of Rome, Florence, Venice and Palermo. His writings have gained international recognition. He has also been actively involved in professional work both in Italy and internationally. He is the author of the Master Plan for the conservation of the historic Centre of Bologna and of Plans for several other Italian historic cities.

[58] Bandarin, Francesco. *The Bologna Experience*. Appleyard, Donald (ed.), 1979: 178–202.

[59] In France the urban morphological approach was developed by the School of Architecture of Versailles. Notably, urban typo-morphological analysis has been used to interpret the structure of the Arab historic cities within activities of the Aga Khan's Program on Islamic Architecture of MIT and the Aga Khan Trust for Culture's 'Historic Cities Support Program'. Important contributions on the use of typology and morphology as tools for the interpretation of the dynamics of cities came also from architects such as Aldo Rossi (1978) and Carlo Aymonino (2000). However, their interpretation was based on a different approach, based on the concept of type as a subjective tool for design, rather than an objective element of the urban context. Rossi's work, because of its rich analysis of the historic city, became very popular internationally, in spite of the lack of a clear methodology (Jencks and Kropf, 2006).

of many disciplines, from geography to psychology. New perspectives were developed by those who tried to renew the discipline of urban conservation by using 'perception' as a tool of interpretation and design of space. While these explorations are mainly focused on the design process, they contain important elements for a new interpretation of the urban experience linked to the historic city. In this field, two figures stand out for the importance of what they achieved: Gordon Cullen[60] in Great Britain and Kevin Lynch[61] in the USA.

Cullen's main interest was the visual impact of the city on the human mind, a process that cannot easily be explained by traditional scientific tools of the discipline, but that requires an analysis of the individual's memory and sensorial experiences (Cullen, 1961). As the city is a particular form of landscape, his analysis involved all the elements that make up the environment: buildings, trees, nature, water, traffic, etc. The scope of the analysis was to define a design methodology that extends beyond the mere 'technical' aspects of city making and defines an 'art' that is able to integrate building and environment.

In Cullen's discourse modern planning (in particular for the New Towns) and its technical statutes do not allow seeing the city as a unitary space (a townscape). In his view, by ignoring the lessons that can be learned from the historical spatial layering of the historic city, planning limits its ability to produce quality spaces.

The clear relationship with the 'aesthetic' approach of the nineteenth century and in particular with Sitte's work does not curtail the interest of a view intended to overcome the specialised practice of planning and to propose an innovative vision of integrated city planning and conservation.

While the work of Kevin Lynch is based on similar concerns, his aim is to define a systematic theory of the city. His ground-breaking work, *The Image of the City* (Lynch, 1960), defines a new object of research for the planner: the mental image. To obtain this, Lynch studies the interaction between individuals and the environment, something that belongs to all the inhabitants, and does not require the mediation of a technical expert.

Relying on interviews and maps drawn by the inhabitants, Lynch developed a classification of the 'elements of city image', a new form of urban morphology derived from the individual's view, in which the time dimension of the urban experience has a fundamental role.

Building on lessons learned from the application of this methodology, the author subsequently developed an overall urban design theory (Lynch,

---

[60]Gordon Cullen (1914–1994) was a British architect and urban designer who had a large influence on planning and architecture with his writings and projects. His book, *The Concise Townscape*, first published in 1961, became one of the most popular urban design books of the twentieth century.
[61]Kevin Lynch (1918–1984) was an American architect and city planner, and Professor at MIT, where he conducted innovative research in the field of city planning. His main focus was on how individuals perceive and navigate the urban landscape. He was also actively involved in professional work.

1981) which also led to a broader reflection on the process of change of the environment (Lynch, 1972).

In this work, Lynch questions some fundamental axioms of conservation (What to preserve? Why? How should change be managed?), observing that often the reasons for conservation are linked to social and institutional conventions that are not compatible with the changing needs of society.

He concluded that the ability to select the elements to be preserved and to manage change is preferable to an inflexible reverence for the past. In a way, preservation choices should be informed more by concern for the future rather than for the past.

Box 1.4 Cologne Cathedral (Germany)

The cathedral is Cologne's signature landmark, a Gothic masterpiece built over the course of seven centuries (1248–1880). The Cathedral's prominent place and symbolic function were severely compromised by the city's High-rise Master Plan (*Hochhauskonzept*), which was approved and publicised by local authorities in 2003, foreseeing the construction of a series of high-rise buildings in different parts of the city. One of the locations included the Deutz Quarter located on the right bank of the Rhine and in the Cathedral's view axis, adding to a number of other view axes that had already been blocked by skyscrapers in past years. After an intense debate, which was dominated by the potential deterioration and loss of the historical landmark function of the Cathedral, the World Heritage Committee decided in 2004 to include the property in the List of World Heritage in Danger. The project gave rise to divergent opinions between the city authorities and local preservation bodies over the city's urban development plans, in particular the economic rationale for the high-rise constructions. The threat of a complete delisting resulted in the cancellation of the Deutz Quarter project, after which Cologne Cathedral was reinstated on the World Heritage List in 2006.

Source: World Heritage Committee State of Conservation Report 30 COM 7A.30

While the typo-morphological approach proved to be a useful interpretative tool to guide urban conservation and planning, to many of those interested in the historic context the method has appeared too deterministic and its application excessively mechanistic, and loaded with the same risks that had negatively marked the experience of the Modern Movement.

Another vision that emerged from CIAM was the impetus to update the old idea of *genius loci*, the '*spirit of place*', already embraced by Geddes. This approach found its greatest exponent in the Norwegian architect and theoretician Christian Norberg-Schulz,[62] who adopted Heidegger's phenomenology as a philosophical approach to define the *genius loci* as an existential space, being the relationship of man with the environment (Norberg-Schulz, 1980).

---

[62] Christian Norberg-Schulz (1926–2000), a Norwegian architect, was a member of the CIAM and participated in the last phase of the movement. He based his research and writings on Heidegger's philosophy, developing a complete theory of phenomenology of place.

In this approach, which resembles contemporary definitions of intangible heritage, what matters is not the physical nature of the space, whether built or natural, but rather what happens when the place is 'inhabited'. In this way, existential spaces are shaped not only by those who build them, but also by those who inhabit them (Turgeon, 2009), as the creation of the meaning of a space and of its spiritual qualities can be derived only from those who live in the place.

Clearly, this relationship is dynamic and evolves with time, as it involves living human beings. Norberg-Schulz recalls Heidegger's concept of *Räumlichkeit*, which he translates as 'presence', a space of everyday life where all the 'places' collaborate in the creation of the environmental whole. The 'world of life' is a basic concept used by Norberg-Schulz, which embraces not only the settlements, but also their natural environment. In his view, a space changes from being a '*situs*' to a '*locus*', because life 'takes place' there. The contribution of Norberg-Schulz to the contemporary debate on urban conservation is very significant, since the evolution of the concept of heritage implies recognition of the value of elements to be preserved, while the physical structures are seen as supports.

Although context is a defining concept for planning and architecture, it came to the forefront of the discussion only in the post-war period, also as a reaction to the crisis of Modernism. The discussion of context took many directions. Maurice Culot[63] and Leon Krier[64] criticised the destruction of the historic city brought about by modern developments, and supported instead the use of styles inspired by the traditional city (Culot, 1980; Krier, 1978).

Culot was active in developing a movement to oppose the destruction of historic centres. Krier later provided the intellectual framework for proposals put forward by the Prince of Wales to return to the traditional language of architecture in the development of new plans, as well as for intervention in the historic city (Jencks, 1988).

Out of these positions, the New Urbanism movement emerged, with great appeal especially in the USA (Katz, 1994), a theory that recalls the traditions of Civic Art and the teaching of Hegemann in proposing planning inspired by traditional models. While these positions have garnered wide support among the public and intellectuals, they have never been able to express an architectural language independent from the vernacular or one that simply replicates historical models.

[63] Maurice Culot (1937–) is a Belgian architect, urban planner and architectural historian, specialising in particular in Art Nouveau and Art Deco. He is the founder of the *Archives d'Architecture Moderne (A.A.M.)*, one of the largest European architectural archives and libraries. Culot is one of the most important personalities of the European urban renaissance movement, a champion of the importance of the traditional urban environment for sustainable development and balanced economic growth.

[64] Leon Krier (1946–) is an architect, architectural theorist and urban planner from Luxembourg, and among the most influential representatives of the New Urbanism movement both in Europe and in the USA. He designed the urban area of Poundbury, UK, under the guidance of the Prince of Wales. He is an active practitioner.

During the same period, Colin Rowe[65] published his landmark work, 'Collage City', an influential theoretical essay pointing to the need to end the opposition between conservation and design, and to find a 'workable détente' between the existing and new forms. The new buildings must therefore relate 'to the known, perhaps mundane and, necessarily, memory-laden context from which they emerge'.[66] Rowe's approach proposed an analytical and design method, the *collage*, aimed at establishing a methodological symmetry between old and new, to allow the necessary mediation between change and the existing fabric. In this approach, the historic city is but a fragment, itself fragmented by the historical layering process.

Context was also at the heart of the theoretical work of one of the most innovative American architects of the post-war period, Robert Venturi.[67] Context is important because it expresses meaning, and because it acknowledges the quality of a place, beyond the single building (Venturi, 1966 and 2004).

Venturi opposed the replication of styles, and supported a modern design vocabulary that could ensure harmony between the different elements of the context. As shown by his extensive research on the historic fabric, Venturi supported dissonance as a part of architectural language, as an expression of the complexity of the physical layering process.

Within the approach developed by Rowe and Venturi, a successful formulation was developed by Thomas Schumacher when he coined the term '*Contextualism*' (Schumacher, 1971), an attempt to define a middle ground between the 'freezing' of the historic city and its complete removal and substitution.

Schumacher analyses the way in which the historic city is gradually formed by accretion, and uses this process to define a methodology to guide the new urban design, without any nostalgia for the vernacular. Along with Rowe and Venturi, architects and planners were realising, at that time, that the modern 'dream' of managing and controlling urban processes was a utopia, or even an ideology, and looked for alternative models for interpreting the fragmented and contradictory form of the city.

This research is epitomised in one of the most provocative contemporary interpretations of the city, Rem Koolhaas'[68] *Delirious New York*. Looking at

---

[65] Colin Rowe (1920–1999) was a British-born American architectural historian, theoretician and teacher. He was among the most influential intellectuals in architecture and urban planning, particularly in the field of urban regeneration. Rowe was among the first critics of the failures of the Modern Movement in architecture and developed a theory aimed at harmonising modern buildings and traditional architecture and urban forms. He was a Professor of Architecture at Cornell University.

[66] Rowe and Koetter, 1978: 49. See also: Isenstadt, Sandy. 'Contested Contexts', in Burns and Kahn, 2005: 163.

[67] Robert Venturi (1925–) is an American architect and one of the major figures in the architecture of the twentieth century. Together with his wife and partner, Denise Scott Brown, he contributed to shaping the contemporary discourse on architecture. Venturi was awarded the Pritzker Prize in Architecture in 1991.

[68] Rem Koolhaas (1944–) is a Dutch architect, architectural theorist, urban planner and Professor at the Graduate School of Design at Harvard University, USA. He is the founder of the

an existing complex, modern and historical city, Koolhaas proposed a 'retroactive manifesto' which sought to recompose the fragments of the city into a coherent and consistent interpretation. By simulating a hypothetical 'programme' for Manhattan, this intellectual exercise reveals the complex web of strategies, programmes and theories that make up through time the urban fabric and its contradictions. This facilitates the identification of 'ideal states' (blueprints), the archetypes that constitute the sequenced and overlapped visions of the city (Koolhaas, 1978).

In the past three decades, the attention of the architectural profession has undoubtedly shifted away from urbanism, and has focused more on the 'objects' of design. The contrast between conservation of the existing city and new design has become increasingly strident and has sparked fiery discussions among professionals and institutions (Frampton, 1983).

However, in spite of a dominant culture that dismisses the appreciation of the context in the design process, many architects and urban planners have tried to redefine systemic approaches to the management of the urban development process. These approaches are based on the definition of large operation scales that embrace all the elements of the area, including the historical, the natural features and all the functions of the territory.

A similar perspective had already been put forward in the post-war period[69] and in particular by Vittorio Gregotti[70] (1966) and Ian McHarg[71] (1969). These authors start from different points of view and have different aims, as Gregotti is interested in the integration of architecture into the development of a territory, the urbanised region, while McHarg aims at defining a method to harmoniously integrate urbanisation into the biosphere.

Gregotti tried to establish a neo-rationalist approach, which integrated the concepts of *genius loci* and place, in order to create an 'architecture of place' as part of a rational dialogue between built and natural forms. He aimed to construct a landscape, in the pure classical tradition that – although by no means absent – had been put aside by Modernism. In recognising the discontinuity of space as a value for architecture, Gregotti defined the

---

Office for Metropolitan Architecture, or OMA, and of its research-oriented counterpart AMO (*Architectuur Metropolitaanse Officie*), based in Rotterdam, the Netherlands. He is the author of many award-winning projects and urban design schemes, as well as the coordinator of innovative research programmes. In 2000 Rem Koolhaas was awarded the Pritzker Prize.

[69]Frampton, Kenneth. 'Architecture in the age of globalisation'. International Architecture Biennale Rotterdam, 2007: 171–178.

[70]Vittorio Gregotti (1927–) is an Italian architect and theoretician. He has been Professor of Architecture at the Universities of Venice, Milan and Palermo, and has taught extensively internationally. He directed the Italian architectural Review *Casabella* from 1955 to 1963. He is the author of several important architectural and urban design projects in Italy and abroad and is considered among the masters of his generation.

[71]Ian McHarg (1920–2001) was a British-born landscape architect and a renowned writer on regional planning using natural systems. He was the founder of the Department of Landscape Architecture at the University of Pennsylvania. His book, *Design with Nature*, pioneered the concept of ecological planning.

design process as a web of relationships and meanings that must find its own balance in a scale larger than the one of the project (Gregotti, 1966).

McHarg defined a different, perhaps opposite, approach that gave priority to nature in the definition of the human environment. He took his views beyond the Western 'opposition' of the two concepts, in order to lay the foundation of 'ecological' planning, which integrated all the variables of the natural environment into a new 'Human Ecological Planning', based on the large design scale, both metropolitan and regional (McHarg, 1981).

While these approaches are very different in their scope and methodology, they both addressed issues that have become extremely relevant today. The need to ensure 'sustainability' of development has reopened not only a reflection on the historic city as a 'model' (historic cities are low-energy products and are designed for the long term), but also on the relationship of the city to its territorial and environmental context.

The reconstruction of a unitary discourse on the built environment, able to take into account the needs of urban conservation and those of urban development, has been, and remains today, *the* central issue in the contemporary debate on architecture and urban planning.

As the account of the theories developed in the post-war period shows, the architects' and planners' approaches to urban conservation have been enormously enriched. No single 'school' can claim to have prevailed, and this is indeed evidence of the need to adapt theories and practice to the values of the context, to the forms of society's appreciation of heritage, and to the pattern of social change.

Modern conservation approaches, however, have provided the basis for the development of a wide range of experiments, which in different degrees reflect the many principles expressed by modern architects. An important new dimension of conservation policies is, for instance, the role played by individual and social perceptions of heritage and of its process of change in planning and design choices, an approach that reverses the traditional, elitist, top-down view on heritage values.

The very nature of the historic city, of its meaning and of its historical formation, has been revealed through the analysis of its structural aspects, of its layering processes, and of the formation of collective and individual value systems through time.

Finally, the awareness of the importance of the physical context, built and natural, in the urban conservation and management process has enabled a redefinition both at the micro and the macro scale to ensure a proper understanding of the relationship between the component parts of the city and its region, a necessary step to ensure quality of urban spaces and respect for social needs.

Contemporary historic conservation approaches have been based on these principles, which one can find reflected in the existing charters and documents and implemented in policies and planning frameworks adopted in all regions of the world today. After over a century of theoretical and empirical tests, urban conservation has indeed emerged as a key area of public policy.

2. Urban Conservation as International Public Policy

Venice is like eating an entire box of chocolate liqueurs in one go.

Truman Capote

Urban Conservation Policies after the Second World War

The post-Second-World-War period has seen extensive planned destruction of historic urban areas in all parts of the world. This was linked to the need to respond to high rural–urban migration flows, increasing private-car ownership and investment pressure for residential and commercial developments (Freestone, 2000).

Cities in Europe and North America were the first to suffer from this process in the 1950s and 1960s (Appleyard, 1979), followed by the historic cities of the Arab World and Latin America in the 1960s and 1970s, and later by Asian cities, where that process is still under way at present (Tung, 2001).

The reaction of conservators, planners and architects to the destruction of the historic cities generated in many countries an awareness of the importance of protecting historic urban values and spurred the emergence of policies and legislation aimed at ensuring a future for the historic city in times of great economic and social change.

Good examples of conservation policies exist in many countries, which reflect the different planning traditions. The *secteurs sauvegardés* (conservation areas) that were established in France in 1962; the Law for the Protection of the Historic Centres of 1973 in Italy; and the Civic Amenities Act of 1967 in the United Kingdom are just some of the many examples of planning laws that supported the urban conservation objectives defined in the first part of the twentieth century (Larkham, 1996; Giambruno, 2007; Roberts and Sykes, 2000; Tiesdell et al., 1996; Cohen, 1999). The main emphasis of these programmes was – as it may be expected – on conservation of the physical fabric and the monuments of the city, in recognition of

The Historic Urban Landscape: Managing Heritage in an Urban Century, First Edition. Francesco Bandarin, Ron van Oers.

their continued relevance to society and as a way to maintain the values linked to identity and place.

While many conservation policies successfully pursued the goal of safeguarding the historic urban fabric, the preservation of the social structure has proven much more difficult to achieve. In the post-war period, most historic cities witnessed processes of intense social transformation, which were first linked to the out-migration of a part of the population, usually middle-income and higher-middle-income classes, in search of better housing and living conditions, followed by an influx of the poorer classes, including immigrants, who occupied vacant homes and spaces in the inner city.

A decade or two later, and often coinciding with the first successful results of inner-city conservation and revitalisation, higher-income groups moved in again in search of central residential space, pushing the 'original' residents out and leading in many cases to 'gentrification' processes of the historic city (Bidou-Zachariasen, 2003). The growth of tourism, the rise in local prices and the demand for second homes increased pressure on local populations and accelerated the process of social transformation, which is still ongoing in practically all parts of the world today.

The post-war period has been very important for the growth of the conservation movement at the international level and the establishment of major governmental and non-governmental organisations for heritage conservation. The creation of UNESCO in 1945 and the international heritage safeguarding campaigns developed in the 1950s and 1960s (such as Venice, 1966; Kathmandu, 1979; Havana, 1980; Sana'a 1984) created a favourable context for the launching of important urban conservation initiatives. Meanwhile, the establishment of the main international conservation organisations, such as ICOMOS,[1] ICOM[2] and ICCROM,[3] contributed substantially

---

[1] ICOMOS (International Council on Monuments and Sites) is an international non-governmental organisation created in 1965 at the initiative of UNESCO at the Second Congress of Architects and Specialists of Historic Buildings, held in Venice, Italy. ICOMOS is an association of professionals that currently brings together approximately 9,500 members in 110 countries. Its international secretariat is located in Paris. Its work is based on the principles enshrined in the 1964 International Charter on the Conservation and Restoration of Monuments and Sites (the Venice Charter).

[2] ICOM (International Council of Museums) is an international non-governmental organisation created in 1946 by museum professionals. ICOM is formally associated with UNESCO and has consultative status at the United Nations Economic and Social Council (ECOSOC). Its international secretariat is located in Paris. ICOM has 26,000 members in 151 countries, 118 National Committees, 30 International Scientific Committees and 17 affiliated organisations.

[3] ICCROM (International Centre for the Study of the Preservation and Restoration of Cultural Property) is an intergovernmental organisation (IGO) dedicated to the conservation of cultural heritage, established and located in Rome in 1959, following the adoption of the proposal by the UNESCO General Conference held in New Delhi in 1956. It has 129 Member Countries.

to the development and internationalisation of the debate on urban conservation.

Urban Conservation in International Charters and Standard-Setting Instruments

These processes made it possible to frame the issue of urban conservation within a system of international principles and charters, the founding document of which was certainly the 1964 *International Charter for the Conservation and Restoration of Monuments and Sites* (Venice Charter), adopted by ICOMOS in 1965. This document, which was the culminating point of a long debate on heritage conservation spanning the first half of the twentieth century, focused on the conservation of historic monuments and their setting, and the need to preserve their authenticity from changes to their physical structure.[4]

It is important to note that this document makes no reference to the historic city, other than as a 'setting' for monuments. This is certainly not due to a lack of awareness of the problems facing the historic city, but rather to the fact that the original drafters were restorers and art historians, and not specialists in urban conservation.

Other texts that deal indirectly with the historic city were adopted at that time. Of particular note is the 1962 UNESCO *Recommendation concerning the Safeguarding of the Beauty and Character of Landscapes and Sites*,[5] which is a far-sighted document that focuses the attention of the

---

[4] 1964 ICOMOS Venice Charter, Article 1: '*The concept of a historic monument embraces not only the single architectural work but also the urban or rural setting in which is found the evidence of a particular civilization, a significant development or a historic event. This applies not only to great works of art but also to more modest works of the past, which have acquired cultural significance with the passing of time.*'

[5] The Definition and General Principles of the Recommendation Concerning the Safeguarding of the Beauty and Character of Landscapes and Sites are as follows:

I. Definition
  1. *For the recommendation, the safeguarding of the beauty and character of landscapes and sites is taken to mean the preservation and, where possible, the restoration of the aspect of natural, rural and urban landscapes and sites, whether natural or man-made, which have a cultural or aesthetic interest or form typical natural surroundings.*
  2. *The provisions of this recommendation are also intended to supplement measures for the protection of nature.*

II. General principles
  3. *The studies and measures to be adopted with a view to the safeguarding of landscapes and sites should extend to the whole territory of a State, and should not be confined to certain selected landscapes or sites.*
  4. *In choosing the measures to be adopted, due account should be taken of the relative significance of the landscapes and sites concerned. These measures might vary in accordance with the character and size of the landscapes and sites, their location and the nature of the dangers with which they are threatened.*
  5. *Protection should not be limited to natural landscapes and sites, but should also extend to landscapes and sites whose formation is due wholly or in part to the work of man. Thus, special provisions should be made to ensure the safeguarding of certain urban landscapes and sites which are, in general, the most threatened, especially by building operations and land speculation. Special protection should be accorded to the approaches to monuments.*'

international community on the dangers of spoiling not only the natural beauty of places, but also the beauty of man-made landscapes, and specifically urban landscapes. Also in the spirit of that time is the 1968 UNESCO *Recommendation concerning the Preservation of Cultural Property Endangered by Public or Private Works.*[6] This Recommendation is, unlike previous texts, quite detailed in recommending the administrative and financial measures needed for the proper preservation of properties. Although not exclusively addressed to urban historic areas, the Recommendation provides detailed study of their management, pointing to the need to develop both adequate planning tools and more detailed management regulations.

Some of the limitations of this first phase of preparation of the standard-setting instruments for heritage conservation were addressed in two important standard-setting instruments issued by UNESCO in the 1970s: the *Convention concerning the Protection of the World Cultural and Natural Heritage* (World Heritage Convention) of 1972 and the *Recommendation concerning the Safeguarding and Contemporary Role of Historic Areas* ('Nairobi' Recommendation) of 1976.

The World Heritage Convention (UNESCO, 2005) makes no direct reference to historic cities, but defines them as part of the category of 'groups of buildings', a definition which is still in use today.

The *Operational Guidelines for the Implementation of the World Heritage Convention*, however, added a more complete definition of

---

[6]The Recommendation Concerning the Preservation of Cultural Property Endangered by Public or Private Works offers a detailed set of definitions and prescriptions for the conservation of historic areas, as exemplified by the paragraph dealing with historic centres:

'24. Important archaeological sites, and, in particular, prehistoric sites as they are difficult to recognize, historic quarters in urban or rural areas, groups of traditional structures, ethnological structures of previous cultures and other immovable cultural property which would otherwise be endangered by public or private works should be protected by zoning or scheduling:

(a) Archaeological reserves should be zoned or scheduled and, if necessary, immovable property purchased, to permit thorough excavation or the preservation of the ruins found at the site.

(b) Historic quarters in urban or rural centres and groups of traditional structures should be zoned and appropriate regulations adopted to preserve their setting and character, such as the imposition of controls on the degree to which historically or artistically important structures can be renovated and the type and design of new structures which can be introduced. The preservation of monuments should be an absolute requirement of any well-designed plan for urban redevelopment especially in historic cities or districts. Similar regulations should cover the area surrounding a scheduled monument or site and its setting to preserve its association and character. Due allowance should be made for the modification of ordinary regulations applicable to new construction; these should be placed in abeyance when new structures are introduced into an historical zone. Ordinary types of commercial advertising by means of posters and illuminated announcements should be forbidden, but commercial establishments could be allowed to indicate their presence by means of judiciously presented signs.'

historic cities[7] by listing three main types: a) towns no longer inhabited; b) inhabited historic towns; c) new towns of the twentieth century. These definitions are aimed at guiding the process of inscription of properties on the World Heritage List (types of physical structure to be considered, perimeters, etc.), and do not contain recommendations or policy prescriptions.

In spite of these limitations, the 1972 World Heritage Convention represents a 'quantum leap' in the field of conservation for three reasons. Firstly, for the first time in history, the principles that had been debated among experts for nearly a century became the object of an international legal system. Secondly, the Convention brought together principles that were previously separated into different categories relating to the natural and cultural realms. Thirdly, it established a system of international responsibility in conserving and monitoring the evolution of sites deemed to be of 'Outstanding Universal Value' (OUV).[8]

---

[7]1972 World Heritage Convention's Operational Guidelines, Annex 3, paragraph 14:

(ii) *Inhabited historic towns: in case of inhabited historic towns the difficulties are numerous, largely owing to the fragility of their urban fabric (which has in many cases been seriously disrupted since the advent of the industrial era) and the runaway speed with which their surroundings have been urbanized. To qualify for inscription, towns should compel recognition because of their architectural interest and should not be considered only on the intellectual grounds of the role they may have played in the past or their value as historical symbols under criterion (vi) for the inscription of cultural properties on the World Heritage List (see Paragraph 77 (vi) of the Operational Guidelines). To be eligible for inscription in the List, the spatial organization, structure, materials, forms and, where possible, functions of a group of buildings should essentially reflect the civilization or succession of civilizations which have prompted the nomination of the property. Four categories can be distinguished:*

a) *Towns which are typical of a specific period or culture, which have been almost wholly preserved and which have remained largely unaffected by subsequent developments. Here the property to be listed is the entire town together with its surroundings, which must also be protected;*

b) *Towns that have evolved along characteristic lines and have preserved, sometimes in the midst of exceptional natural surroundings, spatial arrangements and structures that are typical of the successive stages in their history. Here the clearly defined historic part takes precedence over the contemporary environment;*

c) *Historic centres that cover exactly the same area as ancient towns and are now enclosed within modern cities. Here it is necessary to determine the precise limits of the property in its widest historical dimensions and to make appropriate provision for its immediate surroundings;*

d) *Sectors, areas or isolated units which, even in the residual state in which they have survived, provide coherent evidence of the character of a historic town which has disappeared. In such cases surviving areas and buildings should bear sufficient testimony to the former whole.*

Historic centres and historic areas should be listed only where they contain a large number of ancient buildings of monumental importance which provide a direct indication of the characteristic features of a town of exceptional interest. Nominations of several isolated and unrelated buildings, which allegedly represent in themselves a town whose urban fabric has ceased to be discernible, should not be encouraged.

However, nominations could be made regarding properties that occupy a limited space but have had a major influence on the history of town planning. In such cases, the nomination should make it clear that it is the monumental group that is to be listed and that the town is mentioned only incidentally as the place where the property is located. Similarly, if a building of clearly outstanding universal value is located in severely degraded or insufficiently representative urban surroundings, it should, of course, be listed without any special reference to the town.'

[8]Outstanding Universal Value means cultural and/or natural significance which is so exceptional as to transcend national boundaries and to be of common importance for present and future generations of all humanity (UNESCO, 2008).

Algiers

Valparaiso

Lalibela

Edinburgh

The inscription of over 250 cities in the World Heritage List marks the high point of the recognition of the historic city as heritage in all regions of the world. Their variety and diversity, however, challenge the traditional conservation frameworks.

If the World Heritage Convention did not bring about a major conceptual innovation in the field of urban conservation, it certainly fostered the development of methodological approaches in the definition and management of urban heritage,[9] and it helped to establish this category as one of the most important in all regions of the world.[10] Urban conservation received far greater attention during the European Architectural Heritage Year in 1975, when two milestone documents were issued, namely the *Declaration of Amsterdam*[11] and the *European Charter of the Architectural Heritage*.[12]

---

[9]The Operational Guidelines of the World Heritage Convention ask for several 'tests' for the inscription of a property into the World Heritage List, the most important ones being the tests of authenticity and integrity. The application of these principles (clearly inspired by the Venice Charter and derived from the field of monuments conservation) to the historic city has always been a difficult and contentious endeavour, showing the contradictions of this 'translation'. See paragraph 89 of the Operational Guidelines:

> *'For properties nominated under criteria (i) to (vi), the physical fabric of the property and/or its significant features should be in good condition, and the impact of deterioration processes controlled. A significant proportion of the elements necessary to convey the totality of the value conveyed by the property should be included. Relationships and dynamic functions present in cultural landscapes, historic towns or other living properties essential to their distinctive character should also be maintained.'*

[10]At the 40th anniversary of the Convention, over 250 historic cities and historic urban areas are represented in the World Heritage List, making up a third of the sites inscribed.

[11]The Declaration of Amsterdam, issued by the Congress on the Architectural Heritage (21 to 25 October 1975) includes the following points:

a. *'Apart from its priceless cultural value, Europe's architectural heritage gives to her peoples the consciousness of their common history and common future. Its preservation is, therefore, a matter of vital importance.*

b. *The architectural heritage includes not only individual. buildings of exceptional quality and their surroundings, but also all areas of towns or villages of historic or cultural interest.*

c. *Since these treasures are the joint possession of all the peoples of Europe, they have a joint responsibility to protect them against the growing dangers with which they are threatened – neglect and decay, deliberate demolition, incongruous new construction and excessive traffic.*

d. *Architectural conservation must be considered, not as a marginal issue, but as a major objective of town and country planning.*

e. *Local authorities, with whom most of the important planning decisions rest, have a special responsibility for the protection of the architectural heritage and should assist one another by the exchange of ideas and information.*

f. *The rehabilitation of old areas should be conceived and carried out in such a way as to ensure that, where possible, this does not necessitate a major change in the social composition of the residents, all sections of society should share in the benefits of restoration financed by public funds.*

g. *The legislative and administrative measures required should be strengthened and made more effective in all countries.*

h. *To help meet the cost of restoration, adaptation and maintenance of buildings and areas of architectural or historic interest, adequate financial assistance should be made available to local authorities and financial support and fiscal relief should likewise be made available to private owners.*

i. *The architectural heritage will survive only if it is appreciated by the public and in particular by the younger generation. Educational programmes for all ages should, therefore, give increased attention to this subject.*

j. *Encouragement should be given to independent organizations – international, national and local – which help to awaken public interest.*

k. *Since the new buildings of today will be the heritage of tomorrow, every effort must be made to ensure that contemporary architecture is of a high quality.'*

[12]The issues addressed by the European Charter of the Architectural Heritage adopted by the Council of Europe in October 1975 are the following:

1. The European architectural heritage consists not only of our most important monuments: it also includes the groups of lesser buildings in our old towns and characteristic villages in their natural or man-made settings.

These documents clearly establish the link between conservation and urban planning and point to urban heritage, including the 'lesser' fabric of its vernacular expressions, as a key component of all conservation policies. They also refer to the need to protect the social structure of historic cities as part of the conservation process. Urban heritage is seen – in ways that reflect the experiments that were conducted at the time in several countries – as cultural 'capital' to be valued both for its uses and as a source of inspiration for education and social development.

Finally, the documents also make reference to the role of contemporary architecture in historic areas. These principles were later included in the Council of Europe's *Convention for the Protection of the Architectural Heritage* of Europe adopted in Granada in 1985.[13]

The importance of historic urban areas, however, was clear in the policy debates among experts and officials and, shortly after, UNESCO prepared and adopted what is – to this day – regarded as the fundamental text on urban conservation, the *Recommendation concerning the Safeguarding and Contemporary Role of Historic Areas*, which was adopted in Nairobi in November 1976.

While not dealing exclusively with urban areas,[14] this document includes all the elements relevant to urban conservation. This Recommendation established the following important definitions and guidelines:

---

2. The past as embodied in the architectural heritage provides the sort of environment indispensable to a balanced and complete life.
3. The architectural heritage is a capital of irreplaceable spiritual, cultural, social and economic value.
4. The structure of historic centres and sites is conducive to a harmonious social balance.
5. The architectural heritage has an important part to play in education.
6. This heritage is in danger.
7. Integrated conservation averts these dangers.
8. Integrated conservation depends on legal, administrative, financial and technical support.

[13] The Convention for the Protection of the Architectural Heritage of Europe, Granada, 1985; see, in particular, Article 10:

'Each Party undertakes to adopt integrated conservation policies which:
1. include the protection of the architectural heritage as an essential town and country planning objective and ensure that this requirement is taken into account at all stages both in the drawing up of development plans and in the procedures for authorising work;
2. promote programmes for the restoration and maintenance of the architectural heritage;
3. make the conservation, promotion and enhancement of the architectural heritage a major feature of cultural, environmental and planning policies;
4. facilitate whenever possible in the town and country planning process the conservation and use of certain buildings whose intrinsic importance would not warrant protection within the meaning of Article 3, paragraph 1, of this Convention but which are of interest from the point of view of their setting in the urban or rural environment and of the quality of life;
5. foster, as being essential to the future of the architectural heritage, the application and development of traditional skills and materials.'

[14] The definition of historic areas in the 1976 Nairobi Recommendation is the following:

'(a) 'Historic and architectural (including vernacular) areas' shall be taken to mean any groups of buildings, structures and open spaces including archaeological and paleontological sites, constituting human settlements in an urban or rural environment, the cohesion and value of which, from the archaeological, architectural, prehistoric, historic, aesthetic or socio-cultural point of view are recognized. Among these 'areas', which are very varied in nature, it is possible to distinguish the following in particular: prehistoric sites, historic towns, old urban quarters, villages and hamlets as well as homogeneous monumental groups, it being understood that the latter should as a rule be carefully preserved unchanged.'

- The concept that historic areas represent the living presence of the past in modern life and that they are expressions of the cultural diversity of human societies in time and space, as well as a powerful factor of identity for individuals and societies;
- The need to consider historic areas and their surroundings as a totality and coherent whole, whose protection and conservation are a collective responsibility and should be the object of public policies and ad hoc legislation;
- The need to preserve the character of the setting of historic areas and to adapt new interventions to the urban context;
- The need to associate cultural and social revitalisation to physical conservation, in order to preserve the traditional social fabric and functions of the historic areas;
- The need to develop and implement appropriate measures for the conservation of historic areas, including land-use controls, building regulations, conservation plans, traffic-management schemes, pollution controls, appropriate funding and subsidy mechanisms, participatory frameworks and public awareness and education activities.

Box 2.1 Samarkand – Crossroads of Cultures (Uzbekistan)

Samarkand, with its many masterpieces of Islamic architecture, has been a crossroads of cultures through the ages. The site had been well preserved despite the absence of specific regulation tools. However, during the last decade the authorities have embarked on an almost complete substitution of traditional building materials with modern ones, with the loss of traditional construction practices. This situation was aggravated by various urban development restoration projects, which have caused a serious loss of authenticity and integrity in the thirteenth-century townscape. Moreover, the construction of a four-lane highway right through the World Heritage property in 2006 further fuelled discussions between the local authorities and the World Heritage Committee as regards the elaboration of a Management Plan with a strengthening of the property's governance. To facilitate a cooperation project with the local authorities and other partners, international assistance was made available to the State Party for the implementation of a strategic approach to urban conservation.

Sources: World Heritage Committee State of Conservation Reports 32 COM 7B.79 and 33 COM 7B.84

The 1976 Recommendation represented an advanced point in the international debate on urban conservation, especially as it laid out in great detail the standards and policies to be followed by practitioners and governments. In this sense, it still remains a document of great modernity and relevance for urban conservation. At the same time, it reflects the spirit of an age that had greater confidence in the power of public planning, with an overly optimistic view of public funding capacities.

The document proves particularly weak in the sections dealing with social and economic measures, as it had a fundamentally 'static' view of social processes and foresaw the transfer to the public of the extra costs of restoration. Furthermore, it underestimated two of the main processes that have affected urban conservation processes in the past 30 years, i.e. the gentrification process and the development of a dominant tourism industry.

In order to address the specific character of urban conservation and to fill the gaps existing in the Venice Charter, ICOMOS decided in 1987 to issue a specific document, the *Charter for the Conservation of Historic Towns and Urban Areas*, known as the Washington Charter.[15]

This Charter is the first international document exclusively dedicated to historic urban areas and their conservation. In this regard, it presents many important innovations in the definition of urban heritage, as it links its 'authenticity' not only to the physical structures and their relationships, but also to the setting and surroundings, as well as the functions acquired by the city over time.[16]

The Charter defines the historic city in its complexity and specificity, reflecting also the main findings of the post-war architects and planners: cities are seen in relation to their surrounding environment, and attention is given to social values and participation. The Charter also points to the main problems planners and conservators had to deal with in the urban conservation and management process: automobile traffic, infrastructure and the restructuring of economic activity such as the shift from manufacturing to services.

---

[15] The ICOMOS Washington Charter was first elaborated in the town of Eger in Hungary in 1986, but later reformulated and issued in 1987 as the Washington Charter at the ICOMOS 8th General Assembly.

[16] Excerpts from the Charter for the Conservation of Historic Towns and Urban Areas:

'2. Qualities to be preserved include the historic character of the town or urban area and all those material and spiritual elements that express this character, especially:

a) *Urban patterns as defined by lots and streets;*
b) *Relationships between buildings and green and open spaces;*
c) *The formal appearance, interior and exterior, of buildings as defined by scale, size, style, construction, materials, colour and decoration;*
d) *The relationship between the town or urban area and its surrounding setting, both natural and man-made; and:*
e) *The various functions that the town or urban area has acquired over time. Any threat to these qualities would compromise the authenticity of the historic town or urban area.'*

This document focuses principally on the physical aspects of urban conservation, and it relies essentially on a form of local plan, the 'conservation plan', as the main tool for guiding the process, leaving aside considerations of national and local policies that are needed to support the conservation effort. While many of the processes responsible for the physical and social transformation of historic cities, such as the demise of traditional activities, gentrification, and the impact of tourism, are taken into consideration, the Washington Charter advocates public intervention as the main mechanism for controlling social and economic processes, which reflects the planning culture of the times.

Similarly, the need to link economic productivity to the conservation process is not fully acknowledged, nor is the need to ensure sustainability in maintenance and conservation cycles. In the decades following the adoption of the UNESCO Nairobi Recommendation and the ICOMOS Washington Charter, no other international text concerning historic cities was issued. And yet, discussion of the concept of heritage and its management needs was very intense, reflecting in part the advancement of the discipline, and the need to move away from an excessively 'Eurocentric' framework that had been dominant for a century.

The 1994 *Nara Document on Authenticity* is defined as an extension of the Venice Charter, one which allows it to adapt to the expanding scope of heritage in the contemporary world. The Document defines heritage as an expression of the diversity of cultures and links conservation practices to the values attributed to heritage by each culture. In this respect, the concept of authenticity, as defined by the Venice Charter, needs to be understood in relation to criteria which originate in their respective cultural spheres.

Article 13 of the Nara Document states: '*Depending on the nature of the cultural heritage, its cultural context, and its evolution through time, authenticity judgements may be linked to the worth of a great variety of sources of information. Aspects of the sources may include form and design, materials and substance, use and function, traditions and techniques, location and setting, and spirit and feeling, and other internal and external factors. The use of these sources permits elaboration of the specific artistic, historic, social, and scientific dimensions of the cultural heritage being examined.*'

These documents are symptomatic of the evolution of the concept of heritage that has taken place in recent decades, which is also reflected in the introduction of 'Cultural Landscape' as a category in the World Heritage Convention in 1992.

Awareness of the role of intangible values in the international conservation community was enhanced by the adoption by the General Conference of UNESCO in 2003 of the *Convention for the Safeguarding of the Intangible Cultural Heritage*, an important new addition to existing international standard-setting instruments for heritage conservation that complements the action of the World Heritage Convention in an area of great public international interest.

The 2003 Convention, among other conceptual contributions, facilitates the recognition of the role of multiple layers of identity and other associated intangible aspects in cultural landscapes and historic urban landscapes, among others.[17]

The subsequent *Yamato Declaration on Integrated Approaches for Safeguarding Tangible and Intangible Cultural Heritage* (2004) promoted a comprehensive approach linking the 1972 World Heritage Convention and the 2003 Convention.[18] Finally, the importance of cultural diversity in the definition of heritage values has been reaffirmed with the adoption of the UNESCO *Universal Declaration on Cultural Diversity*[19] in 2001, and of the UNESCO *Convention on the Protection and Promotion of the Diversity of Cultural Expressions*[20] in 2005.

Regional Charters

In addition to the international charters and standard-setting instruments, other noteworthy texts include a group of regional charters, such as the

---

[17] The Convention for the Safeguarding of the Intangible Cultural Heritage, in its Article 2, defines Intangible Heritage as follows:

'1. The "intangible cultural heritage" means the practices, representations, expressions, knowledge, skills – as well as the instruments, objects, artefacts and cultural spaces associated therewith – that communities, groups and , in some cases, individuals recognize as part of their cultural heritage. This intangible cultural heritage, transmitted from generation to generation, is constantly recreated by communities and groups in response to their environment, their interaction with nature and their history, and provides them with a sense of identity and continuity, thus promoting respect for cultural diversity and human creativity. For the purposes of this Convention, consideration will be given solely to such intangible cultural heritage as is compatible with existing international human rights instruments, as well as with the requirements of mutual respect among communities, groups and individuals, and of sustainable development.'

[18] The Yamato Declaration on Integrated Approaches for Safeguarding Tangible and Intangible Cultural Heritage states in its Article 11:

'taking into account the interdependence, as well as the differences between tangible and intangible cultural heritage, and between the approaches for their safeguarding, we deem it appropriate that, wherever possible, integrated approaches be elaborated to the effect that the safeguarding of the tangible and intangible heritage of communities and groups is consistent and mutually beneficial and reinforcing.'

[19] The Universal Declaration on Cultural Diversity, in its Article 7, defines Cultural Heritage as the wellspring of creativity:

'Creation draws on the roots of cultural tradition, but flourishes in contact with other cultures. For this reason, heritage in all its forms must be preserved, enhanced and handed on to future generations as a record of human experience and aspirations, so as to foster creativity in all its diversity and to inspire genuine dialogue among cultures'.

[20] The Convention on the Protection and Promotion of the Diversity of Cultural Expressions states (Article 4.1):

'Cultural diversity' refers to the manifold ways in which the cultures of groups and societies find expression. These expressions are passed on within and among groups and societies. Cultural diversity is made manifest not only through the varied ways in which the cultural heritage of humanity is expressed, augmented and transmitted through the variety of cultural expressions, but also through diverse modes of artistic creation, production, dissemination, distribution and enjoyment, whatever the means and technologies used.

ICOMOS Australia *Burra Charter* of 1979, the ICOMOS Brazil *Itaipava Charter* of 1987, the ICOMOS Japan *Machi-nami Charter* of 2000, as well as the *Aalborg Charter* of 1994. Besides these regional charters, the ICOMOS *Xi'an Declaration* of 2005 is also an important document which has enriched the 'doctrine' in past decades.

The 1979 (revised in 1999) Australia ICOMOS *Charter for Places of Cultural Significance*, or *Burra Charter*, although it refers to a national situation, is important as it introduces the concept of 'places of cultural significance'. It establishes a distinction between the values to be preserved (significance) and the place itself, defined as its fabric, setting, use, associations, meanings, records, related places and related objects.

The Charter brings to the fore a set of values, of intangible, symbolic or spiritual nature, which are normally not found in the traditional 'Western' charters, and addresses important issues for conservation and management. Article 2.2 states that 'the aim of conservation is to retain the cultural significance of a place', while 'conservation is an integral part of good management of places of cultural significance' (Article 2.3). Moreover, continued use is seen as a main feature of the cultural significance of a place.

The First Brazilian Seminar on the Preservation and Revitalization of Historic Centers, in Itaipava in July 1987, issued the Brazil ICOMOS *Itaipava Charter*, which also presents interesting perspectives on urban heritage, as it sees the city not only as a physical artefact, comprising built and natural features, but also as a 'living' heritage made up of the 'experience' of its inhabitants.

Under its Basic Principles, the Charter states: '*urban historical sites may be considered as those spaces where manifold evidences (sic) of the city's cultural production concentrate. They are to be circumscribed rather in terms of their operational value as "critical areas" than in opposition to the city's non-historical places, since the city in its totality is a historical entity (I)*'. Furthermore, '*Urban historical sites are part of a wider totality, comprising the natural and the built environment and the everyday living experience of their dwellers as well. Within this wider space, enriched with values of remote or recent origin and permanently undergoing a dynamic process of successive transformations, new urban spaces may be considered as environmental evidences in their formative stages (II)*'. These principles stress the importance of residents and traditional activities in historic urban sites, and see revitalisation as a continuous and permanent process, where the social values of an urban property should prevail over its market value.

The Japan ICOMOS *Charter for the Conservation of Historical Towns and Settlements of Japan* (*Machi-nami Charter*) of 2000 refers to the historic urban core in both its tangible and intangible components, as well as its physical and spiritual aspects (Machi-nami). The Association for Machi-nami Conservation and Regeneration was founded in 1974 as a liaison and cooperation organisation for local residents' movements, in all regions of Japan, to promote the conservation of historic towns. The Charter contains the idea of a community's surrounding natural and

Box 2.2 Historic Centre of Salvador de Bahia (Brazil)

The old town, founded in 1549 and inscribed on the World Heritage List in 1985, was the first slave market in the New World and includes many outstanding colonial monuments and buildings. In 1993 the World Heritage Committee expressed concern about the renewal works and relocation of the inhabitants as part of a Rehabilitation Project, launched by the state government a year earlier. The project intended to reverse the economic decline and physical degradation process based on three intervention guidelines established by Bahia's Artistic and Cultural Heritage Institute: the physical and territorial structure, the social and economic development process, and the juridical and institutional framework, especially in terms of property ownership in the area of intervention. The plan consisted of a renewal of the use of the city blocks' cores, altering the design and arrangement of the backyards to turn them into courtyards, for which some buildings had to be demolished to provide space for new commercial and touristic uses. The project is still under implementation (the seventh phase) and has been financed by the Brazilian Ministry of Culture and the Inter-American Development Bank (IDB). The project, which was strongly criticised during its initial phases because of the lack of analytical studies and the relocation of its poorest inhabitants, has shown important conservation improvements, especially in its current phase. After a revision of the first six phases of the project, in 2000, changes were made to the scope and focus of the plan as regards the following seventh phase. Consequently, many programmes have been created to support the site's rehabilitation in terms of housing. Furthermore, in 2009 the legal framework at the municipal level was strengthened and guidelines were established for urban intervention at the social and urban scales, emphasising management and the involvement of local stakeholders. Positive effects have been observed through the introduction of new dynamics in the local economy. This has resulted in a mix of diversified uses in the downtown area, while still remaining attractive in terms of housing and business investment, after almost 20 years of being focused on tourism, entertainment, and recreation.

Source: Zancheti Mendes, 2010

cultural environment, stating that 'the aim of conserving the historic town is not only to save groups of houses and the surrounding landscape as material objects, but to attempt to reconstruct the relationships between the daily life of the residents, the houses and the surrounding settings' (paragraph 3). Furthermore, paragraph 6 on The Importance of Conservation explains that the typical lifespan of traditional Japanese houses is short, due to topographical, climatic and seismic conditions, and the fact that architectural structures are built of mainly natural materials, all of which make them accident-prone. 'In spite of this, what has formed historic towns rich in local character, is a continuous practice of conservation, which includes the transmission of techniques to replace decayed material with new material, and is the result of a cycle that has been repeated many times over the course of centuries. Moreover, techniques, customs, and a set of values locally held in common, are integrated into daily life and the traditional events of the year'. This particular practice of conservation formed the basis of the discussion on authenticity in Nara in 1994.

Luang Prabang

Sichuan Village in the Danba Region

Village in Southern Arabia

Tripoli

Timbuktu

Zanzibar

Paramaribo

Quito

Bordeaux

Reine in the Lofoten Islands

Recognising and valuing regional diversity of urban heritage is at the heart of the Historic Urban Landscape approach. This diversity is the result of the layering of tangible and intangible expressions and should inform policies and strategies for urban preservation.

In 1994 at the European Conference on Sustainable Cities and Towns, in Aalborg (Denmark), the *Charter of European Cities and Towns towards Sustainability* (*Aalborg Charter*) was adopted, which affirmed the enduring role of cities as centres of social life, economic drivers, and guardians of culture, heritage and tradition, as well as of industry, craft, trade, education and government. It acknowledged the relationship between today's urban lifestyle – especially the separation of functions, patterns of transport, industrial production, agriculture, consumption and leisure activities – and the environmental problems and lack of social equity that humankind is facing. It recognised the limits of the world's natural resources, the need to live within the carrying capacity of nature, as well as the vital role that cities as centres of consumption have to play in addressing global warming and achieving environmental sustainability.[21]

The Aalborg Charter defined sustainability as a creative, local, balance-seeking process that is central to the responsible management of cities, and insisted that decision-making processes must prioritise the conservation and replenishment of the natural capital of cities, their quality of life, sustainable land use and mobility patterns – including reducing the need for movement by encouraging mixed-use, higher-density neighbourhoods – and the use of renewable energy sources.

The Charter promoted the idea of equitable regional interdependency, to balance the flows between city and countryside and prevent cities from merely exploiting the resources of surrounding areas. It also urged an ecosystem approach to urban management and envisioned a greatly increased role for citizens in establishing and implementing long-term local action plans.

These documents represent an important evolution in concepts of heritage, in that they contain new points of departure, such as retaining the cultural significance of a place, introducing systemic dynamics with the recognition of places as living heritage, or emphasising specific

---

[21] The Aalborg Charter's definition of sustainability is the following:

'I.2   The Notion and Principles of Sustainability

We, cities & towns, understand that the idea of sustainable development helps us to base our standard of living on the carrying capacity of nature. We seek to achieve social justice, sustainable economies, and environmental sustainability. Social justice will necessarily have to be based on economic sustainability and equity, which require environmental sustainability. Environmental sustainability means maintaining the natural capital. It demands from us that the rate at which we consume renewable material, water and energy resources does not exceed the rate at which the natural systems can replenish them, and that the rate at which we consume non-renewable resources does not exceed the rate at which sustainable renewable resources are replaced. Environmental sustainability also means that the rate of emitted pollutants does not exceed the capacity of the air, water, and soil to absorb and process them.

Furthermore, environmental sustainability entails the maintenance of biodiversity; human health; as well as air, water, and soil qualities at standards sufficient to sustain human life and well-being, as well as animal and plant life, for all time.

I.3   Local Strategies Towards Sustainability

We are convinced that the city or town is both the largest unit capable of initially addressing the many urban architectural, social, economic, political, natural resource and environmental imbalances damaging our modern world and the smallest scale at which problems can be meaningfully resolved in an integrated, holistic and sustainable fashion. As each city is different, we have to find our individual ways towards sustainability. We shall integrate the principles of sustainability in all our policies to make the respective strengths of our cities and towns the basis of locally appropriate strategies.'

cultural contexts, such as *Machi-nami*, standing for the mix of tangible and intangible components that make up the whole, including physical settlement, residents, and the natural and cultural environment, which are inseparable.

Future work on the definition of urban heritage and on its conservation principles and practices will be based on the intellectual history of conservation, and will have to build on these innovative approaches.

Box 2.3 The Belvedere Strategy in the Netherlands

The Amsterdam *Waterlinie* (the historical military defence line of the city) is a national project in the Belvedere Policy document, which aims to 'preserve through development'.

In 1999, the government of the Netherlands adopted the Belvedere Memorandum, a policy document aimed at promoting culture-oriented sustainable development programmes.

The objective of the Belvedere strategy is to promote a respectful approach in regard to cultural and historic values within spatial development. This is to be accomplished neither by vetoing change nor by burying the past, but by seeking effective ways to create win–win situations: to use space in such a way that an object of cultural and/or historic importance is given a place and will contribute to the quality of its newly created surroundings.

Cultural-historic identity is to be seen as a determining factor in the future spatial design of the Netherlands, for which government policy shall aim to create appropriate conditions.

This central objective can be seen in terms of the following subsidiary aims:

- To recognise, and to maintain the recognisability of, cultural-historic identity in both rural and urban areas, as a quality and basic starting point for further developments.

- To strengthen and exploit cultural-historic identity and the qualities which go to define such identity, in those areas of the Netherlands which are most valuable in terms of cultural history, the so-called *Belvedere areas*.
- To create appropriate conditions for the initiatives of third parties aimed at a thematic strengthening of cultural history.
- To disseminate knowledge concerning cultural history and to promote opportunities whereby cultural history can be used as a source of inspiration in spatial planning and design.
- To promote cooperation between citizens, organisations, local and regional authorities and government.
- To improve the practicality and use of existing instruments.

The Belvedere strategy also advocates presenting 'the past' (i.e. heritage) as a single, undivided concern. Instead of considering buried archaeological sites, historic buildings and historically important landscapes as separate entities, they should be seen as a single integrated public concern: cultural heritage.

The Belvedere Memorandum has been applied for a ten-year period, from 2000 to 2010, with an annual budget of approximately €7,500,000. For the first five years, more than half of this amount was dedicated to a subsidy scheme in which provinces, municipalities and private organisations had access to funding for research, information gathering and planning processes at the local and regional level. During the first seven years, more than 300 projects were subsidised by Belvedere funding. A carry-over effect has also been evident in national and provincial spatial policies. Making use of cultural heritage in development plans is being considered everywhere in the Netherlands: from the 'national landscapes' to urban restructuring projects, and from water-management plans to education. The tasks for the future will be aimed at consolidating the successes achieved so far by continuing to develop specific, usable information and instruments while reaching new target groups.

Source: Netherlands State Government, 1999

Rethinking Urban Conservation[22]

In the first decade of this new century, UNESCO and other conservation and professional organisations[23] have opened a discussion on the principles of urban conservation established during the previous half-century, which aimed at assessing the viability of these principles in relation to the new challenges that have been unleashed by the forces of globalisation. While this discussion and the revision of the principles are still under way, some important points have surfaced in recent documents and declarations.

[22] Part of this paragraph is adapted from Bandarin, 2011a.
[23] The following organisations have been involved in the Historic Urban Landscape initiative: ICOMOS (International Council on Monuments and Sites), IUCN (International Union for the Conservation of Nature), ICCROM (International Centre for the Study of Preservation and Restoration of Cultural Property), UIA (International Union of Architects), IFLA (International Federation of Landscape Architects), IFHP (International Federation for Housing and Planning), OWHC (Organization of World Heritage Cities), the Aga Khan Trust for Culture, IAIA (International Association of Impact Assessment), UN-Habitat, the World Bank, the Inter-American Development Bank, OECD (Organisation for Economic Cooperation and Development), ISOCARP (International Society of City and Regional Planners), DOCOMOMO (International Committee for Documentation and Conservation of the Buildings, Sites and Neighbourhoods of the Modern Movement), the Getty Conservation Institute.

Among these, the 2005 *Vienna Memorandum* probably constituted the first overall attempt in twenty years to revise and update the modern urban conservation paradigm. It originated from a conference held in Vienna in May 2005 at the request of the World Heritage Committee,[24] which had expressed concern at the frequency of cases of modern or high-rise construction inside, or near, the perimeters of historic cities that were threatening the 'visual integrity' of inscribed properties.[25]

The World Heritage Committee had come to realise the limits of the existing tools – its own Operational Guidelines as well as the various international Charters and Recommendations – to cope with the challenges arising from contemporary development pressure.

The *Vienna Memorandum on World Heritage and Contemporary Architecture* proposed the notion of Historic Urban Landscape (HUL): '*The historic urban landscape, building on the 1976 UNESCO Recommendation concerning the Safeguarding and Contemporary Role of Historic Areas, refers to ensembles of any group of buildings, structures and open spaces, in their natural and ecological context, including archaeological and paleontological sites, constituting human settlements in an urban environment over a relevant period of time, the cohesion and value of which are recognized from the archaeological, architectural, prehistoric, historic, scientific, aesthetic, socio-cultural or ecological point of view. This landscape has shaped modern society and has great value for our understanding of how we live today*' (Article 7). '*The historic urban landscape is embedded with current and past social expressions and developments that are place-based. It is composed of character-defining elements that include land uses and patterns, spatial organization, visual relationships, topography and soils, vegetation, and all elements of the technical infrastructure, including small scale objects and details of construction (curbs, paving, drain gutters, lights, etc.)*' (Article 8).

Although the notion has been discussed and has undergone several revisions (see Annex 1), Historic Urban Landscape was proposed – and has been retained – as a tool to reinterpret the values of urban heritage. This clearly reflects the need to identify new approaches and tools for urban conservation.

The Memorandum was welcomed by the World Heritage Committee at its 29th session in 2005, and formed the basis for *the Declaration on the Conservation of the Historic Urban Landscape*, adopted by the 15th General Assembly of States Parties to the World Heritage Convention in October 2005.[26]

---

[24] The international conference 'World Heritage and Contemporary Architecture – Managing the Historic Urban Landscape' was organised by the UNESCO World Heritage Centre in cooperation with ICOMOS and the City of Vienna (Austria).

[25] Among the cases examined by the World Heritage Committee at the time were: Potsdam, Vienna, Cologne, St Petersburg, Bordeaux, Esphahan, Istanbul, Dresden, Riga, Vilnius, Sevilla, Avila, Graz, Liverpool and Tallinn.

[26] Resolution 15 GA 7.

The Memorandum and the Declaration reflect a change towards sustainable development in the governance of historic cities, as well as a broader vision of the nature of urban heritage.[27] In particular, the Vienna Memorandum aimed to address some of the limitations of the traditional approach, by defining historic urban areas not as a 'sum' of monuments and urban fabric, but as a comprehensive system, marked by historical, geomorphologic and social relationships with its setting and its environment, and characterised by a complex layering of meanings and expressions.

The Vienna Memorandum identifies historic urban areas as the result of long-term dynamics which are still ongoing, and conceives of change – social, economic and physical – as a variable to be managed and understood, not just as a source of contrast. 'Urban landscape' is not a new concept: it is used, for instance, in urban geography and is commonly invoked by historians and planners.[28]

The drafters of the Vienna Memorandum tried to enrich the concept, in order to bring in new aspects of urban conservation. Historic Urban Landscape, according to the Vienna Memorandum definition, stresses the link between physical forms and social evolution, defining historic cities as a system that integrates natural and man-made elements, in an historical continuum, representing a layering of expressions throughout history. Recognition of the value of the diversity of cultural expressions is the basis of the Historic Urban Landscape, as well as a positive interpretation of social and economic dynamics as factors of change and adaptation of values and urban forms.

Following the adoption of the Declaration, an important international discussion forum was initiated by ICOMOS on the subject of Historic Urban Landscape.[29] This discussion reviewed current urban conservation methodologies and identified gaps between urban conservation practice and existing doctrinal texts, and concluded that *'while the existing methodology is essentially valid, increased development pressures in urban areas and the resultant changes in both the quantity and scale of the proposed interventions now require the development of management tools that may help to identify, assess and mitigate the impact of proposed policies, plans and*

---

[27] Following this reflection, the World Heritage Committee decided also to discuss the functions and the nature of the buffer zones.

[28] See, for instance: Schuyler, 1986; Relph, 1987; Whitehand, 1992; Waller, 2000; Sanson, 2007; Tatom and Stauber, 2009.

[29] Within ICOMOS, two International Scientific Committees lead the discussion on HUL, namely, the Committee on Historic Towns and Villages (CIVVIH) and the ICOMOS-IFLA Committee on Cultural Landscapes, which exists online since late 2006.

During the summer of 2007 this was expanded to five Internet discussion groups, totalling some 150 members of various disciplines: a USA-ICOMOS group moderated by Gustavo Araoz; an Ibero-American group moderated by Pedro de Manuel; an Australian group moderated by Sue Jackson-Stepowski; a Finnish group moderated by Leena Makkonen and Marianne Lehtimaki, and a Japanese group moderated by Yukio Nishimura. Three further ICOMOS initiatives facilitated the discussion: CIVVIH dedicated its 2007 annual meeting to a discussion on HUL; the ICOMOS Asia-Pacific chapter dedicated its 4th annual meeting in Seoul to the subject; and a small group of International Scientific Committee members met to propose a revision of the Vienna Memorandum.

interventions on the historic urban complex' (Firestone, 2007). This review process by ICOMOS also constituted the basis for the updating of their 1987 Washington Charter, which is currently under way.

To address some of the issues raised by the World Heritage Committee, as well as by the initiative of the elaboration of the Vienna Memorandum, ICOMOS dedicated two General Assemblies (its 15th in Xi'an, China in 2005, and its 16th in Quebec, Canada in 2008) to themes of great importance for a modern reinterpretation of heritage values, applicable in general but with a specific interest for urban heritage sites: the 'setting' and the 'spirit of place' (*genius loci*).

The 2005 *Xi'an Declaration on the Conservation of the Setting of Heritage Structures, Sites and Areas* defines 'setting' in Article 1 as '*the immediate and extended environment that is part of, or contributes to, its significance and distinctive character*'.

The *Xi'an Declaration* focuses on the need to protect the setting of heritage in view of rapid urban development in many regions of the world. This document is important as it defines 'setting' not only as a physical area, but also as the interaction with the natural environment. Furthermore, setting includes social and spiritual practices and the intangible heritage aspects in general that contribute to constituting the space, as well as the social and economic context.[30] This Declaration also promotes the development of planning tools and strategies for the conservation and management of the areas forming the setting.

The 2008 *Quebec Declaration on the Preservation of the Spirit of Place*[31] attempts to define an approach to the interpretation of the value and meaning of a place based on the interaction and mutual construction between the tangible and the intangible elements. In its first part, *Rethinking the Spirit of Place*, it states:

'*1. Recognizing that the spirit of place is made up of tangible (sites, buildings, landscapes, routes, objects) as well as intangible elements (memories, narratives, written documents, festivals, commemorations, rituals, traditional knowledge, values, textures, colours, odours, etc.), which all significantly contribute to making place and to giving it spirit, we declare*

---

[30] The Xi'an Declaration on the Conservation of the Setting of Heritage Structures, Sites and Areas, was adopted in Xi'an, China, by the 15th General Assembly of ICOMOS on 21 October 2005. The contribution of setting to the value of heritage is so defined:

'1. The setting of a heritage structure, site or area is defined as the immediate and extended environment that is part of, or contributes to, its significance and distinctive character.
    Beyond the physical and visual aspects, the setting includes interaction with the natural environment; past or present social or spiritual practices, customs, traditional knowledge, use or activities and other forms of intangible cultural heritage aspects that created and form the space as well as the current and dynamic cultural, social and economic context.
2. Heritage structures, sites or areas of various scales, including individual buildings or designed spaces, historic cities or urban landscapes, landscapes, seascapes, cultural routes and archaeological sites, derive their significance and distinctive character from their perceived social and spiritual, historic, artistic, aesthetic, natural, scientific, or other cultural values. They also derive their significance and distinctive character from their meaningful relationships with their physical, visual, spiritual and other cultural context and settings.'

[31] The Quebec Declaration on the Spirit of Place was adopted in Quebec City, Canada, on 4 October 2008, by the 16th General Assembly of ICOMOS.

that intangible cultural heritage gives a richer and more complete meaning to heritage as a whole and it must be taken into account in all legislation concerning cultural heritage, and in all conservation and restoration projects for monuments, sites, landscapes, routes and collections of objects. . . .

3. Since the spirit of place is a process, continuously reconstructed, in response to the needs of change and continuity of communities, we uphold that it can vary in time and from one culture to another according to their practices of memory, and that a place can have several spirits and be shared by different groups.'

Towards a New Urban Conservation Paradigm

The new approaches developed in the past decade and the attempts to redefine scopes, processes and values of urban conservation at the international level confirm that a new paradigm is gradually taking shape. Underlying this effort is an awareness of the nature of the challenges facing urban heritage in the new century, which is summarised in the UNESCO document (UNESCO, 2009) that discussed the possibility of a new Recommendation on the Historic Urban Landscape.[32] The following chapter will look at these challenges in more detail.

---

[32] UNESCO Executive Board Document 181 EX/29, April 2009. The document identified the following list of 'new' threats for the conservation of urban historic areas:

'*Growing pressure of urbanization*

12. *More than half of the Earth's population now lives in an urban area. Alterations to the historic urban fabric are frequently associated with increasing uniformity of architecture, decline of public spaces, and fragmentation and commercialization of historic centres. The role of historic areas in promoting the diversity of cultural values, ways of life and social relationships is being increasingly challenged. The weakening of traditional territorial communities, the gentrification and suburbanization of urban areas are also taking place. Urban growth is significantly transforming the face of historic cities and their setting. The capacity of historic cities to accommodate and benefit from the radical and rapid changes that accompany urban growth while maintaining heritage values is becoming a critical factor.*

    Tensions between globalization and local development.

13. *Global processes have a direct impact on the identity and "visual integrity" of historic cities and their broader setting, as well as on the people who live in them. While some cities are growing exponentially, others are shrinking and being radically restructured as a result of shifting economic processes and new patterns of migration. To address these issues, local urban strategies are becoming the key component of urban development planning. The increasing globalization of the economy is radically transforming many contemporary cities, benefiting some groups, whilst marginalizing others. In some countries, centrally controlled planning has given way to decentralization and market-oriented approaches. The result is that cities, and their planning processes, have become increasingly fragmented, while inequality and environmental degradation has increased.*

    Incompatible new development.

14. *With investment in urban real estate, infrastructure and renovation becoming the driving force behind urban transformations, the physical landscape of the historic city is being severely altered. Within a real estate development process that is increasingly market-driven, contemporary architecture in historic cites has taken on an increasingly important role. However, the quality of these interventions in terms of scale, context, sustainable materials, maintenance, comfort, etc., has not always been a priority for decision-makers. This placed the issue of the harmonization of contemporary expressions within the context and setting of historic urban landscapes at the core of the discipline and practice of urban heritage conservation. Contemporary interventions in historic cities, such as new housing to cater for increased population needs, high-rise iconic buildings, projects related to hydroelectricity, energy resource and industrial developments as well as waste disposal,*

Box 2.4 Historic Landscape Characterisation in England

The Historic Landscape Characterisation (HLC) programme was defined and launched by English Heritage in the 1990s, in order to support conservation of historical dimensions within a sustainability framework. The HLC supports the principle that conservation should be based on 'management of change' and in the integration of plans and processes of all stakeholders. The basis of the programme is the 'Atlas' that defines 'character areas' using the pattern of historic settlements. This programme allowed the creation, for the first time in England, of a detailed view of the archaeological, historical and cultural interest of the landscape. HLC has therefore become a central element of historic environment conservation and of spatial planning. The concepts which underpin the HLC programme are the following:

- Conservation must be concerned with present-day landscape, to help management of change. It also has to identify the historic character of that landscape, by developing a comprehensive view of the area and its environment.
- Historic landscape character is the result of the interaction through time of people and their environment, and it is the result of a process of change in the past. Time-depth of cultural and historical processes is the key to understand the character of the landscape and to manage its changes.
- Historic landscape character is a function of perception and understanding. Landscape is a cultural construct that links the various component parts via comprehensive meaning which helps define present-day cultural attitudes.
- Historic landscape character is dynamic and living. Conservation needs to understand how changes over time have affected the landscape patterns and take this into account when guiding present processes.
- Historic landscape characterisation is based on a process of democratic participation in managing change. Landscape as a cultural construct reflects people's perceptions and values, and therefore the process of change management needs to take into account the spectrum of views.

These principles permit the definition of a working method based on maps that define the character of the landscape as a whole, not as a collection of individual sites. The method does not create a single definition of landscape history, but rather a set of interpretations and ideas – a resource base – that can be used to define different narratives. The resulting attributes of the landscape form the basis of the management process. Historic Landscape Characterisation has become in England the main delivery mechanism for conservation and change management in historic environments. It has also become a key component of sustainable development processes, and one of the driving forces of the European Landscape Convention.

Source: Fairclough, Graham. 'Cultural Landscape, Sustainability, and Living with Change?'. Teutonico and Matero, 2003: 23–46

Efforts undertaken so far have yielded interesting results. However, a number of issues need to be addressed to make the approach truly global, one that reflects the diversity of value systems and practices.

In this sense, the discussion on the Historic Urban Landscape represents an attempt to address the need for a renewed approach to urban conservation – perhaps also to go beyond 'urban conservation' as a specialised practice – and to reframe the conservation process within the broader context of urban management and development. The issues that have been put at the centre of the discussion can be summarised as follows.

---

are all increasing in scale and might have detrimental and irreversible effects on the historic city's physical and visual aspect, as well as on their social and cultural values.

Unsustainable tourism.

15. The growth of tourism in historic cities has become one of the major concerns of urban conservators. While tourism can bring benefits to the preservation of cultural heritage, through improved infrastructures and enhanced understanding of the value of culture and traditions, it can also represent a challenge to its physical, environmental and social integrity. Given the expected increase of international tourism in the coming decades there is a need to develop sustainable tourism methodologies, in order to better protect the heritage values of historic urban landscapes.

Environmental degradation including climate change.

16. The impact of environmental factors affecting physical heritage, such as pollution, vehicle traffic and congestion, garbage and industrial waste, acid rain, have all dramatically increased in recent decades. In parallel, countering the negative effects of climate change has emerged as one of the most daunting tasks of our time. Many historic cities are particularly vulnerable to climate change. While cities and human settlements have adapted through history to climatic mutations, the intensity and speed of present climate change is unprecedented and requires immediate action. A number of key strategies called for the integration of climate change mitigation and adaptation into country policies and programmes, triggering a series of regulations and governmental policy instruments at all levels. Numerous international conferences, protocols and initiatives emanating from the United Nations, have mobilized technical, financial and human resources and fostered the establishment of specialized institutions dealing with these issues. These fundamental tools prepared the ground for integrating environmental sustainability in relation to heritage values into the planning and management of the built environment. With initial focus on the nature and scale of the risks posed to World Heritage properties, the World Heritage Committee promoted discussion on lessons learned addressing climate change impacts.

17. The direct impacts of climate change endangering historic urban landscape may include: rising sea levels, alterations of the cycles of wet and dry seasons, more frequent intense rainfall and extreme weather, and changes in hydrology and vegetation patterns. Existing knowledge and the development of research on the predictable impacts of climate change on urban areas have led to the implementation of new policies, especially at the local level. The increasing relevance of impacts of climate change on built and natural environments within historic cities underlines the need to consolidate an integrated approach to historic urban landscape conservation internationally.'

Values and Meaning

A reflection on the values of urban heritage is the starting point for the redefinition of the global approach to urban conservation. In this respect, the significance of creating universally recognised policies and practices of urban conservation needs to be understood in its historical dimension (Choay, 1992). Understanding changes in the values associated with urban heritage conservation is critical to our definition of the present and future value system. In the nineteenth century, the perception of the value of heritage was mainly linked to its monumental value, i.e. its educational and identity functions.

In the twentieth century, the social conservation element was added to these functions while the historic city was better understood in its morphological and typological dimensions. Today, the perception of the values of the historic city has broadened to include the aesthetic and symbolic values of places, and to a new use and enjoyment of the urban space that defines the city as 'living heritage'. Even the meaning of 'urban community' has changed, with the emergence of a multiplicity of communities of urban users, not necessarily of a permanent type, which contribute to a reinterpretation of the values of the historic city.

Authenticity and Integrity of Historic Urban Areas

The existence of a plurality of urban transformation and conservation models has important implications for any discussion of urban conservation and management. In fact, it may be impossible to adopt a unique definition of authenticity and integrity, as local value systems have had a significant influence on conservation policies and practices. The complexity of the global situation cannot be understood unless a bigger role is assigned to cultural diversity as a defining factor of urban heritage conservation. Furthermore, it is important to define authenticity and integrity with respect to the specific definition of the values of urban heritage. The statements concerning values to be preserved should originate from the communities of users (bottom-up) and not only from the experts (top-down).

In other words, the definition of a city, or part of it, as 'heritage' should not be simply seen as the creation of a special district, inside which special regulations apply. On the contrary, it should be seen as a policy statement that determines the dynamics of the city in the long term by defining strategies and tools. The presence of a long-term heritage policy is indeed more important than detailed building regulations, for instance, as it can more reliably ensure the preservation of those values deemed critical by the communities concerned and by the experts.

Layers of Significance

The city is a layering of significance, originating both from natural and man-made features. While the view of the historic city as a complex formation has always been integrated into conservation policies, other aspects (such as the relationship with geological and natural forms, special visual or symbolic axes, the symbolic or spiritual value of places) have normally been associated more with cultural landscapes than with historic areas, where the architectural aspects have always played a predominant role. Viewing the city as a layering of significance makes it possible to identify the conservation policies and trade-offs between conservation and development facing communities and decision-makers. It brings to an end the conceptual and operational separation of the old city and its modern developments, which have often acquired historical and memory value without being properly identified as areas of special interest. Furthermore, it creates linkages between the historic patterns and modern development or redevelopment areas.

The Management of Change

The conservation of the historic city has always encountered difficulties in interpreting change. Social, economic and physical changes tend to be seen as an alteration of the values to be preserved. As a consequence, both principles and practices are not adequately equipped to define the limits of acceptable change, and the assessments tend to be ad hoc and subjective. A specific approach has to be developed to define the role of contemporary architecture and cultural creation in historic places, as the need to respect a continuum has been frequently disregarded or misunderstood. Specific approaches need to be developed for the management of change in the fields of architecture, infrastructure, public space and uses of existing buildings. In this respect, management plans should be seen as strategic documents linking the different areas of management.

Social and Economic Development

Socio-economic dynamics have fuelled the change of the role of the historic city in modern societies. Yet, this role is poorly understood in terms of urban management and is mostly seen in conservative terms, i.e. as something to regulate. A reflection on the changing role of historic urban areas and on how to synergise socio-economic development and conservation strategies is necessary, in order to identify new roles and resource streams necessary to maintain the historic urban landscape in a sustainable way – a goal that has been elusive thus far.

Environmental Sustainability

The reflection on the city includes increasing concern on the part of society about the sustainability of economic development. The growing influence of the environmental movement, the emergence of new issues (such as energy production and conservation, climate change) and the overall impact of global development processes have significantly modified views

Box 2.5 A Dilemma: Venice or Varanasi?

Venice

Varanasi

Venice is today the extreme example of an historic city that has been preserved in its full physical authenticity, with an approach that fully matches the established conservation principles. It also provides a model case of a city that is looking at the challenges of the future and developing responses to climate change.

At the same time, Venice exemplifies the almost complete loss of social and cultural values, clearly reflected in the out-migration and substitution of most of the population, and in the dominance of a single economic activity: tourism. In this sense, Venice has not been preserved as an historic urban entity.

And yet, a new social structure, based on the presence of non-permanent population groups (commuters, students, tourists, etc.), has created new social dimensions, enriched by the importance of its global cultural events.

While only a small part of the cultural product is generated locally, the historic city has become the scene for global cultural representations that support and complement its iconic heritage image. Seen from the viewpoint of the socially conscious urban conservation principles, Venice is a failure. However, it is difficult to say that its universal significance has been lost, as is proven by the unique character of its urban form, the enduring importance of its artistic achievements and by its success as a global centre for tourism and for the arts.

Varanasi, the most venerated city by Hindus and by followers of other faiths such as Buddhists, Jains and Senthoo, has remained in the past three millennia as the sacred place where people come in mass pilgrimage to bathe in the sacred Ganges river, and where they want to be cremated upon dying. It is one of the most significant sacred cities in the world, loaded with spiritual and cultural values. Its religious and political importance has led, over the millennia, to much destruction and alteration: present-day Varanasi is essentially a structure that originated in the sixteenth century.

While the traditional values associated with religion and spirituality are authentic and intact, the same cannot be said of the urban and architectural fabric, which has been continuously transformed and altered to adapt the structures and spaces to the new uses demanded by pilgrims, visitors and tourists. In fact, very little of the physical fabric has remained intact, despite the fact that the overall urban landscape is unchanged, marked on one side of the river by the great system of the Ghats, and overlooking a completely non-built area on the other side. In spite of the lack of (physical) authenticity and integrity, the values of Varanasi as an historic city and spiritual centre are totally intact.

So here is the dilemma: when choosing the city that best exemplifies our contemporary concept of heritage, should it be Venice or Varanasi?

on the urban environment, its economy and its form. Concepts of sustainability have been applied to the historic environment, revealing its important long-term contribution, as well as its vulnerability to global changes. This cultural transition has also affected perspectives on urban conservation, and requires an update of approaches and visions.

New Urban Conservation Tools

Over time an elaborate toolkit has been developed for the conservation of the historic city. There is a need to assess the effectiveness, and to check the coherence, of the different policy and management practices as they relate to overall goals of conservation. Furthermore, new tools need to be defined, which can contribute to the management of the processes for identifying and preserving urban values. This could include tools to involve the participation of the communities of stakeholders in the definition of the value system of an historic place; tools to define and protect the integrity of the urban fabric and the urban landscape; tools to identify the trade-offs and the limits of acceptable change in an historic context; or tools to better integrate built and natural dimensions of the cityscape and to ensure models of sustainable development.

The Historic Urban Landscape Approach

Undoubtedly, modern 'urban' conservation principles suffer from being derived from 'architectural' conservation principles. In the 1964 Charter of Venice, the founding document of modern international conservation, the focus is almost exclusively on the monument and its restoration. In fact, it was this limitation that prompted ICOMOS to formulate a specific complementary Charter for Urban Conservation, the 1987 Washington Charter, a document that substantially enriches the international toolkit in this field, including elements such as urban patterns, public spaces, natural and man-made settings.

This approach has certainly played an extremely important role in the creation of urban historic conservation as a field of public policy and city planning, but presents – as we have shown – weaknesses and limitations that have pushed practitioners to explore new avenues, and take into account many innovative views expressed in past decades.

In this respect, the discussion originated by the UNESCO World Heritage Committee in 2003 and the Vienna Memorandum issued in 2005 constitute the first attempt in twenty years to revise and update the modern urban conservation paradigm.

The Vienna Memorandum – in itself a document still largely grounded in the traditional disciplinary approach – aimed at discussing some of the limitations of the traditional approach, by defining urban historic areas not as a 'sum' of monuments and urban fabric, but as a comprehensive system, marked by historical, geomorphologic and social relationships with its setting and its environment, and characterised by a complex layering of meanings and expressions.

The Vienna Memorandum sees urban historic areas as the result of long-term – and still ongoing – dynamics and conceives of change – social, economic and physical – as a variable to be understood and managed, not just as a source of contrast.

Historic Urban Landscape, in the definition given by the Vienna Memorandum, stresses the link between physical forms and social evolution, defining historic cities as a system integrating natural and man-made elements, in an historical continuum, representing a layering of expressions throughout history. Recognition of the value of the diversity of cultural expressions is the basis of the 'Historic Urban Landscape', as well as a positive interpretation of social and economic dynamics as a factor of change and an adaptation of values and urban forms.

The recognition of the cultural value of contemporary architectural creation in historic areas, something which sparks heated debate among conservators, follows from this approach, as historic cities are seen as a layering of significance that cannot per se exclude modern contributions. What is expressed clearly is the need to respect integrity and the continuity of the design features of a given place, a basic 'rule' of intervention in historical settings that is often ignored by contemporary architectural creativity.

The Vienna Memorandum calls for a more integrated approach to conservation of the values of natural and man-made features. While most of the existing Charters speak about the need to preserve 'settings' and 'surroundings', the Historic Urban Landscape approach sees the natural features as generating factors of the urban values, intrinsically linked to their constitution and expression.

Historic Urban Landscape does not constitute a separate 'heritage category'. On the contrary, the concept is inscribed within the established concept of urban historic areas, while at the same time adding a new lens to the practice of urban conservation: a broader 'territorial' view of heritage, accompanied by a greater consideration of the social and economic functions of an historic city, an approach to managing change that tries to cope with modern developments, and finally a re-evaluation of modern contributions to historic values. It is a tool to project the ideas of urban conservation in the twenty-first century.

3. The Changing Context of Urban Heritage Management

Clearly, then, the city is not a concrete jungle, it is a human zoo.

Desmond Morris

Introducing External and Internal Forces of Change

The emergence of an international conservation movement was outlined in the previous chapter, along with the development of international standard-setting instruments for urban conservation.

The development of the discipline, which allowed a broader definition of cultural heritage – from monuments and sites to practically the entire built environment including its intangible dimensions – was accompanied by the framing of conventions, charters and recommendations that cover virtually all new categories and every aspect of heritage. In that respect the cultural heritage preservation movement of the twentieth century has registered some remarkable successes.

However, while breaking this new ground, the old and familiar world was transforming in a way that often outpaced our ability to understand the changes.

Thus, while the discipline was debating the meaning and extent of intangible heritage, authenticity, and the statement of outstanding universal value, some profound changes have come about that have significantly impacted, and continue to impact, the ways and means of conservation itself. Since the adoption of the last international instrument on the conservation of heritage more than thirty years ago, which was the UNESCO *Recommendation concerning the Safeguarding and Contemporary Role of Historic Areas* in 1976, the world has witnessed, among others, the following external changes of relevance to the conservation of historic cities:

- Exponential increase in urbanisation on a global scale;
- Growing concern for the environment and the sustainability of urban development;

The Historic Urban Landscape: Managing Heritage in an Urban Century, First Edition. Francesco Bandarin, Ron van Oers.

- The vulnerability of cities in terms of the impact of climate change;
- The changing role of cities, with ongoing market liberalisation, decentralisation and privatisation as new drivers of development;
- The emergence of tourism as one of the largest industries in the world;
- And as an internal force of change came a broader understanding and appreciation of the concept of cultural heritage, including the essence of the 'urban condition' in relation to urban heritage values to be protected.

In the following sections these six phenomena – five that emerged from outside the realm of urban conservation and one generated from within – will be examined in terms of their role as change drivers for the discipline of conservation.

Exponential Increase in Urbanisation on a Global Scale

Since the late-1960s the migration of people from rural to urban areas has increased exponentially and given rise to the worldwide transformation of villages into cities, and to the emergence of metropolises and mega-cities. Metropolises, or cities with a population of one million or more, have increased from 11 in 1900 to 100 in 1980, and are estimated at more than 500 today.

At the beginning of the 1980s there were just three cities with more than 10 million inhabitants, the definition of a mega-city: Mexico City, New York City and Tokyo. During the period from 1990 to 2010 the number of people living in urban areas increased by 12 per cent, and accounted for 59.8 per cent of the total global population in 2010. In 2030 this percentage is expected to increase to 67.5 per cent, or the equivalent of 4.8 billion people worldwide, up from 2.9 billion in 2000.

Practically all this growth will be concentrated in cities, adding to the number of 500-plus metropolises and 20 mega-cities in existence today, which include Lagos, Jakarta, Manila, Mumbai, Bangkok, Osaka-Kobe, Shanghai, Rio de Janeiro and Sao Paulo. While Europe and North America are already highly urbanised – 69.7 per cent of their total population in 2010 – certain areas in Central and Eastern Europe are currently experiencing declines due to ongoing socio-economic restructuring. Even for these regions an overall increase of 5.2 per cent to 74.9 per cent is forecast for 2030.[1]

The cities of the developing world are absorbing virtually all of this urban population growth, with an unprecedented average rate of one million new inhabitants every week. In addition to the growing number of metropolises, in developing countries the majority of urban residents will live in secondary cities, or, in other words, those cities with fewer than 200,000 people. Acting as the link between rural and urban areas, such secondary cities will provide the greatest future challenge and opportunity as they continue to

[1] UN-Habitat's Global Urban Indicators database at: www.UN-HABITAT.org/stats/default.aspx

Seoul

Maputo

Asia and Sub-Saharan Africa are experiencing exponential urban growth. This process offers opportunities for poverty alleviation, but also threatens the preservation of historic urban landscapes.

grow and multiply exponentially. Statistics suggest that while the population of Sub-Saharan Africa doubled in the period from 1950 to 1980, its urban population increased fivefold (Yacoob and Margo, 1999).

While mega-cities host just 10 per cent of all urban residents, cities with fewer than one million people account for close to two-thirds of the total.

Next to Sub-Saharan Africa, India and China in particular are experiencing phenomenal growth rates. India's urban population increased from 26 per cent in 1990 to 30.1 per cent in 2010, and is forecast to grow to 40.6 per cent in 2030. China's urban dwellers stood at 27 per cent in 1990, and jumped to 44.9 per cent in 2010, with 2030 expected to bring an increase to 60.3 per cent. By 2030 Asia will rank first, and Africa second, in terms of the total number of urbanites: almost seven out of every ten urban dwellers in the world will be living in either of these two regions (De Mulder and Kraas, 2008).

With urbanisation and urban development often being confused, it is important to clarify the distinction between the two. According to Alan Gilbert, urban development or growth means an increase in the number of people living in urban areas, and insofar as urbanisation is used as an analogy for urban development, it means precisely that. *'But urbanization also has a more subtle meaning that conveys something about economic, social and cultural change. It's part and parcel of the process of modernization – a phenomenon involving a shift from agricultural to urban forms of work, a change in social relationships, and important modifications in family life. People change their lifestyles when they move from the countryside to the city'.*[2]

Since the advent of industrialisation, urbanisation has been viewed as key to economic growth and social development. In general, urban residents have higher rates of literacy, lower rates of fertility, and more economic opportunity.

Urbanisation creates opportunities to enhance the quality of life for city dwellers through economies of scale, access to services, agglomeration, transfer of technology, proximity and productivity (Lanzafame and Quartesan, 2009).

However, when the growth of cities is rapid and unmanaged, as has been shown during the past fifty years of urban development, several 'externalities' occur. These include environmental stress, such as pollution and land consumption, pressures on housing and urban services, such as electricity, piped water, sewerage and solid-waste management (accompanied by an increasing number of urban dwellers living in slum conditions) and growing income gaps and social inequalities, which can precipitate conflict, crime and violence in societies that are increasingly fragmented in spatial and political terms.

The competition for urban land for housing, infrastructure and services is particularly intense in inner-city areas, where skyscrapers are the resulting building form if outward extension is not possible anymore or urban sprawl

[2]Gilbert, 'Urbanization and Security'. Rosan et al., 1999: 75.

Alexandria

People bring their value and belief systems with them when they move from the countryside to the city, which are gradually being replaced by new, urban lifestyles.

is restricted. These downtown areas and key nodes in metropolises receive huge investments in real estate and telecommunications, while other parts of the city are neglected when their location is less central and accessible (Sassen, 2001). As a result, historic inner cities around the globe are the focus of urban development and regeneration processes, which more often

Box 3.1 Historic Centre of Vienna (Austria)

The historic centre of Vienna, registered on the World Heritage List in 2001, is rich in architectural ensembles varying from Baroque castles and gardens to the *Ringstrasse* monuments and parks dating from the late-nineteenth century. The visual integrity of the property was threatened in 2002 by a development project involving 4 towers of more than 100 metres, planned to be built next to the World Heritage property (*Wien-Mitte* Project). Owing to the proximity to the historic centre, the towers would have had a significant impact on the historic urban landscape of the city, which had maintained a high degree of integrity since the famous *veduta* painted by Bellotto in the eighteenth century from the Belvedere. Strong public opposition to the project forced the city's authorities to reconsider the design solution. While one of the towers was already under construction (the Vienna City Tower), the World Heritage Committee opened a debate on the possible delisting of the property in the event that the full project would be completed. Owing to these pressures, the Municipality decided to cancel the original project and to reformulate the programme in order to avoid a negative visual impact.

Source: World Heritage Committee State of Conservation Report 28 COM 15B.83

than not lead to conflict over the preservation of their urban heritage values.

In recent years the number and intensity of debates at the annual sessions of the World Heritage Committee have increased significantly, suggesting that the current framework is inadequate for addressing matters of contemporary development within historic urban contexts. In 2007 at its 31st session the World Heritage Committee reviewed a total of 33 'state of conservation' reports for cultural properties that focused on potential harmful

Box 3.2 Historic Centre of Riga (Latvia)

The historic centre of Riga, inscribed on the World Heritage List since 1997, has retained its medieval fabric, while its surrounding suburbs display an unparalleled collection of nineteenth-century buildings in neoclassical style and Jugendstil/Art Nouveau. However, in 2003, development activities in Kipsala Island – which constitutes part of the buffer zone on the opposite side of the River Daugva – threatened to damage the visual integrity of the site and revealed an insufficiency of the legal framework for the preservation of the historic centre. In fact, Riga had adopted in 2004 an instrument for management of the World Heritage site, the Riga Historic Centre Preservation and Development Plan. However, this instrument did not prevent the large-scale redevelopment of the areas in front of the World Heritage property on the other side of the river. In spite of the recommendations issued by the World Heritage Committee, the redevelopment plan of Kipsala Island was carried out with significant impacts on the historic urban landscape of Riga.

Source: World Heritage Committee State of Conservation Report 28 COM 15B.74

impacts of urban development and regeneration projects, which included threats posed by infrastructure projects, contemporary architecture and tall buildings – 39 per cent of the total of cultural World Heritage sites reported to the Committee (Van Oers, 2008), which is clearly only the tip of the iceberg if the global situation of historic cities is taken into consideration.

What has become clear from all these debates at the World Heritage Committee sessions is that responsible authorities encounter difficulties in addressing the issue of urban development and modernisation of historic cities and the preservation of their inherited qualities and values in mutually satisfactory ways – in both developed, and developing, countries, and on all continents. The reconciliation of development and conservation of protected sites needs a new and strong impetus, with updated strategies and tools for local communities and decision-makers (including the World Heritage Committee).

Environmental Concerns and the Sustainability of Urban Development

Concern for the environment and the sustainability of urban development increased in parallel with the extraordinary population growth of urban areas throughout the world. According to Adams, the idea of sustainability goes back more than forty years to the new mandate adopted by the International Union for the Conservation of Nature (IUCN) in 1969. This mandate spoke of '*the perpetuation and enhancement of the living world – man's natural environment – and the natural resources on which all living things depend*', referring to management of '*air, water, soils, minerals and living species including man, so as to achieve the highest sustainable quality of life*' (Adams, 2006).

The theme of sustainability was central to the United Nations Conference on the Human Environment, in Stockholm (Sweden) in 1972. Subsequently, the concept of sustainable development was 'mainstreamed' through the World Conservation Strategy (IUCN, 1980), which emphasised the need to maintain essential ecological processes and life-support systems, to preserve genetic diversity, and to ensure the sustainable utilisation of species and ecosystems; the Brundtland Report of 1987,[3] which delivered the key message that economic growth without environmental damage was possible, and necessary if future generations were to be allowed the means to achieve their own development; the United Nations Conference on Environment and Development in Rio de Janeiro in 1992 that adopted Agenda 21; and the World Summit on Sustainable Development in Johannesburg in 2002, which was preceded by the United Nations Millennium Summit in 2000 that issued the 'Millennium Declaration' with the development agenda of the United Nations for the next 15 to 20 years in the form

---

[3]United Nations World Commission on Environment and Development, 1987 – online at: http://ourcommonfuture.org/

of eight Millennium Development Goals,[4] among which was Environmental Sustainability.

The 2005 Millennium Ecosystem Assessment,[5] more than thirty years after the term sustainable development was launched, provided a sobering insight into the state of planet Earth and the sustainability of the management of its resources by man. Next to negative impacts on the biosphere around the globe due to human activity, with declines in regulating ecosystem services, the level of poverty has remained high, while inequality has grown.[6] In the context of the United Nations International Year of Biodiversity (2010), the third edition of the Global Biodiversity Outlook (GBO-3) was released on 10 May 2010 by the Secretariat of the Convention on Biological Diversity (CBD), the broadest international treaty for the conservation and sustainable use of biodiversity that has been ratified by 193 Parties.

The report concluded that the world has failed to meet its target to achieve a significant reduction in the rate of biodiversity loss by 2010 and that natural systems that support economies, lives, livelihoods and poverty eradication across the planet are at risk of rapid degradation and collapse, unless there is swift, radical and creative action to conserve and sustainably use Earth's resources.[7]

From 1981 to 2005, the global Gross Domestic Product more than doubled, in contrast to the 60 per cent of the world's ecosystems being degraded or used in an unsustainable manner. Only a fraction of national income is spent on the environment.

Global annual spending on the environment is estimated at best at US$ 10 billion per year, while some US$ 60–90 billion is needed for those environmental investments that contribute directly to poverty reduction alone.[8] In more than three decades of development, which has been driven globally by cities and urbanisation primarily, it seems that for both the environment and development the target of sustainability has not been met.

Yet despite the negative image of most cities when it comes to the environment, urban areas have a crucial role to play in promoting sustainable development, as advocated by UNESCO's Man and the Biosphere (MAB) Programme.

---

[4] Available at: http://www.un.org/millenniumgoals/

[5] Available at: http://www.millenniumassessment.org/en/index.aspx

[6] Global improvements in levels of poverty reduction are skewed by rapid economic growth in India and China. Poverty elsewhere, especially in Sub-Saharan Africa, is profound and persistent. In: Adams, 2006, pp. 5–6.

[7] See: http://gbo3.cbd.int/home.aspx

[8] Taken from: UNEP, 2008 on-line at: http://www.unep.org/documents.multilingual/default.asp?documentid=548&articleid=5957&l=en.

Cape Town

New York City

Cape Town and New York City are case studies in the Man and the Biosphere Programme of UNESCO, to promote sustainability through the conservation of cultural and biological diversity in large metropolitan areas.

Established in 1971, MAB was one of the first international efforts to study cities as ecological systems. Research is conducted in dozens of places around the world, encompassing a variety of biophysical and socio-economic situations that range from small, rural settlements to some of the largest mega-cities in the world. MAB adopted an ecological approach to improve understanding of the system, notably the complexity of the inter-relationship and interactions within urban systems themselves, and between urban systems and their hinterlands (Von Droste, 1991).

In 1990 the Organization for Economic Co-operation and Development (OECD) put forward the *Urban Environmental Policies for the 1990s* to promote sustainable urban development.[9]

Their suggestions included taking an interdisciplinary approach, facilitating cooperation and coordination within, and between, public and private sectors, enforcing environmental standards and promoting recycling and the use of renewable resources.

At the dawn of this century most of these had been incorporated into national development strategies. However, at the same time it had become apparent that sustainable development had become an empty shell, a convenient container for almost any idea or vision related to economic and environmental management, since 'the concept is holistic, attractive and elastic, but imprecise'.[10]

But instead of discarding it, it would be more effective to re-orient the concept and re-emphasise its meaning in clear and unambiguous terms, as argued by Adams, since sustainability is widely used, and it has taken more than 15 years to build the concept into the mindset of local and national governments, business and industry, as well as schools and universities.

Moreover, two other aspects need to be discussed. The first is the conventional model of the 'three pillars' of sustainability, encompassing its environmental, social and economic dimensions, which lacks the all-pervasive role of culture. At the Intergovernmental Conference on Cultural Policies for Development, in Stockholm in April 1998, UNESCO's Action Plan on Cultural Policies for Development was adopted, which stipulated in its first principle that sustainable development and the blossoming of culture are interdependent.[11]

A few years earlier, the World Commission on Culture and Development had argued that *'cultures cannot survive if the environment on which they depend is laid to waste or impoverished. Humanity's relation to the natural environment has so far been seen predominantly in biophysical*

---

[9]Simonis and Hahn, 1990 – online at: http://www.biopolitics.gr/HTML/PUBS/VOL3/qi-sim.htm
[10]Adams, 2006: 3.
[11]The Stockholm Conference adopted the following five policy objectives:

Objective 1: To make cultural policy one of the key components of development strategy;
Objective 2: Promote creativity and participation in cultural life;
Objective 3: Reinforce policy and practice to safeguard and enhance the cultural heritage, tangible and intangible, movable and immovable, and to promote cultural industries;
Objective 4: Promote cultural and linguistic diversity in and for the information Society;
Objective 5: Make more human and financial resources available for cultural development.

terms; but there is now a growing recognition that societies themselves have created elaborate procedures to protect and manage their resources. These procedures are rooted in cultural values that have to be taken into account if sustainable and equitable human development is to become a reality'.[12]

At the United Nations Meeting on the 10-year Review of the Barbados Plan of Action for the Sustainable Development of Small Island Developing States (SIDS), held in Mauritius in January 2005, UNESCO convened an international panel to debate the role of culture in the sustainable development of SIDS. At the meeting culture was endorsed as the fourth pillar of sustainability.[13]

Above all, as Keith Nurse has argued, culture should not just be added as a fourth pillar, but become the central pillar that is fully integrated into the economic, social and environmental pillars: because culture is at the root of peoples' identities and thereby determines their communication and signifying systems, their world views and cognitive frameworks that shape the perception and understanding of, and actions in, the environment, including the social and economic systems (Nurse, 2007).

This argument was put forward by UNESCO during the 2010 Millennium Development Goals (MDG) Review Summit at UN Headquarters in New York. The principal aim was to ensure that when in 2015 the world's leaders decide on the follow-up to the MDG's, culture will be included as one of the main policy frameworks for consideration to focus programmes and actions. For this to happen it will be essential to demonstrate the role of culture and of cultural diversity in achieving sustainable development, through job creation and revenue generation (through tangible and intangible cultural heritage, cultural industries and cultural institutions), by fostering social cohesion and peace-building, and through its role in shaping environmental awareness and actions.

The Resolution adopted by the UN General Assembly in December 2010 on this matter established for the first time a clear role for culture in the development process and has opened the way to a new consideration of cultural heritage, cultural creativity and cultural institutions in the Millennium Development Goals' framework of activities.[14]

---

[12]UNESCO, 1996: 17.
[13]For this discussion, see: http://www.unesco.org/csi/B10/mim/Panel3sum_English.pdf
[14]UN resolution 65/166, Culture and Development, 20 December 2010

'1. Emphasizes the important contribution of culture for sustainable development and the achievement of national development objectives and internationally agreed development goals, including the Millennium Development Goals;
2. Invites all Member States, intergovernmental bodies, organizations of the United Nations system and relevant non-governmental organizations:
  (a) To raise public awareness of the importance of cultural diversity for sustainable development, promoting its positive value through education and media tools;
  (b) To ensure a more visible and effective integration and mainstreaming of culture into development policies and strategies at all levels;
  (c) To promote capacity-building, where appropriate, at all levels for the development of a dynamic cultural and creative sector, in particular by encouraging creativity, innovation and entrepreneurship, supporting the development of sustainable cultural institutions and cultural industries,

Box 3.3 Medina of Marrakesh (Morocco)

The Medina of Marrakesh has been an important political and cultural centre since its foundation in 1070, and to this day remains the core of local identity and traditional activities. Listed as a World Heritage site in 1985 for its outstanding monuments, while its main square, the Jamâa el Fna, was proclaimed a Masterpiece of the Intangible Heritage of Humanity in 2001, this vibrant urban space has become a renowned international tourist destination. A study, highlighted in the 2008 policy note on 'Development Strategy for Morocco's Historic Towns', carried out at the request of the Moroccan Ministry of Housing, Urban and Regional Planning, and in cooperation with the World Bank and the Italian Culture and Sustainable Development Trust Fund, analyses the Marrakesh renewal strategy and its challenges. The city's main economic potential for development derives from its cultural assets. The creation of a university and the development of the local economy, based on local arts and crafts and the tourist industry in close collaboration with local society, are some of the factors that have enhanced the preservation of Marrakesh's cultural heritage. Additional activities such as the Urban Landscape Improvement Program, the creation of the Marrakesh city label campaign, the promotion of the region's agricultural products and diverse building rehabilitation for tourism are among the achievements of the expansion of the tourist economy. However, the site is going through rapid urban and economic changes that may be inappropriate for the Medina and the traditional activities of the inhabitants. Therefore, effective institutional participation and the approval of a management plan are still needed in order to improve social distribution, enhance the property's authenticity and consequently foster the city's sustainable future.

Source: Bigio, 2010

providing technical and vocational training for culture professionals and increasing employment opportunities in the cultural and creative sector for sustained, inclusive and equitable economic growth and development;

(d) To actively support the emergence of local markets for cultural goods and services and to facilitate the effective and licit access of such goods and services to international markets, taking into account the expanding range of cultural consumption and, for States Parties to it, the

The second aspect is the idea that trade-offs can be made among the different pillars. This leads in practice to development decisions being taken that put the greatest emphasis on the economy, often resulting in 'business as usual'.

Recently, an important case was discussed involving the Black Sea in Europe, where an intricate array of human pressures have cumulatively damaged a complex ecosystem with a huge catchment area involving 16 different countries. During the 1970s and 1980s intense fishing activity had eliminated a number of important species, notably tuna and sword-fish, while introduced species of jellyfish had out-competed and preyed upon smaller fish. Furthermore, agricultural pollution led to prolific algae blooms, which diminished the level of oxygen in the water leading to the collapse of seabed habitats. With the fall of the Soviet Union in the early 1990s and the subsequent economic collapse of the socialist republics, agricultural activity slowed down significantly, which actually provided an opportunity for the Black Sea ecosystem to begin its recovery. A recent European-Commission-supported study, cited in an article, suggests that social and environmental needs must be prioritised alongside, or above, immediate, local, economic needs if the Black Sea is to fully recover.[15]

The prioritisation of economics over other concerns is also apparent in the development of urban projects and architectural interventions in historic cities. Where currently new buildings in general comply with the latest regulations on energy efficiency, achieving environmental sustainability through environmental design that involves the latest technology, this is rarely the case when it comes to cultural sustainability, i.e. ensuring continuity and compatibility with the historic setting in terms of form and function. And more often than not the economic dimension overrides other considerations, for instance, arguing in favour of the building of skyscrapers in historic inner cities, while such economic necessity has never been clearly demonstrated. To achieve true sustainable development, the range of factors to be taken into account has increased significantly and currently requires a complex urban-management agenda.

---

provisions of the Convention on the Protection and Promotion of the Diversity of Cultural Expressions;

(e) *To preserve and maintain local and indigenous traditional knowledge and community practices of environmental management, which are valuable examples of culture as a vehicle for environmental sustainability and sustainable development, and to foster synergies between modern science and local and indigenous knowledge;*

(f) *To support national legal frameworks and policies for the protection and preservation of cultural heritage and cultural property, the fight against illicit trafficking in cultural property and the return of cultural property, in accordance with national legislation and applicable international legal frameworks, including by promoting international cooperation to prevent the misappropriation of cultural heritage and products, recognizing the importance of intellectual property rights in sustaining those involved in cultural creativity'.*

[15] See: http://ec.europa.eu/environment/integration/research/newsalert/pdf/22si.pdf

Box 3.4 Vilnius Historic Centre (Lithuania)

Vilnius represents an important stage in architectural development in Eastern Europe. It has preserved an important complex of buildings from the thirteenth century to the end of the eighteenth century, as well as its medieval layout and natural setting. The property's integrity was challenged by a development project called 'Detailed Plan of Vilnius' that could have impacted the visual integrity of the site, not only because of its planned high-rise constructions, but also because it required the demolition of wooden heritage located within the buffer zone. After these issues were discussed at the World Heritage Committee in 2005, the Lithuanian Government called on different experts to review the plan, in order to take into account the site's Outstanding Universal Value. In addition, measures were adopted at the local level to ensure the property's protection: among these, a new law that became effective in 2005, and a Plan of Action concerning the revision of the buffer zone, which resulted in a draft project for the Vilnius Historic Centre buffer zone. As a result of the visual-impact assessments, there are no new high-rise developments threatening the property. However, a fully integrated management plan is still needed.

Source: World Heritage Committee State of Conservation Report 30 COM 7B.86

The Impact of Climate Change

In addition to the environmental considerations, there is growing concern, albeit rather late, over the implications of climate change on the historic built environment. The potential impact of climate change as the partial result of human influence, in particular the vulnerability of coastal regions, was already under political scrutiny in the late 1980s with the passing of Resolution 44/206 on the possible adverse effects of sea-level rise on islands and coastal areas at the 44th session of the UN General Assembly in 1989,[16] and the Small States Conference on Sea Level Rise hosted by the Government of the Maldives in November 1989 (which adopted the Male Declaration on Global Warming and Sea Level Rise).[17]

It gained momentum during the 1992 UN Conference on Environment and Development, held in Rio de Janeiro (Brazil), with the adoption of Agenda 21, a programme of action for sustainable development, followed by the meeting of the United Nations Framework Convention on Climate Change (UNFCCC, or FCCC) in Japan in December 1997, which adopted the Kyoto Protocol.[18]

The Kyoto Protocol treaty came into force in February 2005 and as of November 2009 it had been signed and ratified by 187 states. The major feature of the Kyoto Protocol is that it sets binding targets for 37 industrialised countries and the European Community for reducing greenhouse-gas emissions by 5.2 per cent compared to the year 1990 (but note that, compared to the emissions' levels that would be expected by 2010 without the Protocol, this target represents a 29 per cent cut).

---

[16] Earth Negotiations Bulletin, International Institute for Sustainable Development (IISD), Vol. 8, No. 48, online at: http://www.iisd.ca/sids/msi+5/

[17] See: http://www.islandvulnerability.org/slr1989.html

[18] Available at: http://unfccc.int/resource/docs/convkp/kpeng.html

Pristine Amazon rainforest

Los Angeles

Greenhouse-gas emissions of urban areas coupled with deforestation are resulting in negative impacts on the biosphere. Cities can play an important role in mitigating the global human footprint.

In 2005 a group of concerned organisations and individuals brought the issue of climate change and its impact on World Heritage sites to the attention of the World Heritage Committee and its Secretariat. At its 29th session in Durban (South Africa, 2005), the World Heritage Committee requested that the World Heritage Centre convene a broad working group of experts to review the nature and scale of the risks arising from climate change and to prepare a strategy for dealing with the issue.[19]

In general, the expert group established the need for an increase in baseline data, which necessitates the gathering of climate data sets and climate projections from various models for different regions and properties. To facilitate a better understanding of the links between climate change and the impact at the local level, three types of research were identified: 1) research that responds to increased risk factors (such as drought or flooding) to support disaster-management plans; 2) socio-economic research, such as cost-benefit analysis valuing the economic losses from climate change, as well as research into the impact on societies; and 3) research into the nature and sources of other stress factors (such as pollution or deforestation) that can reduce the resilience of properties to impacts from climate change (UNESCO World Heritage Centre, 2008).

In 2007 the Inter-Governmental Panel on Climate Change (IPCC) issued its 4th Assessment Report, 'Climate Change 2007',[20] which unequivocally established the warming of the Earth's climate and acknowledged that this temperature increase since the middle of the twentieth century is very likely caused by human-induced greenhouse gases.

While the IPCC's 4th Assessment Report noted that urban centres are often capable of considerable adaptation, little attention has so far been paid by the decision-makers and planners to adaptation in urban areas, including historic cities. As David Satterthwaite observes, '*adaptation to climate change has to be built into the core of all urban planning and management. It is, however, difficult to get local governments to act on adaptation. There are always other priorities that seem more pressing and, at present, the information base on the likely local impacts of climate change is weak. [...] All cities need effective disaster risk management plans, both to reduce risks and have in place appropriate responses. Good disaster-preparedness is a key part of adaptation*'.[21]

Threats to urban areas and historic cities would include direct impacts, such as more frequent and severe flooding because of extreme weather conditions or rising sea levels. A high proportion of the urban population in low-income and middle-income countries live within the Low-Elevation Coastal Zone (LECZ), the continuous area along the coast that is less than 10 metres above sea level.

---

[19] The group of experts prepared a report on Predicting and Managing the Effects of Climate Change on World Heritage, as well as a Strategy to Assist States Parties to the Convention to Implement Appropriate Management Responses, available at: http://whc.unesco.org/en/climatechange/ and published in the World Heritage Papers Series as no. 22 in English and French.

[20] Available at: http://www1.ipcc.ch/ipccreports/assessments-reports.htm

[21] Satterthwaite, 2008: 2.

Hadramawt

Sana'a, Yemen

Global warming will increase extreme weather phenomena, including flooding, which ravaged the Hadramawt region in Yemen in October 2008.

For China this means some 80 million urban dwellers, and another 30 million in India. But also in the USA this means close to 20 million urbanites, and some 10 million in the Netherlands alone, out of a total population of around 16 million (McGranahan et al., 2007). At the beginning of 2007 the UK announced 15 projects to study ways to reduce urban flooding, conducted in cities including Birmingham, London, Newcastle and Leeds, based on a scenario of more intense rainfall brought on by climate change. [22]

Adaptive policies to increase renewable energy supplies or to reduce the demand for energy could generate a variety of indirect impacts. While policies to reduce the demand for energy could have a broadly beneficial effect on the historic environment, they could equally have a detrimental impact if energy-saving measures are poorly designed or inappropriate for historic buildings.[23] For cultural heritage in general, five themes of research and investigation are therefore relevant: understanding the vulnerability of materials; the monitoring of change; the modelling and projection of climate behaviour; the management of cultural heritage; and damage prevention.

The major scientific research projects on the impact of climate change on cultural heritage, to date, are Engineering Historic Futures by the United Kingdom (2006),[24] which focused on moisture-related climate change, and Global Climate Change Impact on Built Heritage and Cultural Landscapes by the European Union.[25]

In an increasingly urban world, the most innovative ideas in the fight against global climate change are being generated by cities and local initiatives.

The report, 'Our Urban Future', by the Washington-based Worldwatch Institute, an environmental think-tank, noted that efforts by cities and other local governments are only part of the picture, but can be instrumental, particularly in the developing world where local efforts can have a quicker impact than national plans that have little support. While our understanding of the potential and imminent impact of a changing climate on our built environment may only be in the early phase, nevertheless, cities and local governments will lead the way in combating the effects of global warming (Worldwatch Institute, 2007).

The Changing Role of Cities as Drivers of Development

A major impetus for the rural-to-urban migration has been economic restructuring. Many countries have reoriented their economies towards

---

[22]'Programs to monitor Earth at risk, panel says' by Andrew C. Revkin, *International Herald Tribune*, 16 January 2007.

[23]Taken from: *Climate Change and the Historic Environment*, Statement by English Heritage, published in January 2006, available at: www.helm.org.uk

[24]Available at: http://www.ucl.ac.uk/sustainableheritage/historic_futures.htm

[25]Available at: http://noahsark.isac.cnr.it/

more free market activity. Although it would be difficult to argue that this trend is universal, nevertheless, in important ways the shift is under way, and population redistribution is an important consequence. The most notable case is China, but countries like Vietnam, Ethiopia, Mexico and Brazil have also seen economic restructuring leading to internal migration. This leads not only to people moving to new locations, but it also generates different rates of economic growth by region, which produces opportunities for work to which workers respond.[26]

At the start of the new millennium the World Bank noted that cities and towns were growing not only in size and number, but were also gaining new influence. Globalisation was leading to major restructuring within countries, shifting trade and manufacturing away from many traditional urban centres toward cities and towns that could demonstrate market advantage.

The industrial and commercial activities are primarily located – and serviced, marketed and financed – in urban areas, accounting for one-half to four-fifths of Gross Domestic Product in most countries. The role of national governments is being refocused to facilitate markets, promote economic and social stability, and ensure equity (World Bank, 2000b).

It also observed that distinctions among cities, towns and rural areas had become almost obsolete, as economic activity spreads outward into major semi-urbanised and rural industrialised regions, of which the Pearl River Delta in China is perhaps the most striking example. As such, 'urban' and 'rural' do not signify closed systems within a country anymore, but rather a seamless continuum of economic activities and settlements distinguished by degrees of density, by dependence on agriculture or production, and by social organisation.

The development of urban areas, therefore, is closely tied to the rural economy through exchanges of goods, labour, services, capital, social transactions, information and technology, benefiting residents in both locations. In response to this vanishing dichotomy, the Bank's Strategic View of Urban and Local Government Issues refers to the 'city' as *an urban economic area that represents an integral market, but typically extends beyond formal administrative boundaries to encompass closely neighboring sub-regions, which may include smaller cities, peri-urban, or even adjacent rural areas*.[27]

This definition presents a close analogy with the concept of Historic Urban Landscape in relation to urban conservation, as discussed in the previous chapter.

To optimise potential, policies and strategies for urban development need to be implemented differently in different places, with a focus on the level of political commitment and institutional and technical capacities that exist in particular locales. Cities that have become key nodes in their regional economies have invested heavily in improving local conditions,

---

[26]White, M.J., 'Migration, Urbanization, and Social Adjustment'. Rosan et al., 1999: 21.
[27]World Bank, 2000b: 22.

Outside Kampala, Uganda

Zanzibar

The urban economy stretches beyond the city limits to include hinterlands that provide urban areas with land, labour and produce.

such as ensuring an efficient network of technical infrastructure and offering a high-quality urban environment in terms of social and cultural services and facilities.

Transferring significant measures of autonomy from national to city governments, or decentralisation, allows the planning and design of these specific attributes at the local level, which boosts the performance of cities. In addition, place marketing and place branding for cities and regions have emerged in recent years to manage internal and external opportunities and to transform them into competitive advantage.

The 2007 (First) Global Report on Decentralization and Local Democracy in the World summarises several distinct directions that have been taken by nations in pursuit of decentralisation, '*with different objectives – some political, others more economic, still others give more weight to better services or democracy*'. But in spite of the lack of a single normative framework guiding the formulation and implementation of decentralised governance, many states have chosen to engage in the process of decentralisation, which in itself constitutes '*a remarkable phenomenon*'.[28]

This drive is linked to underlying structural factors that are engulfing the globe, namely, the obsolescence of the central state model since the collapse of the Soviet Union; the process of regionalisation in Europe; and the spread of democracy in Africa, Asia and Latin America. Decentralisation primarily involves the delegation of power, a transfer of functions and responsibilities from a higher, national level, to a lower, municipal level. With decentralisation, however, comes a need for central monitoring – hence the steady growth worldwide of central services in the past few decades, both in the governmental and corporate realms.

In the competition for economic market share and direct investments, cities have appropriated more power and become more autonomous, which in turn has had dramatic effects on other socio-cultural aspects that were previously the primary concern of national governments.[29] In general, with economic restructuring and decentralisation came a rapid privatisation and commercialisation of space, and commoditisation of culture and heritage, which is glaringly visible in historic inner cities today. Much of the historic fabric has been altered or disfigured by aggressive advertisements, new franchises and theme-park developments, often lamented as the 'Disney-fication' of heritage, '*which involves a filtering and packaging operation to eliminate unpleasantness, tragedy, time and blemish*' (Rowe and Koetter, 1978: 48).

---

[28] UCLG, 2007: 283.

[29] One such aspect is the preservation of World Heritage sites. The removal from the World Heritage List in 2009 of the Elbe Valley Cultural Landscape in Dresden (Germany) is a case in point.

Furthermore, '*it not only provides a fictional and often nostalgic identity, but – its critics claim – also is purposely designed to break the contingency of public space that is characteristic of urban culture, replacing it with a domesticated family-friendly scenography of – often commercially controlled – pseudo-public spaces*'.[30]

In addition to a loss of authenticity, cultural diversity has also fallen victim to large, international corporations with powerful brands that replace local shops and their products – from coffee bars and sandwich shops, to restaurants and hotels. Historic inner cities have become more uniform in the range of products and services they offer nowadays, which significantly diminishes the cultural-historic value of the place, and thus the visitor experience.

Moreover, the socio-economic effects on the local community are often devastating. They are either directly or indirectly removed from the place, evicted or driven out by higher rents and rising costs of living, or otherwise denied access when public space is privatised, in the form of terraces or shopping plazas for instance. But however unpleasant, it is important to point out that the problem lies not with globalisation itself, but more with the way in which globalisation has been managed, with unregulated market forces driving the process.

While big corporations are capable of producing goods and services for the mass market at a price and standard that smaller businesses cannot manage anymore in our socially and technologically complex societies, it should also be acknowledged that the architectural reconfiguration of historic cities and towns into a mono-culture of shopping plazas, strip malls and theme parks has been driven by these same big corporations, which are neither place-bound nor community-bound, in a non-participatory way by the handing down of planning and design decisions from above by a team of corporate experts (Kaplan, 2000).

In the coming decades the fate of nations will largely depend on their network of increasingly autonomous cities, how coherently and effectively they interact with each other and with other networks in order to identify complementary action and high standards of performance in the socio-economic realm, as well as in cultural continuity. Cultural continuity is a defining element of identity and urban pride, both of which are equally important assets in determining competitiveness and building resilience (Campbell, 2003).

Moreover, municipalities and city governments are in closer proximity to their citizens than are national governments, and thus more sensitive to their social and cultural needs. As such they are ideally suited to lead reform of the globalisation process to address socio-economic imbalances and cultural differences. Cities can harness local civil society for

---

[30]De Waal, Martijn. 'Powerifications', in: International Architecture Biennale Rotterdam, 2007: 228.

Prague

Luxor

Management excesses: a 'sanitised' public space in Prague, Czech Republic, at one end of the spectrum, and aggressive advertising in Luxor, Egypt, on the other.

capacity building, and take into account local labour, cultural expressions, languages, businesses and communities at all levels of decision making, thereby strengthening and enhancing social sustainability and democracy.

City governments and their mayors are constantly expanding their responsibilities and reach in relation to the citizens – 'paradoxically, in the global era, the one socio-political unit growing in power is the city'.[31]

The Emergence of the Tourism Industry

The World Tourism Organization (UNWTO) states that over the past six decades tourism has experienced continued growth and diversification to become one of the largest and fastest-growing economic sectors in the world.

International tourist arrivals have grown steadily and significantly: from 25 million in 1950, to 277 million in 1980, to 438 million in 1990, to 684 million in 2000, and reaching 922 million in 2008. By 2020 international arrivals are expected to reach 1.6 billion. As growth has been particularly brisk in the world's emerging regions, the share in international tourist arrivals received by developing countries has steadily risen, from 31 per cent in 1990 to 45 per cent in 2008. International tourism receipts rose by 1.7 per cent in real terms to US$ 944 billion (642 billion euros) in 2008.[32]

While these overall facts and figures are already impressive, the visitor numbers at individual iconic or World Heritage sites can be mind-numbing, as demonstrated in the case of the Galapagos Islands (Ecuador), Venice (Italy) or Hangzhou (China). The Galapagos Islands were among the first sites to be inscribed onto the World Heritage List in 1978, when around 9,000 tourists paid a visit.

This number grew to 50,000 in 1996 and then tripled to 150,000 in 2007 – the year when the World Heritage Committee decided to inscribe the site onto the List of World Heritage in Danger due to a series of persistent negative impacts, including a rapid increase in the number of invasive species and ongoing uncontrolled fishing and poaching.

For the category of historic cities, the Venice-city region is widely quoted to be among the most visited tourist destinations in the world, with in 2008 a staggering 39.5 million visitors (OECD, 2010).

However, China is expected to eclipse these numbers in the coming years, as it experiences in particular a rapid national growth of its tourism market. The city of Hangzhou in Zhejiang Province is home to the 5.66-square-kilometre West Lake and scenic area, which is famous for its

---

[31] Savir, 2003: 30.
[32] Source: World Tourism Organization at http://unwto.org/facts/menu.html

Box 3.5 Historic Town of Zabid (Yemen)

The historic town of Zabid was inscribed onto the World Heritage List in 1993 because of its great importance and influence in the Arab and Muslim world over centuries. During the Rasulid period (thirteenth to fifteenth centuries) it was the capital of Yemen and its vernacular architecture is the most characteristic example of the Tihama style of courtyard house. At the time of inscription ICOMOS stated that the lack of proper conservation and management programmes for Zabid was a cause for alarm, since the town was clearly threatened at the time. In 2000 it was inscribed onto the List of World Heritage in Danger, owing to a persistent process of decline and degradation. The city has been losing its authenticity as a result of a lack of maintenance and building regulations, which resulted in the construction of new concrete buildings within the city's historic perimeter. According to a 2008 architectural survey, 70 per cent of the domestic and military architecture that constitutes an outstanding urban pattern is still present, although in a poor state of conservation, causing a gradual decline in the original values for which the site was inscribed. An Action Plan was developed by the German Development Agency (GTZ, now GIZ) and the local authorities to avoid the definitive delisting of the property. The project's approach, which consists of keeping the site's authenticity through individual buildings rather than its urban fabric, has slowed down the process of deterioration. However, the project's biggest challenge is to improve economic opportunities and local capacities for Zabid's inhabitants, while fostering the conservation of the city's cultural heritage as a basis for socio-economic development.

Source: World Heritage Committee State of Conservation Report 30 COM 7A.21

influences on art and landscape architecture throughout East Asia. Last year it reportedly was visited by 20 million tourists and one can only wonder what will happen after its 2011 nomination to the World Heritage List. All this growth is facilitated by the rapid development of, and cost reduction in, transportation technology, and by improved standards of living, its citizens having more disposable income and paid vacation time. As such it becomes clear that a large part of the world's population does not engage in tourism as tourists, despite the fact that tourism has become a global phenomenon.

As many have pointed out, tourism is a double-edged sword because of the paradoxes built into its organisation and operation. Three main tensions can be identified (Robinson and Picard, 2006). Firstly, tourism is a typical exponent of globalisation as it is an industry that is highly structured and globally interconnected, which operates in a world of transnational capital flows, multinational companies and organisations, and the free movement of people.

At the same time, however, this industry is still built around the nineteenth-century concept of the nation state, with its own institutions, political systems, economic needs, and all in competition with each other to attract large numbers of people.

Secondly, tourism is on the one hand strongly dependent on the public sector for the provision of infrastructure, such as roads, airports, water – and heritage as well – while on the other hand it generally consists of a multitude of fragmented small and medium-sized, privately owned and operated businesses, which make it difficult to coordinate and legislate for.

Thirdly, and certainly the most visible issue in the mass media, is the dual capacity of tourism to generate significant benefits, in terms of direct revenues and employment, while at the same time creating pressures and problems associated with large numbers of visitors overrunning local populations, altering or destroying their environment and traditional livelihoods.

Yet, in spite of these paradoxes and tensions, UNESCO promotes tourism because it is such a powerful tool to bring people and communities into contact, which plays an important role in facilitating dialogue among cultures and civilisations – the core of the Organization's mandate.

This dialogue creates cross-cultural awareness and understanding, thereby diminishing the likelihood of conflicts and tensions that are often the product of poor communication and a basic lack of knowledge of why and how cultures are different. As with globalisation in general, the benefits of tourism and their fair distribution depend heavily upon the quality of the design and implementation of its policies and activities. In large parts of the world it has become an essential part of national and regional economies. When managed successfully, tourism can capture the economic characteristics of heritage and harness these for conservation by generating funding, educating the community and influencing policy.[33]

The United Nations Environment Programme (UNEP) and the World Tourism Organization jointly published a guidebook stating that *'sustainable tourism development guidelines and management practices are applicable to all forms of tourism in all types of destinations, including mass tourism and the various niche tourism segments'*.[34] It identifies three conditions that have to be met to make tourism sustainable.

Firstly, the environmental resources that constitute a key component in the development of tourism have to be used in an optimal way to maintain essential ecological processes and to help conserve natural resources and biological diversity.

Secondly, the cultural authenticity and social integrity of host communities need to be respected to conserve their built and living cultural heritage with their traditional values, and to contribute to inter-cultural understanding and tolerance.

Thirdly, viable long-term economic activities must exist to provide socio-economic benefits to all who are involved, including stable employment and other income-earning opportunities and social services to host communities, which are fairly distributed and contribute to poverty alleviation. In addition to these, the report further states that a meaningful experience

[33] ICOMOS International Cultural Tourism Charter of 1999. ICOMOS, 2001: 115.
[34] UNEP, 2005: 11.

102

Hangzhou's West Lake

Hangzhou, the ancient capital of the Song Dynasty, is today a bustling industrial city with a strong tourist appeal for all East Asia, further boosted by its inscription onto the World Heritage List.

should be provided for the visitors, with a high level of tourism satisfaction, to raise their awareness about issues of sustainability and to promote sustainable tourism practices among them.

Only a handful of historic cities have tourism-management and public-use plans in place to effectively deal with the increase in visitor numbers and related impacts. Public use includes, among others, site interpretation and visitor experience, business planning, and setting standards for, and monitoring, the impact of increased visitation through methodologies based on the limits of acceptable change for the historic city. There is a need to 'mainstream' such tourism-management and public-use plans as a tool for better site protection and conservation, and to enhance local economic development and community empowerment. In addition, systematic approaches to engage the tourism industry to work with urban managers on destination management are vital and just beginning.

The process of engaging and mobilising the tourism industry to contribute to monitoring and mitigation of negative impacts on the environment and culture, and to local capacity building, is still in its infancy. This hampers the effective delivery of economic benefits to local communities and the urban periphery, but has great potential given the growing network of

Box 3.6 Luang Prabang (Laos)

Luang Prabang's particular townscape is the result of a fusion of traditional Laotian architecture with European colonial structures. The listing as a World Heritage site in 1995 propelled the city to become a popular tourist destination, which brought changes such as reversing a depopulation process dating back to 1985, and new urban morphologies and typologies that threatened to interfere with the traditional social and spatial structures. In 1996, a programme of decentralised cooperation was established by UNESCO with the French city of Chinon. The programme, funded by the French Development Agency (AFD) with 7.1 million euros, was developed in several phases aiming to raise local awareness of heritage conservation and to create new Laotian administrative structures, including the Local Heritage Committee and a Heritage House. The Local Heritage Committee involves the local population in the city's conservation and planning, while the Heritage House is in charge of the implementation of Luang Prabang's Safeguarding and Preservation Plan, which was elaborated from 1999 to 2001. In addition, different pilot restoration projects were implemented with French technical supervision and in collaboration with local NGOs, such as the restoration of the city's humid zones, which was funded by the European Commission. After several years of cooperation and the restoration of many historic buildings and urban facilities, as well as the construction of the Bona Kang Bung eco-museum, which was designed by the Heritage House architects based on the local typology, local awareness of heritage conservation has increased significantly. The participation of the local population has been enhanced by the Population Aid Fund, which through allocations helps inhabitants to restore their traditional houses. In 2004 the AFD further financed the elaboration of a Territorial Development Plan, a tool which aims to ensure the uniformity of territorial development in harmony with the site's character and identity in the future, highlighting the inhabitants' vision of Luang Prabang as a green heritage city. The decentralised cooperation programme, with its interdisciplinary approach, based on a solid knowledge of the site's characteristics, has become a model for international cooperation.

Source: Savourey, 2005

stakeholders involved in tourism development including local, national and international organisations eager to assist in making tourism a force for sustaining and developing local cultures and economies (Robinson and Picard, 2006).

Broadening Perceptions and Urban Heritage Values

Broadening Perceptions of Cultural Heritage

While all five previously discussed forces of change emerged from outside the realm of heritage conservation, the broadening of the understanding and appreciation of the concept itself was generated from within.

In the early years of the implementation of the World Heritage Convention, during the 1970s and 1980s, a 'monumental' approach was taken towards the identification and conservation of cultural properties as a direct result of the evolution of the discipline, as outlined in Chapter 1.

This meant for historic ensembles, districts and larger urban sites that the 'picturesque' value played an important role in their designation as protected areas and consequently in the decision-making concerning their conservation and management. The emphasis was very much on the aspects of beauty and visual harmony in formal terms according to the canon of architecture as part of fine arts (Van Oers, 2007a).

Moreover, the *Operational Guidelines for the Implementation of the World Heritage Convention* positioned historic districts and city centres in the category of 'groups of buildings'. This further hampered the recognition of the social richness and cultural diversity harboured by historic cities, and reduced the multiplicity of their values, some intangible and living, to mere architectural and urban form.

Along with the debates on the Global Strategy at the World Heritage Committee,[35] which began in the 1980s when growing imbalances between inscribed cultural and natural properties on the World Heritage List became apparent, a steady broadening of meaning and interpretation of heritage has taken place.

As a result ICOMOS put forward the following comprehensive statement that captures this process: *'Heritage is a broad concept and includes the natural as well as the cultural environment. It encompasses landscapes, historic places, sites and built environments, as well as bio-diversity, collections, past and continuing cultural practices, knowledge and living experiences. It records and expresses the long processes of historic development, forming the essence of diverse national, regional, indigenous and local identities and is an integral part of modern life. It is a dynamic reference*

---

[35] The Global Strategy for a Balanced, Representative and Credible World Heritage List was adopted by the World Heritage Committee in 1994. It is an action programme designed to identify and fill the major gaps in the World Heritage List and it relies on regional and thematic definitions and analyses of categories of heritage of outstanding universal value.

point and positive instrument for growth and change. The particular herit-age and collective memory of each locality or community is irreplaceable and an important foundation for development, both now and into the future'.[36]

Thanks to the Global Strategy, a series of complementary concepts was articulated, or reinterpreted during the 1990s and the early years of this century, most notably:

- The new category of Cultural Landscapes.[37]
- The Nara Document on Authenticity in 1994.[38]
- The programme on Modern Heritage launched by UNESCO in 2001 for the identification and protection of built heritage from the modern era.[39]
- The 2003 Convention for the Safeguarding of the Intangible Heritage.[40]
- The 2005 Convention on the Protection and Promotion of the Diversity of Cultural Expressions.[41]
- The Historic Urban Landscape initiative initiated by UNESCO in 2005.[42]

Urban Heritage Values

At the international workshop Partnerships for World Heritage Cities – Culture as a Vector for Sustainable Urban Development, organised by the World Heritage Centre and local authorities in Urbino (Italy) in November 2002, participants concluded that urban heritage is a human and social cultural element that goes beyond the static notion of 'groups of buildings', as cities are witness to the fact that the accumulation of cultures and traditions, recognised as such in their diversity, are the basis of heritage values in the areas and towns that these cultures have pro-duced or reused. These 'urban heritage values' must be made clear from the outset and be used to define urban development strategies and poli-cies, with related programmes and actions (UNESCO World Heritage Centre, 2004).

What are then these urban heritage values? To get a handle on this complex issue, it is useful to first look into the essence of the urban condition.

---

[36] ICOMOS International Tourism Charter of 1999, ICOMOS 2001: 115.
[37] See: http://whc.unesco.org/en/culturallandscapes
[38] See: http://whc.unesco.org/archive/nara94.htm
[39] See: http://whc.unesco.org/en/activities/38/
[40] See: http://www.unesco.org/culture/ich/index.php?pg=00006
[41] See: http://unesdoc.unesco.org/images/0014/001429/142919e.pdf
[42] See: http://whc.unesco.org/uploads/activities/documents/activity-47-11.pdf

The notion of 'urban' is related to the Latin term *urbs*, which referred to the delimitation of the city of Rome and to the word *urbum* (plough). In ancient times the Romans used a plough to trace the limits of a settlement. Tracing this boundary, an area was delimited from a previously open and free field into a confined area to be constructed (Rykwert, 1989).[43]

As such, an emphasis can be put on context and (rural or natural) setting of urban heritage – the city and its territorial dimension – while at the same time recognising the importance of social and cultural processes, such as the sacred act of city demarcation in ancient times, that shaped – and are still shaping – the city. It is important to underline that urban heritage values are as much about buildings and spaces, as about rituals and traditions that people bring to the city.

An important determinant of any culture – also urban culture – is spirit of place (Durrell, 1969; Norberg-Schulz, 1980). Sense of place is the contemporary equivalent of the *genius loci* of ancient times, which was the guardian divinity of a place, its 'genius' or protective spirit (Rykwert, 1989). Dissociated from its spiritual and symbolic meaning today, sense of place is rather simplified and refers to the character or quality of a place as can be perceived when visiting it.

But as explained by Smith, the sense of place cannot be observed,[44] nor instantly created for that matter, by present-day urban planning practices as part of the fashion of 'place-making' in new developments. It is typically the aggregate of individual perceptions, which is expressed collectively, from the community that lives, works and socializes in a place, rather than the limited knowledge and perceptions acquired by transient visitors.

Fundamentally, it is local communities who make places – not architects or designers. Local communities integrate natural and cultural components of any given locale through their daily practices and behaviour, their beliefs, traditions and value systems, into a singular experience, which can only be truly appreciated when participating in that practice.

A place acquires its identity through the continuous historic process of negotiating between different groups and communities. Olivier Mongin (2005) observes that the urban condition since ancient times has been determined by two interrelated and complementary factors: a physical entity, *urbs*, or its Greek equivalent of *polis*, being the town proper, and its symbolic counterpart of the political institution, *civitas*, which is the collective agreement by a community to inhabit and coexist in a given place, and is generally associated with citizenship.

---

[43] See also: Jokilehto, Jukka. 'Reflection on Historic Urban Landscapes as a tool for Conservation'. Van Oers, 2010: 53–63.

[44] Smith, J., 'The Marrying of the Old with the New in Historic Urban Landscapes'. Van Oers, 2010: 45–52.

Living in a city, or city-state, and having citizenship were considered a privilege in ancient times, since much of the environment was either rural (mired in poverty) or wilderness (outright dangerous). Citizenship was foremost determined by one's conduct and behaviour and was guided by a set of unwritten rules, among which were the *mores* (societal norms, customs, virtues or values) governing the population of an urbanised society – of their own choice and free will. In his view, therefore, the urban condition is also strongly associated with democracy (Mongin, 2005).

Urban heritage values thus pertain to built and non-built spaces in a historic city, and to their formal function and informal use, by residing communities and visitors alike, which can create different geographies of the city.

It is as much about the urban form and architecture, which make a crucial contribution to its character and articulation, as about social patterns and cultural traditions embedded in the historic city. Because our communication rests upon it, tradition is considered indispensable (Hobsbawm, 1983), and this, in turn, is related to a felt need for a structured social environment – of which the historic city must be the epitome.

Often there is more than one community, each with its own traditions and customs; all of them put their mark on the town to create a dynamic melting pot of experiences that are enhanced by site-specific qualities, such as geography and topography, and local flora and fauna, to name but a few. Many historic cities have started surveying their built environment, assembling lists of historic monuments and important places, primarily to serve the tourism industry. However, very few have engaged in broader cultural mapping to identify a wider range of attributes, also related to intangible components such as processes and traditions associated with this built environment, which are important to maintain, and where possible to enhance, the historic city's full range of urban heritage values.

The Management of Change

The external and internal forces of change that are affecting urban heritage conservation are the result of processes related to globalisation, which has brought people, places and cultures closer to each other through improvements in transport, communication and information technologies. However, as the German philosopher Rüdiger Safranski has observed in an essay about the impact of globalisation on our consciousness and direct living environment: although we can communicate and travel on a global scale, we can't live globally – our capacity and our willingness to maintain an open attitude towards the world fails or succeeds in particular with an emotional attachment to a place (Safranski, 2007).

This brings us again to the seminal work of Kevin Lynch, *The Image of the City*, where he argues that '*we need an environment which is not simply well organized, but poetic and symbolic as well. It should speak of the individuals and their complex society, of their aspirations and their historical tradition, of the natural setting, and of the complicated functions and*

Havana

Jerusalem

Buildings and spaces, as well as communities' rituals and traditions form part of the city's urban values, which need to be comprehensively mapped and interpreted to serve as guidance for conservation and management.

movements of the city world. But clarity of structure and vividness of iden-
tity are first steps to the development of strong symbols. By appearing as
a remarkable and well-knit place, the city could provide a ground for the
clustering and organization of these meanings and associations. Such a
sense of place in itself enhances every human activity that occurs there,
and encourages the deposit of a memory trace'.[45]

Jeremy Whitehand continues this argument, noting that *'the spirit of a*
society is objectivated in the historico-geographical character of the urban
landscape which enables individuals and groups to take root in an area.
They acquire a sense of the historical dimension of human existence, which
stimulates comparison and encourages a less time-bound and more inte-
grated approach to contemporary problems. Landscapes with a high
degree of expressiveness of past societies exert a particularly strong edu-
cative and regenerative influence'.[46]

The tremendous broadening of perception and appreciation of heritage
over the last decades has been accompanied by an increasing complexity
in the ways and means to identify, protect, conserve, present and transmit
heritage assets, and this complexity continues to grow – albeit on a different plane, as this chapter has aimed to demonstrate. Certainly as regards
the conservation of living historic cities, there is a need to substantially
reform management approaches and practices, because the environmental
and resource-management issues of today cut across traditional sector
boundaries, across social and economic systems, and across political fron-
tiers – furthermore, they have increased in scale and therefore in impact.

It has become clear that despite being unpredictable, and therefore
uncomfortable, the variable of 'change' has to become part of the equation
if we want to take the conservation of historic cities to the next level.
Change has become a formidable force to reckon with and in several critical
ways it is an essential factor affecting urban conservation practice. What is
emerging is a complex management environment, where change can be
plotted along three perpendicular axes that display:

1) living, dynamic cities with a constant need for modernisation and adap-
    tation, in recognition of the life cycles of a city, being growth, maturity,
    stagnation, decline, and regeneration, in which the pace of change
    seems to be increasing all the time;
2) an expansion of interrelationships, bringing with it a widening circle of
    stakeholder groups and interests, which necessitate conflict resolution
    as a key practice;
3) changing notions of what constitutes heritage, through changes in the
    make-up of populations (due to migration, as well as demographic
    changes), bringing with it different value systems of perception and
    appreciation of heritage.

---

[45] Lynch, 1960: 119.
[46] Whitehand, 1992: 6.

With all these changes occurring, at different intervals, at different levels, and with different magnitudes, it can be concluded that urban heritage conservation has become a moving target, to which a static, monumental approach as inherited from the previous century is wholly inadequate, or may become perhaps downright destructive.

When rigid conservation doctrine prioritises authenticity and restoration of the historic fabric over socio-economic functionality, for instance, it may diminish vitality and resilience of the historic city, which could have devastating effects in the long term. In today's world, cities are at the core of economic, social and cultural activity, where the diversity of encounters and interactions generates new initiatives and ideas. In order to sustain this vital function in society, cities have to be replenished and recreated through modernisation, adaptation and regeneration (Roberts and Sykes, 2000), while retaining and further building upon their character and identity.

Thus, change can be for better or for worse, depending on which parameter is chosen; but like it or not, it will happen, whether demographically, climatically or culturally induced, and with this certainty in mind the best strategy seems to be to prepare for it and to anticipate it.

The management of change is a conservation approach to anticipate and regulate, but not to plan, the market-driven processes of urban development in, or adjacent to, historic cities. The notion of change was incidentally introduced into conservation by Alois Riegl and articulated in his fundamental theoretical studies, as discussed in Chapter 1.

In modern times the management of change has been advocated as a process of careful analysis to control and reduce its adverse impacts, instead of being a doctrine of submission (Teutonico and Matero, 2003). However, until very recently the international conservation community had resisted this approach, as it found this difficult to accept in view of the core ideology to preserve monuments and sites as unchanged as possible, but as of October 2010, ICOMOS has embarked on a global exercise to explore issues of change and continuity in the conservation of monuments and sites (Araoz, 2011): an extremely important initiative in view of the multitude of critical cases currently under debate at both the national and international level.

4. New Actors and Approaches to Urban Heritage Management

We should make the old serve the new.

Mao Zedong

The Contemporary Context of Urban Heritage Management

In the previous chapter, six processes were identified as having an impact on the practice of urban conservation. These are urbanisation, urban development, climate change, the changing socio-economic role both of cities and of tourism, and the changing perception of urban heritage values to be protected, as an important factor in transforming the position of the historic city in contemporary societies. These processes overlap and create a complex and dynamic conservation environment with growing interrelationships and a widening circle of stakeholder groups, often with competing interests. At the same time, in many parts of the world the responsibility for action has shifted from the national to the local level, empowering cities and regions to make their own strategies for development. But this increase in tasks and responsibilities at the local level has not always been accompanied by a corresponding increase in capacity, whether institutional, technical or financial. The market will tend to occupy the resulting vacuum, causing distortions and conflicts. But instead of blaming the market, it seems more appropriate to take a critical look at the ways and means of the practice of conservation, with a view to innovate and update existing strategies and tools for urban heritage management in order to cope with increasing complexity and shifting responsibilities.

ICCROM's revised management guidelines for historic towns, for instance, are still a good reference and introduction to the topic (Feilden and Jokilehto, 1998). But as their subject is the relatively small and easy-to-delineate historic town, and their focus is almost solely on the

The Historic Urban Landscape: Managing Heritage in an Urban Century, First Edition. Francesco Bandarin, Ron van Oers.
© 2012 Francesco Bandarin and Ron van Oers. Published 2012 by Blackwell Publishing Ltd.

preservation of its historic fabric, it has become less pertinent for operations in today's dynamic urban environment, where cities and towns are part of a diffuse network irrigated by a continuous flow of capital, goods and services, and as such are affected by it. In order to deal more effectively with current interrelationships and complexities, ICCROM's four pillars of historic city management (typo-morphological analyses, conservative property management, modest rehabilitation schemes and participatory processes to involve inhabitants) should be supplemented by a range of other issues and instruments, which lie at the heart of the Historic Urban Landscape approach.

In order to fully grasp the rationale and substance of the Historic Urban Landscape approach, the overall framework of city management will first be examined. The World Bank, which has become one of the key players in natural and cultural heritage conservation, including historic city regeneration,[1] has recently developed a new urban strategy. This, together with other city strategies under development by key actors in the field, will be discussed in brief.

The Emergence of a New Urban Strategy

The new Urban Strategy of the World Bank labels urbanisation as the defining phenomenon of this century (World Bank, 2009b). It stresses that urbanisation is a force to be harnessed, not to be curbed, in order to facilitate growth and fight poverty. Notwithstanding the fact that rapid urbanisation and accompanying urban development should be situated in a national strategic framework, in the same way that critical policy areas such as land and housing markets are beyond the remit of single city administrations, cities are at the core of a dynamic development environment where the implementation of sector activities interacts with collaboration efforts among communities, different levels of government, and other private-sector and public-sector institutions, which can create agents of sustainable development for the country. In other words: while socio-economic planning needs to take on a national perspective, the onus is on cities to act as trailblazers – they are the engines to drive growth and alleviate poverty, but also to innovate in search of sustainable approaches to policy implementation and localised action. The World Bank proposes five key issues, or 'business lines', to be addressed if cities and towns are to perform this function best. They are:

- **City management, governance, and finance**: ensuring accountability, integrity and transparency of local government action, with inclusion

[1]Since 1971, the World Bank has invested over US$ 4 billion in financing 267 lending and non-lending operations, with currently 120 operations under implementation for an outstanding commitment of more than US$ 2 billion. Of the 267 World Bank projects, more than one-third (101) has focused on World Heritage sites, providing investments, conservation and rehabilitation policies, site management plans, physical improvements and technical assistance. Source: World Bank unpublished portfolio review, 15 September 2010.

and representation of all groups in urban society, as well as sound treatment of revenue sources and expenditure, in particular concerning the necessary fiscal decentralisation that follows an increase in the authority of local governments.

- **Urban poverty**: addressing urban poverty in a wider policy framework than just slum upgrading, through issues such as property rights, land and labour markets, with city-wide and nation-wide investments from both the public and private sector, in services for the poor to ensure decent standards of living and working conditions with specifically designed social safety nets.
- **Cities and economic growth**: ensuring competitiveness to maintain relatively stable levels of employment, income and investment, which includes redevelopment and urban regeneration to transform and adapt derelict or dysfunctional urban areas to new uses, also in partnership with the private sector.
- **City planning, land, and housing**: addressing the challenges of planning for markets, public land management, property rights and housing finance to regulate urban spatial structures. These challenges include land use, density and urban form, notably the need to relieve pressure on the limited availability of urban land, which drives up prices, and the need to anticipate future urban growth.
- **Urban environment, climate change, and disaster management**: focusing on urban form and design to achieve greater efficiency in terms of proximity of facilities and access to services to reduce energy use and greenhouse-gas emissions, including at the site and building level, i.e. compact cities with a small environmental footprint, combined with efforts to strengthen the resilience of cities through climate change adaptation and mitigation planning.

This strategy addresses the overall framework of urban management issues. In the context of this book, the important question to ask is: does cultural heritage conservation cut across these five main strategic priorities of the new urban framework?

When looking at possible linkages and influences, it is important to keep in mind that traditionally culture has been perceived as unproductive, as no quantitative economic measurements were able to demonstrate otherwise. But in reality culture works for many other sectors, such as heritage, which in many countries, including developing countries, constitutes a primary driving force behind the development of the tourism industry (Purchla, 2005). In the words of Ismail Serageldin: *'Many of the benefits of cultural heritage do not enter markets, or do so only imperfectly'*.[2] However, increasingly, studies have appeared that focus on the direct and indirect economic benefits of protected areas, which point to the significant gains to be achieved in particular from a wise utilisation of natural and cultural heritage as part of national programmes of integrated planning and

---

[2] Serageldin, 1999: 24.

Box 4.1 Stone Town of Zanzibar (Tanzania)

In 2006 the European Commission funded a rehabilitation project for Stone Town's port, which was conceived as remedial work for an existing project that had begun prior to the inscription of the site onto the World Heritage List in 2000. However, the rehabilitation project did not include an assessment of the possible impact on the property. A 2008 mission reported that the work included some massive interventions in the port area, including an unauthorised demolition of two protected warehouses from the early-twentieth century, as well as new construction between the jetty and quay. These had an overall negative visual impact on the property's townscape and urban fabric, which retains the site's particular character of fairly homogeneous elements from different cultures spanning more than a millennium, the value for which the site was listed. The project has since been completed without an Environmental Impact Assessment or monitoring component, despite several requests from the World Heritage Committee. But in 2010 a Management Plan was developed with a clear action plan, which included urban conservation, while an inventory of the public spaces in Stone Town is currently under way.

Source: World Heritage Committee State of Conservation Report 31 COM 7B.49

development.[3] Experience shows that culture 'works' in terms of economic performance and human development, not least because cultural resources, once recognised and their creative potential applied, are infinite and omni-present – they cannot, however, be relocated: they are place-bound and community-bound. As part of the preparation of the 2015 Millennium Development Goals Review Summit, discussed in Chapter 3, UNESCO has put in place a special programme on Culture and Development in order to gather the necessary data to demonstrate the role of culture and of cultural diversity in achieving sustainable development.[4]

As regards city management, governance and finance ('business line 1'), in which local revenue mobilisation constitutes an essential component, it is worth recalling that urban heritage areas generate much higher returns than do areas devoid of any cultural-historic significance.[5] Proximity to world-class monuments and sites, because of reasons of visibility and iden-tification, usually draws high-end service-sector businesses and residents, who are willing to pay an inflated price for locations with prestige and status, which is reflected in land and property values. The 250-plus historic cities that have been included in the World Heritage List deliver very sig-nificant socio-economic benefits at the local and national levels, not only through tourism and related goods and services, but also through other functions (Ost, 2009). For instance, Salzburg (Austria) has only 6 per cent of the country's population, but the city contributes 25 per cent of its net economic product. In addition, the Mercer Quality Living Survey, which compares 215 large cities with 39 criteria, rated several World Heritage cities as among the best in 2009: Vienna (ranking 1), Bern (9), Brussels (14), Berlin (16), Luxemburg (19), Paris (33), and Lyon (37). Furthermore, urban heritage areas often require enhanced management, because of more and/ or stricter regulations on controlling and monitoring the built environment of heritage significance, which – if properly done – improves planning and design. This, in turn, increases certainty for investors, including property owners, as regards the general direction of local urban development, which

---

[3] The report 'Economic Activity of Australia's World Heritage Areas' prepared by Gillespie Economics and BDA Group for the Department of Environment, Water and Heritage Affairs in Australia in July 2008 found that Australia's 17 World Heritage properties generate Austral-ian $12 billion annually and sustain more than 120,000 jobs nationally.

[4] Although only the historic centres of some major cities are designated as World Heritage, the economic data on these cities is very revealing. A study by PricewaterhouseCoopers estimated the GDP of Lima in 2005 at US$ 67 billion; for Vienna 93; St Petersburg 85, Lyon 56, Budapest 43, Cairo 98, Rome 123, and Paris 460. See: http://www.citymayors.com/statistics/richest-cities-gdp-intro.html

[5] Reims, a French city with 63 historic monuments, including its famous Cathedral, receives 1.5 million visitors each year for various reasons, which generates 107 million euros – 90 per cent, or 96 million euros, for the Cathedral alone; Rouen, another French city with 50 regis-tered historic monuments and 1,000 ancient timber-framed houses, receives more than 2 million tourists each year, which generates 200 million euros, 80 per cent of which is from its historic monuments. Source: Van den Broucke, 'Les retombées économiques de la sauvegarde et de la valorisation du patrimoine sur un territoire', at:
http://www.fondation-patrimoine.org/read/0/rencontres-colloques/documents/lesretombeeseconomiquesdelasauvegardedupatrimoine-versionintegrale13.pdf

provides safeguards on their investments in the long term (Van Oers, 2007a).

Next to a top-economic performance, France (ranked 3rd by the United Nations in 2009 in terms of trade and development, behind the USA and China) has mastered a niche market in which culture and heritage work together to promote and brand the country's identity, with the city of Paris as one of the crown jewels, synonymous with a particular lifestyle.[6] At the other end of this spectrum we can identify the ongoing erosion of historic landscapes, natural and urban, with corporate enclaves dedicated to global business and that are defended by private security firms adjacent to heavily zoned suburbs.[7]

In the broader perspective, urban heritage often works in synergy with cultural industries, which can create spill-over effects that are beneficial to cities where cultural and trade objectives are intertwined to reinvigorate socio-economic growth, as encompassed by the concept of 'creative cities' (Landry, 2000; Florida, 2002). An idea that emerged in the late 1980s, this term describes an urban complex where cultural activities of various sorts form an integral component of the city's economic and social functioning. Being primarily a management approach, *'such cities tend to be built upon a strong social and cultural infrastructure, to have relatively high concentrations of creative employment, and to be attractive to inward investment because of their well-established cultural facilities. [. . .] The contribution of the creative sector to the economic vitality of cities can be measured in terms of the direct contribution of the sector to output, value added, incomes and employment and further through the indirect and induced effects caused, for example, by the expenditures of tourists visiting the city to experience its cultural attractions. In addition, cities with an active cultural life can attract inward investment in other industries seeking to locate in centres that will provide an enjoyable, stimulating environment for employees'*.[8]

When looking at urban poverty ('business line 2'), cultural heritage and related industries have until now not been systematically looked at as a means to alleviate it – with a notable exception being the Inter-American Development Bank (IDB). Back in the 1970s this bank was already offering loans for projects based on an awareness of the importance of culture and heritage carried out in a variety of domains, ranging from primary rural education to cultural tourism, with as its flagship project the restoration and revitalisation of the historic centre of Quito in Ecuador. An analysis

---

[6]Le Figaro magazine of 24 July 2010 ran an article about how France is drawing not only a majority of tourists to its territory, but also in particular a steady stream of wealthy and famous residents, among others John Malkovich, Brad Pitt and Angelina Jolie, Tony Blair, Mick Jagger, and Elton John, who have decided to make France their home, either primary or secondary, 'Pourquoi ils aiment la France', in: *Le Figaro magazine* of 24 July 2010, pp. 26–36.

[7]Robert Kaplan recalls that during his travels he has looked for cities such as St Louis and Atlanta in the USA and not found them, but 'only hotels and corporate offices with generic architecture, 'nostalgic' tourist bubbles, zoned suburbs, and bleak urban wastelands'; there was nothing distinctive that he could label as 'St Louis' or 'Atlanta', Kaplan, 2000: 84.

[8]UNCTAD, 2008: 17.

produced by IDB provides an overview of the evolution of policies and projects related to urban poverty and underlines in particular the role of cultural heritage in the development and revitalisation of downtown areas, where the rehabilitation of monuments and historical buildings and the establishment of new commercial activities and entertainment venues *'valorizes the inner character of these areas, creating values, whose main 'service' is to attract people and money'.*[9] The urban heritage of Quito was the key component in the large-scale rehabilitation scheme developed for this city, which was among the first sites to be inscribed onto the World Heritage List in 1978. More than 30 years later Quito is a case in point showing that it pays to take urban heritage as an interface, as it has managed to regulate and upgrade its urban affairs, while maintaining an almost-intact historic urban structure despite several natural disasters (among which the severe 1917 earthquake) and man-made pressures that have ravaged other historic cities around the globe. Cultural heritage, tangible and intangible, is, however, still a largely neglected economic resource that can serve as a powerful catalyst for economic and social regeneration, particularly in cities that have few other means of stimulating sustainable economic development.

Quito

Among the first properties to be inscribed onto the World Heritage List in 1978, the historic city has retained its authenticity and integrity to a large extent, which has been used to successfully revitalise the downtown area.

[9]Lanzafame and Quartesan, 2009: 76.

In addition to historic cities, and contrary to popular perception, slums constitute vast economies, albeit informal and unregulated, where in addition to basic necessities such as food, clothing and housing, a variety of cultural industries and services are being produced and delivered, usually on a small-scale artisanal basis, but which add up when considering the sheer size of these areas – 'the fortune at the bottom of the pyramid'.[10] *'The arts and crafts and design [. . .] are indeed the two groups of creative industries of greatest economic and social importance for developing countries. [. . .] While developed countries have dominated both export and import flows, developing countries year after year have increased their share in world markets for creative products, and their exports have risen faster than those from developed countries'*.[11] The creative industries are an essential component for identity formation at the local, regional, national and international levels (for instance, carnival in Brazil, reggae music in Jamaica, or movies in India), and constitute a new dynamic sector in world trade, growing at an annual rate of 8.7 per cent for the period 2000–2005 (and expected to continue throughout the decade). In 2005, total exports of all creative industry products reached US$ 424.4 billion, of which 'heritage goods and services' – the only sector of creative industries in which developing countries have an important participation in world markets – accounted for US$ 26.7 billion, US$16 billion of which was taken up by the developing countries (UNCTAD, 2008). Although it has remained difficult for mainstream (read: Western) investors to tap into the creativity and resourcefulness of slum dwellers – arguably due to a lack of interest and imagination – it would be a mistake to ignore this field or label it as insignificant. Instead, innovative approaches need to be devised in close cooperation with local partners to develop investment opportunities in a manner that actively promotes broad-based economic empowerment and social cohesion, for which both urban heritage sites and the arts-and-crafts sector seem ideally suited.

As for cities and economic growth ('business line 3'), urban heritage preservation has gained widespread recognition already, not only from national and local governments, but also from regional and international lending institutions such as the IDB and the World Bank,[12] as discussed earlier. Regarding investment strategies, such as urban regeneration, it is important to recognise that economic changes and corresponding population flows often lead to increasing polarisation in cities, economically and socially. *'Treating urban areas as a single category conceals the differences which exist both between and within urban areas. Some areas suffer multiple aspects of deprivation. The cumulative spiral of decline that can result leads to greater polarization between cities, but more particularly between*

---

[10]Indian academic C.K. Prahalad quoted in 'From slums into suburbs: how Sao Paulo is showing the way to civilise a megacity', in: *The Financial Times*, 25 August 2006, p. 11.
[11]UNCTAD, 2008: 102–106.
[12]The importance of culture as a factor in economic development was at the centre of the Conference 'Culture Counts', convened in Florence, Italy, in 1999 by the World Bank, UNESCO and the Government of Italy, World Bank, 2000a.

localities within them. Unemployment is often taken as the principal indica-
tor of the economic health of a locality and [. . .] it is inner city areas which
have suffered considerable unemployment',[13] in particular during the 1970s
and 1980s. For historic cities, these are usually the areas of greatest heritage significance, and actions to address the problems of inner cities have
therefore impacted directly on heritage assets.

While the style of approach to urban regeneration has evolved over the
years, reflecting the policy and practice of dominant socio-political attitudes
(Roberts and Sykes, 2000), approaches based on an integrated vision would
seem compatible with the conservation of urban heritage. A key element is
the financing and provision of incentives for the implementation of urban
heritage conservation and regeneration programmes, including knowledge
transfer and capacity building. A large part of such incentives needs to
come from the public sector to bridge short-term (fear of risk and cost) and
long-term (environmental and socio-economic benefits) perspectives.[14]

When examining the business line relating to city planning, land, and
housing ('business line 4'), it needs to be stressed that, in spite of the failure
of centrally planned economies such as those of the communist countries
before the fall of the Berlin Wall in 1989, planning is still an essential component of economic and urban development. In fact, without it the process
of urbanisation would lead to unmanaged growth with many negative side
effects, such as environmental stress, pollution, pressure on housing and
urban services, and serious social inequalities, of which the large slums that
fringe many cities in the developing world are a spatial manifestation. A
careful design of the urban infrastructure systems of water, sanitation,
public health, transport and energy are prerequisites for functioning urban
and regional markets, without which major cities will perform far below
their economic potential, or not at all. It is equally important to acknowledge that such infrastructure systems cannot be put in place by market
forces alone: they require planning and policy integration at the national
level if cities are to fulfil their potential as engines of growth for their
regions (Sachs, 2003).

Within this scheme urban heritage is also part of the infrastructure
system, similar to sanitation or transport. Like those systems, urban heritage cannot be left to market forces alone, as it needs a regulatory framework with incentive tools so that it can maintain, and enhance, its meaning
and significance for local communities, while acting as a catalyst for socio-
economic development via tourism, commercial use, and higher land and
property values. As such, the public and private sectors play a different,
but complementary, role, which is embedded in the concept of Public-
Private-Partnerships (PPPs). Officially they refer to *'innovative methods*
used by the public sector to contract with the private sector, which brings
in their capital and their ability to deliver projects on time and to budget,

---

[13] Roberts and Sykes, 2000: 133.

[14] For this reason, significant parts of economic stimulus packages have also been invested in
heritage preservation; see Van Oers, Ron. 'Sleeping with the Enemy? Private Sector Involvement in World Heritage Preservation'. Descamps, 2009: 57–66.

Box 4.2 Historic Cairo (Egypt)

The rehabilitation of the historic centre of Cairo (Egypt) was designed and implemented by the Aga Khan Trust for Culture. What was conceived in 1984 as an idea to build a new park for the metropolis, near the eastern limits of medieval Cairo, had by 2004 become one of the boldest visionary urban heritage projects in the Middle East, in which the creation of a green public space was used as a catalyst for the social and cultural development of adjacent communities. The site chosen for the new park, the 30-hectare Darassa Hills, had been a rubbish dump for five centuries and was located right beside the historic city walls dating from the Ayyubid period (twelfth – thirteenth centuries), of which only a small part was still visible, the larger part being covered by rubble and debris. On the other side was one of historic Cairo's most economically depressed communities, the neighbourhood of al-Darb al-Ahmar, which nevertheless is endowed with a rich cultural heritage. In a concerted effort among important partners such as the World Monuments Fund, the Ford Foundation, and the Egyptian Swiss Development Fund, the creation of the 74-acre/30-hectare Al-Azhar Park involved the restoration of 1.5 kilometres of the Ayyubid city wall, the socio-economic rehabilitation of Darb al-Ahmar community with US$ 4 million (in grants) in housing projects and restoration and reuse of heritage buildings and sites, with skills-training programmes for masons, carpenters, plumbers and electricians, as well as apprenticeships with local businesses arranged through a stipend system (in total 150 positions) and microcredit programmes (400 borrowers with a near 100 per cent recovery rate on loans in the first 6 months). By 2004, 19 community-owned houses (approximately 70 families), of which seven were part of the initial pilot credit programme, a health centre and a business centre were completed. For the next five years 50 houses annually were planned to be brought into the housing programme. At the peak of the project approximately 400 workers were employed daily on site, through three main contractors, fifteen specialised contractors and many suppliers. Last but not least, the project involved the insertion of high-quality, contemporary architectural expressions in the park for new facilities, while the Park itself has created 250 jobs on site, is receiving now about 2,000 visitors per day, and ran a deficit only in the first three years of operation. Understandably, the project of Al-Azhar Park has become a model of integrated conservation and inner city revitalisation, the lessons of which the Aga Khan Trust for Culture is using for projects in other (World Heritage) historic cities, such as Stone Town in Zanzibar (Tanzania) and Aleppo in Syria.

Source: Bianca and Jodidio, 2004

while the public sector retains the responsibility to provide these services to the public in a way that benefits the public and delivers economic development and an improvement in the quality of life'.[15]

Unofficially there is recognition of the opposing motivations driving each partner. With the private-sector partner being driven by the profit motive (which should not be the case for the public-sector partner), care must be taken not to transfer public-sector funding and/or authority as this could confer an unfair competitive edge while diminishing the public good.

The private-sector partner may invest its own resources in the partnership, because of the goodwill this can generate, or because it can enhance product visibility among potential customers – both may translate into profits later on. The public-sector partner has to be transparent, consistent and clear concerning its policies, whereas the private-sector partner has to recognise the opportunities offered by the choice of a higher-quality built environment and thus adjust its strategy. In the case of cities and their management, however, the public sector should remain the dominant partner, because of the many externalities involved, as mentioned before.

---

[15] UNECE, 2007: 1.

With regard to the regulation of urban spatial structures, which involve – among other things – land use, density and urban form, high-rise construction in inner-city areas demands special attention because of its impact on the historic urban fabric. The popularity of the skyscraper today is undeniable and even under the prevailing global economic conditions, the Council of Tall Buildings and Urban Habitat (CTBUH) reported that 2010 was by far the most active in the history of the skyscraper with more than 100 buildings, 200 metres or taller, completed worldwide.[16]

But in spite of this enormous popularity, the economic rationale for this building form still needs to be demonstrated (apart from situations where serious physical restrictions on surface area exist, such as in Manhattan, NYC, Hong Kong Island, or in Male, capital of the Maldives). Contrary to what politicians and city managers maintain, high-rise construction and tall buildings do not offer a more economic way of urban land use.[17] If they do, it is often at the expense of something else, usually public space and the quality of the living environment in the immediate surroundings (in terms of diminished direct sunlight and green spaces, for instance, or increased wind disturbance) and this is seldom accounted for when presenting the economic arguments. Ever since the first high-rise constructions were erected in Chicago in the late-nineteenth century, skyscrapers have been the preoccupation of architects and developers wanting to build taller and taller, often eagerly supported by politicians and city managers.

Hong Kong

---

[16] From 2012 it is expected that there will be a drop in the number of tall buildings completed due to the global recession, until the worldwide economy recovers; taken from: www. worldarchitecturenews.com

[17] For a different view on this issue, see: Bertaud, 2003.

Male in the Maldives

La Paz

125

High-rise building is a solution for cities with limited surface area. While compactness provides answers to density and offers higher sustainability than sprawl, there is a risk of losing the human dimension.

London

Paris

Rio de Janeiro

Tel Aviv

The choice of location for high-rise buildings is not always respectful of urban form and character. Positioning at a distance from historic areas and clustering is a solution unfortunately rarely considered.

As early as 1929 Walter Gropius developed diagrams that showed the development of a rectangular site with parallel rows of apartment blocks of different heights,[18] demonstrating the need for more non-built surface area when building higher to compensate for loss of open sky and direct sunlight if one aims to maintain an urban environment of high living quality – indeed, something for which the Central Business Districts (CBDs) that were developed in the twentieth century are not particularly famous for.

At the turn of this century the focus of urban planners and designers shifted towards the concept of 'urbanity', understood as a maximum of density and diversity in a minimum of space. The rationale for this is that compact living equals sustainable living, because high-density cities can support closer amenities, and thus encourage reduced transport and commuting times, coupled with the use of public transport, which cuts energy costs and greenhouse-gas emissions. High-density planning can also assist in controlling the suburbanisation process into open lands, improving urban infrastructure efficiency and services to produce environmental benefits, which in turn can lead to a higher quality of life in cities. By understanding the relationship between density, urban form and performance, the encouraging of higher-density urban development has become a major policy goal and a central principle of management programmes used by planners around the world. But instead of focusing on the normative aspect of density alone, the search is on to understanding how variables such as types of urban environment and the amount, size, physical properties and economic values work together to create successful planning and design proposals. This is important in the current debate on urban conservation and development, as it will empower urban planning and spatial development professionals in their confrontation with economists and politicians (Ng, 2009; Berghauser Pont and Haupt, 2010).[19]

Despite all these advances in the practice of urban planning, outdated arguments for high-rise construction in inner cities persist, with recent debates flaring up over the need for skyscrapers in Paris, fuelled by President Nicolas Sarkozy.[20] In St Petersburg, the direct involvement of President Dmitry Medvedev has helped avert the proposal to build the highest tower in Europe (406 metres) in the proximity of the historic centre.[21] If towers were part of the twentieth century, they are no longer part of the

---

[18] Rowe and Koetter, 1978: 57; see also: Pedersen, 2009.

[19] Since 2004 the database of samples used in this book has been accessible online, at http://www.spacecalculator.nl

[20] In his address on 17 September 2007 at the *Cité de l'architecture et du patrimoine* in Paris – see: 'Grand Paris, tours . . . les projets de Sarkozy', in: *Le Figaro*, 18 septembre 2007, p. 28; see also: 'Les tours ressurgissent autour de Paris', in *Le Monde*, 28 novembre 2006, p. 3; 'Les architectes réfléchissent aux futures tours pour Paris', in: *Le Figaro*, 25 octobre 2007, p. 30; 'Pourquoi les touristes ont boudé Paris', in: *Le Journal du Dimanche*, No. 3219, 21 septembre 2008, p. 35.

[21] In: 'Medvedev turns attentive ear to critics of Gazprom tower in St Petersburg', press-release by Itar-Tass, Moscow, 22 May 2010.

twenty-first. Apart from locales with serious physical restrictions where high-rise construction can offer particular solutions, many, if not most, of the towers are erected for the sole purpose of attracting attention, often in a predatory fashion – 'the transformation of many cities into places of spectacle is one of the most distinctive features of the contemporary world'.[22] While there is nothing against high-rise buildings per se, when operating in historic cities, some design criteria have to be respected, as a code of honour, so to speak. Spiro Kostof examines shape, approach and height, when he discusses the urban profile in its relationship to the site, where the general mass and shape of buildings are helpful in distinguishing different competing programmes within one historical frame, such as castle versus city hall, or else where it marks the introduction of a new regime or historical era over the former, like Brunelleschi's cathedral dome in the medieval context of Florence (Kostof, 1991). Significant power shifts are marked by some skyline feature, which is inserted by incoming regimes to set themselves apart from the rest of history. Kostof continues to explain that distinctive landmarks were raised in cities of all descriptions and periods to celebrate faith and power, as well as special achievement. But while these landmarks focus city forms and highlight city portraits, the presentation itself is primarily meant for an external audience. Thus the approach concerns the direct experience of skyline features by the visitor to the city, whether the pilgrim, official visitor, or common tourist. The height of landmark buildings, then, Kostof concludes, is above all relative to a landmark's surroundings. And related to relative height is the consideration of proportion.

In their ground-breaking work, 'Learning from Las Vegas', Venturi, Scott-Brown and Izenour were inspired by the California Electric Sign Association in Los Angeles, who in 1967 had prepared 'Guideline Standards for On Premise Signs' specifically for Community Planning Authorities.[23] They argued that 'learning from the existing landscape is a way of being revolutionary for an architect. Not the obvious way, which is to tear down Paris and begin again, as Le Corbusier suggested in the 1920s, but another, more tolerant way; that is, to question how we look at things'.[24]

Last but not least, the question of urban environment, climate change, and disaster management ('business line 5') has become a major change-driver in politics, according to European Commission directive C (2008) 4598 of 28 August 2008, as energy is at the heart of the climate-mitigation

[22]Urry, John, 2007 'The Power of Spectacle', International Architecture Biennale Rotterdam, 2007: 137.

[23]'No matter what you may call it – beauty, eye appeal, good taste, or architectural compatibility – limiting the size of electrical advertising displays does not ensure any of these. Proper proportions – the relationship of graphic elements to each other – are necessary to good design, whether it be a matter of clothing, art, architecture, or an electrical sign. Relative size, not overall size, is the factor in determining guidelines which will satisfactorily influence attractive appearance' (Venturi, Scott-Brown and Izenour, 1982: 81).

[24]Venturi, Scott-Brown and Izenour, 1982: 3.

agenda. As demand for energy continues to grow, the ability to address energy issues, including energy access, efficiency and use of renewable energy sources, will be paramount in enabling development and climate-change priorities to be met in a mutually reinforcing way. Since urban areas are responsible for more than 75 per cent of global emissions of CO_2, reducing energy use and emissions in cities is fundamental to combating climate change.

Shanghai

The preference given by policy-makers to private transportation over public systems has dominated urban development worldwide over the past century. Sustainable cities will have to shift the balance toward mass transit.

This is the rationale behind the Clinton Climate Initiative, which promotes a series of practical steps to enable city authorities to increase energy efficiency and reduce greenhouse-gas emissions, such as more efficient lighting for traffic and streetlights, more efficient municipal water and sanitation systems, localised cleaner electricity generation, schemes to reduce traffic congestion, and more intelligent design for electric grids.[25] In particular when considering building codes and practices that are more

[25] The Clinton Climate Initiative, online at: http://www.c40cities.org

efficient in energy consumption, cultural heritage properties in historic cities can provide information and inspiration as they were built with traditional building materials and techniques with a low carbon footprint, and used features such as natural ventilation and water-harvesting techniques. These can be adaptively reused, scaled up and replicated to encourage sustainable urban development with lower CO_2 emissions. Furthermore, when comparing the cost of proper maintenance of existing buildings as against the construction of new ones, the former has a better return on investment in real economic terms, as it is nearly always cheaper in terms of cumulative capital expenditure to preserve, maintain, restore and adapt, than to sit idle and then initiate large renewal and replacement schemes. Maintenance and repair are less costly in human, social and economic terms than physical decay, social blight and renewal (Hankey, 1998). This is in itself a solid argument for heritage preservation: it conserves and enhances resources.

Regarding the impact of climate change on built heritage and building materials, the European Commission's Noah's Ark Project has as objectives: 1) to determine the meteorological parameters and changes most critical to built cultural heritage; 2) to research, predict and describe the effects of climate change on Europe's built cultural heritage; 3) to develop mitigation and adaptation strategies for historic buildings, sites, monuments and materials that are likely to be the worst affected by climate change and associated disasters; 4) to disseminate results obtained through a Vulnerability Atlas and Guidelines.[26]

Overall, the issue of resilience has gained more prominence over the last decade, primarily due to a better understanding of how ecosystems respond to internal and external stresses, which has become paramount in the face of natural or man-made disasters befalling societies.

---

[26] Recognising that the impacts of climate change are affecting many World Heritage sites and are likely to affect many more in the future, the Intergovernmental World Heritage Committee asked UNESCO's World Heritage Centre and its advisory bodies to investigate the impacts of climate change on World Heritage and propose strategies to address them. This led to the 2006 study 'Predicting and Managing the Impacts of Climate Change on World Heritage' and a 'Strategy to Assist States Parties to Implement Appropriate Management Responses'. In 2007 a compilation of 26 case studies on the impacts of climate change on World Heritage was prepared and widely distributed as a means of raising awareness. In October 2007, the General Assembly of States Parties to the World Heritage Convention adopted a policy document on the Impacts of Climate Change on World Heritage Properties. The document identifies key research priorities for World Heritage sites, using them as laboratories for long-term climate-change impact monitoring and testing of innovative adaptation solutions, emphasises the importance of building synergies with other international conventions and organisations, and discusses the legal aspects of responding to the challenges. Consequently, concern for climate change has been mainstreamed into the various operational mechanisms and processes of the World Heritage Convention. Information on the UNESCO Strategy for Action on Climate Change, progress on its implementation and results achieved can be found at: www.unesco.org/en/climatechange linked to the Gateway to the United Nations system's work on climate change at: http://www.un.org/climatechange/index.shtml

Box 4.3 Traditional Knowledge Saved the Simeulue Community

Indian Ocean

On 26 December 2004, an earthquake off the Indonesian coast caused a tidal wave, or tsunami, which struck the Indian Ocean coasts from South-East Asia to East Africa, claiming more than 250,000 lives. Soon after, when the international community started calling for a high-tech warning system linked up to satellites, reports circulated about the fate of indigenous communities in the region, who had managed to survive the tidal wave due to their traditional knowledge. Unlike many who were drawn to the beaches by the unusual sight of fish remaining on the sand after the waters had receded, the Moken and Urok Lawai peoples, living on the coasts and islands of Thailand, the Ong, living on the island of Andaman, in India, and the Simeulue community, in Indonesia, all understood that they had to move swiftly inland in order to escape the upcoming, but still out-of-sight, wall of water. The small villages of the Moken and the Ong were totally destroyed, but their inhabitants were unharmed. More surprising was the fact that more than 80,000 Simeulue fled and took refuge in places beyond the reach of the tsunami. Only seven of them lost their lives. This amazingly effective response contrasts with the terribly large number of victims recorded in other parts of Indonesia. Unexpectedly, the tsunami that struck the Indian Ocean drew attention to the traditional knowledge of the indigenous peoples in view of natural-disaster preparedness and potential responses.

Source: Elias, 2005

When addressing urban resilience, a distinction should be made between resilience *in* cities, which concerns sustaining ecosystem services at the city-to-region scale, and resilience *of* cities, which operates at the supra-regional scale of a system of cities. Such a system entails a set of cities that maintain functional relationships of exchange, trade and migration, or others that sustain the flow of energy, matter and information among the cities, as explained in a paper of 29 July 2010 published online by the Royal Swedish Academy of Sciences. The paper put forward compelling arguments for a transition in urban governance to enable cities to navigate change, build capacity to withstand shocks, and use experimentation and innovation to deal with uncertainty. According to its authors, innovation is a key driver of urban growth, and since sustainability and resilience depend on a society's innovative capacity, they see the urban arena as an opportunity *for* sustainability, since experimentation, learning and innovation can take place at such high levels in cities. It would follow, therefore, that the answer to increased resilience might not lie in its ecological dimension, but rather in the social dimension. The authors advocate a change of culture, where 'collaboration' between society and the environment becomes key, instead of mere 'interaction', and a look at how uncertainty and ecosystem services can be integrated into urban planning practices (Ernstson et al., 2010).

A 'collaboration' between communities and their environment is precisely the focus of Goran Gugic's fine study of the living landscape and floodplain ecosystem of the Central Sava River Basin in Croatia. This river basin is subject to flood dynamics and unpredictable periods of inundation, and has nurtured an authentic and traditional system of land use since medieval times, where the local people have adapted to, rather than sought to control, the river's unpredictability and changes through a system of traditional animal husbandry with indigenous breeds of horse, pig, cow and goose. This system of traditional pasturing represents both an ecological and a cultural key process, as the man-made habitats are at least of the same importance for biodiversity conservation as the natural floodplain habitats. Moreover, with a focus on keystone processes, instead of keystone species (which is popular among conservation biologists), the author argues that several advantages become apparent with regard to the conservation management of the protected area. '*It offers the manager the basis of decision-making: as long as the ecological key processes are able to run, there is space for negotiations on possible interventions in the protected area and change might be tolerated. But if an intervention impinges on the ecological key process itself, conservation cannot allow it any scope of space*'.[27] This approach is highly relevant to the management of historic, living cities, where socio-economic vitality and functionality can be considered a key process in conditions of change and unpredictability with space for negotiations on possible interventions in the protected area.

---

[27] Gugic, 2009: 85.

Urban Strategies of International Institutions

Alongside the World Bank, various organisations have programmes in place that address cities and urban issues in a comprehensive manner. A brief outline will be provided of the key organisations working on these issues within the United Nations system, namely, the United Nations Human Settlements Programme (UN-Habitat); the United Nations Development Programme (UNDP); the United Nations Environment Programme (UNEP); and the United Nations Educational, Scientific and Cultural Organization (UNESCO); as well as those of the European Union (EU); and the Organisation for Economic Co-operation and Development (OECD).[28]

UN-Habitat's Strategic Vision

UN-Habitat was established in 1978, first as the United Nations Centre for Human Settlements (UNCHS), as the lead agency in the UN-system for coordinating activities in the field of human settlements with mandates to address policies and strategies, city planning, infrastructure and services, among other areas. It is the focal point for the implementation of the Habitat Agenda, the global action plan adopted by 171 countries at the second United Nations Conference on Human Settlements (Habitat II) in Istanbul, Turkey, in 1996. As a normative and operational agency, UN-Habitat focuses on developing policies, programmes and technical support for urban development policies, capacity building and training. There is an increasing emphasis on networking and knowledge management of the lessons learned, aimed at the development of new tools for sustainable urban development. Poverty eradication and sustainable development in cities, as part of the *Millennium Declaration*, are key themes of UN-Habitat's work. Based on its Medium Term Strategic Plan (MTSP) for 2008–2013, UN-Habitat is strengthening its global programmes, several of which are of relevance to the management of global urban heritage:[29]

- *Urban Governance Programme.* This programme aims to strengthen institutions that deal with urban development, to support participatory processes and the reinforcement of municipal planning and management, to promote good urban governance via support for broadbased action that focuses on participatory context-specific aspects of

---

[28]This section updates and expands an internal UNESCO report *'Cities and Urban Issues in the UN system and Major Cooperation Agencies'*, by Caroline Simonds, SHS, Paris, April 2004.

[29]Source: UN-Habitat's Medium Term Strategic and Institutional Plan 2008–2013 (MTSP), available at: http://www.unhabitat.org/downloads/docs/9304_1_593122.pdf

municipal planning and management. The programme enhances the ability of local authorities to integrate these action plans into strategic urban development plans to stimulate inter-sector synergies. Often these interventions have a well-defined spatial dimension linked to management and reactivation of urban heritage.

- *Urban Environment and Planning.* The main aim is to develop synergies between economic, social and environmental concerns. This programme promotes the sharing of environmental/development information and expertise and develops concerted action for planning and management action at the local level to improve urban resilience and sustainability. Given that core historic parts of cities are often degraded and suffer from severe environmental and social problems, this programme promotes multi-actor partnerships to specifically intervene in these areas. It seeks to develop environmental planning and management capacities, system-wide decision-making, the management of environmental resources for achieving sustainable development, and inter-agency partnerships, which facilitate global exchanges of experience and know-how at the local level.

- *The Slum Upgrading Programme.* This programme seeks to alleviate urban poverty and urban environmental problems in informal as well as in deprived central urban areas where disadvantaged parts of the population tend to live, and to disseminate this knowledge at the city, country, regional and international levels.

- *Local Economic Development.* UN-Habitat works as a catalytic entity to bring together different resources (financial, technical and institutional) to provide local government, communities and business organisations with practical strategies for local economic development. It also aims to reactivate historic and other urban heritage assets to nurture the city's identity and generate comparative advantages that further strengthen the city as a wealth-generating entity.

A new emphasis on partnership forms the core of UN-Habitat's 2008–2013 MTSP. Key partnerships have been developed with UNDP, Multilateral Development Banks, and Local Authorities organisations such as UCLG, while UN-Habitat is also one of the funding members of The Cities Alliance. This partnership and its corollary will be extensively dealt with in the next chapter on Tools for Urban Heritage Management. The Sustainable Urban Development Network (SUD-Net) and the World Urban Campaign (WUC), launched during the Fifth World Urban Forum in Rio de Janeiro (Brazil) on 24 March 2010, are also good expressions of how UN-Habitat promotes partnership networking to bring the public and private sectors together with civil society and local government, to push sustainable urbanisation to the top of the agenda for governments around the world.[30]

---

[30] See: http://www.unhabitat.org/categories.asp?catid=634

Box 4.4 Old Havana and its Fortifications

Havana was founded in 1519 by Spanish colonisers and by the seventeenth century it had become one of the Caribbean's main centres for shipbuilding and commercial activities. Today, it is a sprawling metropolis of 700 square kilometres with 2.2 million inhabitants. The urban structure comprises a system of squares of different sizes and functions, providing a polycentric character dating back to the days of its foundation. After the Cuban Revolution in 1959, an Administrative Plan was developed for Havana which established different areas of development and prioritised improvements for the population in the countryside. As a result, the physical growth of the capital was curtailed and the condition of housing, particularly in Old Havana, deteriorated progressively, with overcrowding, inadequate supplies of running water, and frequent building collapses. In 1967, Dr Eusebio Leal Spengler took the Office of the Havana City Historian and a series of policy instruments and associated conservation actions were put in place as part of integrated planning:

- in 1978: Havana City Historical Centre and its system of fortifications were declared a national monument;
- in 1981: the Cuban State assigned an exclusive budget to the rehabilitation and restoration work in the Historical Centre, thereby starting the first five-year restoration plan. The following year, in 1982, Havana City Historical Centre and its system of fortifications were inscribed onto the UNESCO World Heritage List;
- in 1993: Law Decree No. 143 of the Council of State widened the framework of authority and the jurisdiction of the Office of the City Historian, and the inscribed sector was recognised as a prioritised zone for conservation.

From 1981 onwards, five-year plans were established for the renovation of Old Havana. Increasingly successful, the Cuban government decided to further empower the Office and authorise the creation of an independent executive agency for the development, funding, renovation and restoration of the old walled city. Under this entrepreneurial-capitalist approach, the Office of the Historian of Havana was able to generate funds that served wider socio-cultural interests, supporting urban conservation and broader cultural activities. The results so far have been remarkable, certainly when considering the particular politico-economic situation of Cuba. Since 1994, the exploitation of Havana's cultural, tourism and tertiary resources has generated a profit of US$ 216.8 million. With the implementation of a fiscal policy, an additional US$ 16.2 million have been collected. Economic decentralisation has allowed for the immediate reinvestment of these resources, resulting in visible social and urban improvements in the short term, thereby generating positive externalities attracting more investments and interests, with a corresponding increase in visitors and people requesting services. The reliability of the process stimulated the National Bank to expedite credits of US$ 61.9 million, to be invested in very expensive rehabilitation work, and the State to contribute 321.3 million pesos (equivalent to the US$) from the central budget. With 40 per cent of the budgeted resources allocated to social works (real estate, housing, health and educational institutions), the introduction of social-benefit policies and the rehabilitation of buildings destined for community services of the municipal administration, the mobilisation of US$ 16.1 million from international cooperation projects was made possible through co-financing schemes. In ten years (1994–2004), through its management efforts, the Office had achieved the recovery of 33 per cent of the area of the Historical Centre and implemented five times the number of projects carried out in the previous periods.

Source: Van Oers, Ron. 'Sleeping with the Enemy?'. Descamps, 2009: 57–66

UNDP's Local Governance Focus

As the lead agency on development, the United Nations Development Programme (UNDP) provides a range of services to governments involving five practice areas: Democratic Governance; Poverty Reduction; Crisis Prevention & Recovery; Energy & Environment; and HIV/Aids.[31] UNDP's urban work is located under Democratic Governance and focused primarily on urban governance. In 2002, UNDP and UN-Habitat signed a Memorandum

---

[31] See: http://www.undp.org/.

of Understanding to place national Habitat Programme managers in selected countries where there are, or may be, UN-Habitat activities at national and local levels. The increased presence at the country level will enhance the inclusion of urban policy issues in the national United Nations Development Assistance Framework (UNDAF).

UNEP's Global Green New Deal

In October 2008 the United Nations Environment Programme (UNEP) launched the *Global Green New Deal* as part of the Green Economy Initiative, which originated in a research paper that argued that an investment of one per cent of global Gross Domestic Product (i.e. approximately US$ 750 billion) over 2009 and 2010 could provide the critical mass of green infrastructure needed to seed a significant greening of the global economy. Utilising only a quarter of the total size of proposed fiscal stimulus packages, totalling US$ 3 trillion globally, the Global Green New Deal presented three broad objectives: 1) making a major contribution to reviving the world economy, saving and creating jobs, and protecting vulnerable groups; 2) promoting sustainable and inclusive growth and the achievement of the Millennium Development Goals (MDGs), especially ending extreme poverty by 2015; and 3) reducing carbon dependency and ecosystem degradation. The Policy Brief argued strongly for an active 'greening' of proposed fiscal stimulus packages, backed by necessary changes in international and domestic policies, since the prevailing framework is geared toward reviving an unsustainable 'brown' economy, with significant environmental costs per unit of production, as compared to a green economy where the energy/resource use per unit of production is low. The proposals are grouped under three categories: targeted stimulus spending in 2009–2010; changes in domestic policy; and changes in the international policy architecture.[32]

Section 3.4 Fiscal Stimulus for 2009 and 2010 outlines sectors that are particularly important in terms of their economic, employment and environmental benefits, among which are Energy Efficient Buildings and Sustainable Transport that are noteworthy in the context of the management of urban heritage. Furthermore, Section 3.5 Domestic Policy Initiatives outlines actions to take in the domains of Perverse Subsidies (3.5.1), Incentives and Taxes (3.5.2) and Land Use and Urban Policy (3.5.3), in each of which consideration should be given to the wise use of resources – in our case, the preservation and adaptive reuse of urban heritage. What stands out when we look at some of the general characteristics attributed to 'green cities', such as low energy/resource intensity, reliance on renewables, diversity of activities, compactness, and a knowledge-oriented, smart

---

[32]UNEP, 2009a: 1. Available on-line at: http://www.unep.org/pdf/A_Global_Green_New_ Deal_Policy_Brief.pdf

and wired urban society, is that they are strikingly similar to the attributes of historic cities.

European Union's Urban Initiative

The European Regional Development Fund (ERDF) implements the EU's regional policy by financing projects that either prevent regions from lagging behind or lead to conversion of declining urban industrial areas. Created in 1994, the Urban Initiative focuses on financing projects to regenerate depressed urban areas and it provides for the sharing of experiences and best practices through the European Network for Exchange of Experience, URBACT, in which 255 cities in 29 countries and more than 5,000 participants are active. Integrated urban development is central to URBACT II, whose main vocation is to promote a new 'integrated' approach to urban policy, which considers both the environmental and social impact of urban development.[33] To date, nine thematic areas have been identified under three Thematic Poles, which assemble URBACT projects that are working on similar or complementary projects. In the context of this book, the thematic area of Cultural Heritage and City Development, and in particular the HerO-project, Heritage as Opportunity, is extremely relevant as it seeks to devise integrated systems of cultural heritage management, preserving and developing historic urban landscapes as a key facet of the dynamic multi-functional city.[34]

OECD's Urban Programme

The Organisation for Economic Co-operation and Development (OECD), which groups 32 mainly developed countries sharing a commitment to democracy and the market economy, addresses cities and urban issues in three main areas: the Territorial Development and Public Governance Directorate; the Local Economic and Employment Development Programme (LEED); and the Environment Directorate. Each is similar in its approach of organising conferences, conducting research, publishing papers and offering technical assistance to promote policy dialogue.[35] All three of these groups have the ability to engage with non-member countries and focus on transition economies. LEED focuses on private-sector involvement and employment policies. Through its Forum on Cities and Regions, LEED advises local development agencies to

[33] Taken from: http://urbact.eu/en/header-main/integrated-urban-development/understanding-integrated-urban-development/
[34] See: http://urbact.eu/en/header-main/integrated-urban-development/exploring-our-areas-of-expertise/cultural-heritage-and-city-development/
[35] What distinguishes the OECD's approach from other organisations is the peer review process, i.e. mutual examination by government officials; see also: http://www.oecd.org/dataoecd/9/41/37922614.pdf

encourage holistic strategies for cities and regions and to assess specific policy instruments with an aim to attract private-sector investment. The Territorial Development and Public Governance Directorate is the main area of the OECD that addresses metropolitan issues, and it assesses progress of cities on economic and social criteria. The current Metropolitan Regions Series evaluates metropolitan regions as a whole with a focus on coherence and cooperation between local city and suburban administrations toward a coordinated development strategy. Its main purpose is to inform national-level policy-making, although its city reviews also benefit local administrations.[36] Furthermore, in 2007 it established the OECD Urban Roundtable of Mayors and Ministers, a pre-eminent forum for developing intergovernmental approaches for stronger, more effective urban policy. In May 2010 the Roundtable discussion took place in Paris and focused on 'Cities and Green Growth'.[37]

UNESCO's World Heritage Cities Programme

The global challenges of urbanisation, development, sustainability and climate change have created the need for a strategic framework that views these issues as interrelated in order to work towards the overriding objective of sustaining and enhancing the quality of the human environment. Serving the transformation from an industrial to an ecological civilisation in the twenty-first century, the World Heritage Cities Programme examines the implications of developing a harmonious continuum between the past, present and future through sustainable urban development. Using World Heritage sites as cases, it explores the issues of how to preserve the ecological balance and social identity of urban communities, embedded in natural, cultural and intangible heritage, while at the same time fostering cities as the vanguard of creativity and technology, to increase their productivity and resilience, and thereby improve the welfare and quality of life for citizens.

---

[36] Its work is overseen by high-level representatives of ministries who attend the Territorial Development Policy Committee (TDPC) and the Working Party on Urban Areas (WPURB). These bodies meet twice a year to define the work programme and discuss the OECD's research on regional development. Recently the territorial review of Venice in Italy was completed. The report assesses the city-region's productivity, related to demographics, labour market, entrepreneurial milieu, and industrial infrastructure, and challenges that stem from its spatial structure and vulnerable environment. In this assessment, the cultural-historic value of the built environment is identified as a powerful force, which *endows the region with a distinct identity and instant name recognition. The 39.5 million tourist visits to the city-region in 2008 testify to its appeal, making it one of the most visited destinations on the planet. Venice's architecture, its 150 canals and its 400 bridges offer a built environment that is the envy of other cities, and Venice's image has been appropriated and replicated by cities from Las Vegas to Macau. Demand for housing in Venice is consequently very high, and it has become the most expensive urban real-estate market in Italy'* (OECD, 2010: 14).
[37] See: http://www.oecd.org/urban/2010roundtable

The Programme aims to serve and bring together a broad constituency comprising, *inter alia*, national and local government representatives, non-governmental organisations, development banks and corporations. In particular, the Programme aims to contribute to the implementation of key declarations and resolutions in the field of sustainable urban conservation.

5. Expanding the Toolkit for Management of the Urban Environment

We shape our tools, and thereafter they shape us.

Father John Culkin

Urban Heritage Management: Actors and Tools

In Chapter 3 we observed how urban conservation today has become a moving target due to the emergence of an increasingly complex management environment, where changes occur at different intervals and at different levels and with different magnitudes. This situation poses a major challenge to established management practices. The task of the urban professional or site manager is compounded by an expansion of territory under their surveillance, by the number of stakeholders involved, and by the type of attributes that carry meaning and value. This increase in complexity should be balanced by the forging of new partnerships, better institutional coordination, and more available resources, both technical and financial. As the constituency broadens, it becomes important to clearly define roles and responsibilities of the actors involved in urban heritage management in general, and in the implementation of the Historic Urban Landscape approach in particular. The principal actors in the process of urban heritage management are the following:

- **Governments** that can integrate urban heritage conservation strategies into national development policies and agendas according to the Historic Urban Landscape approach. Within this framework, **local authorities** can prepare urban development plans that are informed by historic forms and practices.
- **Public service providers and the private sector** that can cooperate through partnerships to ensure the successful application of the Historic Urban Landscape approach.

The Historic Urban Landscape: Managing Heritage in an Urban Century, First Edition. Francesco Bandarin, Ron van Oers.
© 2012 Francesco Bandarin and Ron van Oers. Published 2012 by Blackwell Publishing Ltd.

- **International organisations** dealing with sustainable development processes that could integrate the Historic Urban Landscape approach into their strategies, plans and operations.
- **National and international non-governmental organisations** that could participate in developing and disseminating tools and best practices.

Any further refinement in specifying roles and responsibilities would be incompatible with the variety of geo-cultural, institutional and political environments that exist worldwide. In addition, and before discussing ways to update the toolkit for urban heritage management, it is important to emphasise once again that international and regional instruments and tools must be adapted to their local context, with regular and systematic exercises in training and capacity building, and continued efforts to forge partnerships, in order to stay ahead in an increasingly complex and interconnected world.

As cultural diversity is an essential dimension of heritage management, reference has been made, as far as possible, to any interesting initiatives occurring in different geo-cultural regions as they relate to the debate on urban conservation, heritage management and local development.

The successful management of urban heritage in complex environments, for which the Historic Urban Landscape approach has been developed, demands a robust toolkit. It should include a range of interdisciplinary and innovative tools, which can be organised into four different categories, each of which will be discussed by presenting outlines of a range of established approaches, practices and instruments. It should be emphasised that for urban heritage management to succeed, the policies and actions in these four categories need to be addressed simultaneously, as they are interdependent.

- **Regulatory systems** should include special ordinances, acts or decrees to manage tangible and intangible components of the urban heritage, including their social and environmental values. Traditional and customary systems should be recognised and reinforced as necessary.
- **Community engagement tools** should empower a diverse cross-section of stakeholders to identify key values in their urban areas, develop visions, set goals, and agree on actions to safeguard their heritage and promote sustainable development. These tools should facilitate inter-cultural dialogue by learning from communities about their histories, traditions, values, needs and aspirations and by facilitating mediation and negotiation between conflicting interests and groups.
- **Technical tools** should help protect the integrity and authenticity of the architectural and material attributes of urban heritage. They should permit the recognition of cultural significance and diversity, and provide for the monitoring and management of change to improve the quality of life and urban space. Consideration should be given to the mapping

of cultural and natural features, while heritage, social and environmental impact assessments should be used to support sustainability and continuity in planning and design.

- **Financial tools** should aim to improve urban areas while safeguarding their heritage values. They should aim to build capacity and support innovative income-generating development rooted in tradition. In addition to government and global funds from international agencies, financial tools should be deployed to promote private investment at the local level. Also central to making the Historic Urban Landscape approach financially sustainable are micro-credit and other flexible financing mechanisms to support local enterprise, as well as a variety of models of public–private partnerships.

Regulatory Systems

At the highest possible regulatory level the preservation of natural and cultural heritage can be included in a country's Constitution, as India has demonstrated. Among the fundamental duties of Indian citizens under the Constitution of India, article 51A item (f) reads *'to value and preserve the rich heritage of our composite culture'*, while item (g) reads *'to protect and improve the natural environment including forests, lakes, rivers and wild life, and to have compassion for living creatures'*.[1]

Since 1999 the Government of South Africa has implemented a new democratic constitutional framework, which was promulgated in 1996, that changed the role of various government structures, especially municipalities. Under the Constitution's *Schedule 5: Functional Areas of Exclusive Provincial Legislative Competence* both the Minister and Heritage Western Cape are empowered to promulgate regulations in terms of the National Heritage Resources Act, 1999 (Act 25 of 1999) to regulate matters pertaining to heritage resource management in the Western Cape. This introduced an integrated system for the management of heritage resources in South Africa. Section 30(5) of this Act provides that at the time of the compilation or revision of a town or regional planning scheme or a spatial development plan, the planning authority shall compile an inventory of the heritage resources that fall within its area of jurisdiction and submit the draft inventory to the provincial heritage resources authority. In turn, the provincial authority shall list in the provincial Heritage Register those heritage resources that fulfil the assessment criteria set out in the Act and the relevant regulations (conform with the concept of integrated conservation). Since the promulgation of the Municipal Systems Act, both local and district municipalities in South Africa have been tasked to fulfil their mandates as far as Integrated Development Plans are concerned. Central to this is

---

[1]This information was downloaded from the website of the Ministry of Law and Justice (Legislative Department) at http://lawmin.nic.in/coi/coiason29july08.pdf, p. 25.

the consolidation and sustainability of planning, implementation and management skills.[2]

In the first decade of this century China has also strengthened its legislation for cultural relics (the Chinese terminology used for heritage) through its State Administration of Cultural Heritage (SACH) and related administrative departments. From 2002 to 2007 the administrative rules for the protection of cultural relics have been improved and a total of about 23 administrative rules, regulations and regulation files have been promulgated.[3]

In the 1980s the city of Luoyang, which was a capital city for many Chinese dynasties and endowed with an extraordinary array of cultural-historic monuments and underground archaeological sites, became a pioneer in making regulations to protect this legacy: land planning authorities could not proceed with a planning permit for any infrastructure project without review by, and approval of, the department of cultural heritage.

Such regulations, which require strict coordination between cultural heritage authorities and planning authorities, with mutual review and approval, became known as the 'Luoyang method'. More recently, Luoyang embarked on a huge project for the development of the city, with a strong commitment from, and involvement by, the Luoyang Cultural Relics Bureau, as well as several levels of government (municipal, provincial and national). A special plan of protection includes some important objectives, aiming to 'incorporate the protection of great sites into urban planning and rural construction so as to effectively avoid damage to the underground cultural remains by urban and rural infrastructural construction; support the protection of the great sites by strengthening policies and rendering financial support; and put into effect the planning for the protection of the great sites by consistently taking the development of protection planning as the key link and important step for the protection of the great sites'.[4] According to the authors, this project in Luoyang can be considered a 'happy case of strategy of development based on cultural heritage'. Furthermore, the Principles for the Conservation of Heritage Sites in China, or the China Principles, are an integrated and methodological approach to the conservation and management of sites, in compliance with the existing legislation of the People's Republic of China, as they apply to the conservation of ancient wooden architecture and with particular reference to the concepts of authenticity, integrity and reconstruction. They were developed in a collaborative effort involving SACH, ICOMOS-China, the Getty Conservation Institute and the Australian Heritage Commission and promulgated in Chinese in 2000 (Agnew and Demas, 2002).[5]

---

[2] See: http://www.saflii.org/za/legis/num_act/nhra1999278.pdf
[3] Regulations on implementation of the Law of the People's Republic of China on the Protection of Cultural Heritage; Measures for the management of cultural relics programmes; and Measures for the management of protection of World Cultural Heritage promulgated by the Department of Culture of China; see: Guo et al., 2008: 29.
[4] Op. cit. in Guo et al., 2008: 127.
[5] UNESCO maintains a database of national cultural heritage laws, which is available at http://www.unesco.org/culture/natlaws

Mogao Grottoes

Chinese Fortress of the Han Dynasty, Gansu Province

The China Conservation Principles apply to many types of heritage focusing on authenticity, integrity and reconstruction.

147

Within the framework of general State reform, *Réforme générale des politiques publiques* (RGPP), in 2008 the French Government merged two ministries, the Ministry of Public Works (*Ministère de l'équipement*), which was the pillar of construction and planning policies in France, with the fairly new Ministry of the Environment, into a new Ministry of Ecology, *le Ministère de l'écologie, de l'énergie, de développement durable et de l'aménagement du territoire* (since October 2010 renamed *Ministère de l'écologie, du développement durable, des transports et du logement*).

While urban conservation falls under the responsibility of the Ministry of Culture, the 'cultural' novelty for France was to focus on ecology, and less on the traditional sectors of public works and housing, in an attempt at horizontal integration among various sectors of public action focused on a new integrated approach to (urban) development. Integrated Urban Development as a new approach to urban policy emerged in Europe in the early 1990s to break away from a compartmentalised approach to territories, issues and policies, and to promote a more holistic approach that takes into consideration the physical, economic and social dimensions of urban development.[6]

On 19 October 2009 the President of Ecuador, Rafael Correa, inaugurated the former Foreign Minister, Maria Fernanda Espinosa, as Minister of the newly created Ministry for the Coordination of Heritage. After taking office, Fernanda Espinosa told reporters that the new ministry was expected to replace the mercantilist vision of natural, cultural and human resources of the country with a vision of collective and public welfare.[7] The coordination would extend to the Ministry of Culture, Ministry of Sports, Ministry of the Environment, Ministry of Tourism, Ministry of Education and Ministry of Health.[8]

Relying on the cross-cutting extent of a policy issue, government policy managers can organise Inter-Agency Committees or Taskforces to accomplish policy formulation tasks collectively or independently, depending on the case at hand. This is especially important when an issue is first initiated in one sector, but whose solutions require multi-sector efforts or exert impacts on other sectors, as apparent in the previous section. Agencies responsible for policy implementation, monitoring and evaluation should be involved as they can contribute views on the operational practicality of the options to be explored. Formal procedures are, however, necessary to resolve conflicts that might arise from the operation of these mechanisms, and require the establishment of a level of independence upfront. '*Ad hoc policy formulation mechanisms may be supported by long-standing and independent policy communities – networks of actors, governmental or non-governmental, with interest and expertise in a common policy area.*

---

[6]See URBACT of the European Commission, at: http://urbact.eu/en/header-main/integrated-urban-development/understanding-integrated-urban-development/

[7]'Ecuador creates world heritage ministry', as (incorrectly) reported by China's Xinhua News Agency on 21 October 2009, at www.chinaview.cn, edited by Lin Zhi.

[8]New Ministry's website: http://www.ministeriopatrimonio.gov.ec

Box 5.1 Cultural Heritage Strategy for Cape Town

On 31 October 2001 the City of Cape Town formally adopted the first Integrated Metropolitan Environmental Policy (IMEP) along with its implementation strategy, the Integrated Metropolitan Environmental Management Strategy (IMEMS), which is associated with Integrated Development Planning (IDP). This IMEMS required that the City of Cape Town develop detailed sector strategies to meet the commitments made in the sector approaches by giving effect to the environmental principles in IMEP. Cultural heritage was one of the sector approaches of IMEP. The City has committed itself through IMEP to ensuring that the diverse cultural heritage of the City of Cape Town is protected and enhanced. This includes:

- Recognising the rich cultural history of the City of Cape Town;
- Recognising all cultures and religions represented within the City of Cape Town;
- Including cultural values, sites and landscapes of historic significance, areas of scenic beauty and places of spiritual importance in planning and decision-making. This commitment needs to be further augmented by ensuring that the diverse cultural heritage of Cape Town is conserved, and that objects and socio-political dimensions are included. Subsequently, on 19 October 2005 the Cultural Heritage Strategy for the City of Cape Town was approved by the Executive Mayor and Members of the Mayoral Committee. The document sets out a policy and framework for the management and protection of the cultural heritage resources of the City of Cape Town. It also provides a response from the City to the obligations of local government contained in the National Heritage Resources Act (Act 25 of 1999 – see above). Finally, the document provides a framework for cooperation among the national, provincial and local spheres of government in managing and protecting heritage resources in the City of Cape Town.

Source: City of Cape Town, 2005

Members of a policy community adhere to certain core shared values, even though they may disagree over details'.[9]

In June 2006 Japan enacted the Law on the Promotion of International Co-operation for Protection of Cultural Heritage Abroad. This law seeks to contribute to the advancement of diverse cultures throughout the world by further promoting international cooperation on cultural heritage. It established the Japan Consortium for International Co-operation in Cultural Heritage (JCIC-Heritage), bringing together a variety of institutes and individuals, with the aim of creating a common base for coordinated and collaborative international cooperation.[10]

City-to-City Cooperation is a framework in which a variety of policy considerations can be implemented, ranging from governance, infrastructure development and rural–urban integration, to cultural heritage and tourism management. A variety of forms of city-to-city cooperation have already begun to take root through the work of various local governments, NGOs and international institutions. International institutions are beginning to see benefits that the city-to-city approach offers: efficiency of resources; proximity to the needs of people; and sustainability beyond the scope of a given programme. '*As a locally rooted approach, city-to-city co-operation offers a cost-efficient and high-quality alternative to many existing programs that are constrained by heavy bureaucracy and far-removed centres of decision-making. However, in order to fulfil its potential, this approach must be fully adopted by the international community as a mainstream modality for international co-operation*'.[11] An example of a near-nationwide city-to-city cooperation scheme, which was brokered by the UNESCO Office in New Delhi, involves French–Indian decentralised cooperation for urban management. Currently in India there is no legal and institutional framework to facilitate urban conservation, as only 'monuments' can be protected. Consequently, city administrators seeking to develop conservation initiatives have to operate in a vacuum. Therefore, developing the legal and policy framework for urban conservation, and facilitating this through contacts with homologues in other countries, such as France, could prove very useful.[12]

---

[9]UNEP, 2009b.

[10]http://www.jcic-heritage.jp/

[11]Savir, Uri, 2003: 31.

[12]Under the supervision of the Ministry of Urban Development of the Government of India and with the participation of 80 French professionals from over 40 French local governments, in January 2010 political approval was granted at the Union level for states and municipalities to engage in cooperation with French (or other) local governments. Results achieved included:

1. At the Central-Union level, India and France will cooperate on capacity building for city administrators through development of short-term courses on urban governance and technical issues, notably through the provision of French experts to teach at training institutions that belong to, or are affiliated with, the Ministry of Urban Development. The content will be developed jointly between French and Indian expert institutions (on the Indian side it will involve the National Institute of Urban Affairs);

In addition, a Good Practice Compilation was produced by the European Union's HerO project, Heritage as Opportunity–Sustainable Management Strategies for Vital Historic Urban Landscapes, in which the network invited partners to identify and present tools and practices adopted in their cities in response to questions of Protecting Visual Integrity and Applying Integrated Revitalisation Approaches. The document brings together 18 good practices on these issues, derived from nine city partners. The compilation of 2–3-page résumés (Liverpool, Regensburg, Valetta, Vilnius, Lublin, Poitiers, Graz, Sighisoara and Naples) allows for an immediate overview of the challenge faced by each city and the planned, implemented or ongoing actions. Each case has links to relevant contact persons so that those who wish to know more can have a direct contact with informed local representatives.[13]

Similarly, ongoing cooperation between UNESCO's World Heritage Centre in Paris, the European Commission in Brussels, the Organization of World Heritage Cities in Quebec, the Getty Conservation Institute in Los Angeles and the city of Lyon on the development of a best-practice guide aims to make an important contribution in facilitating direct city-to-city cooperation on matters of urban heritage management. Since 2008 a bottom-up approach has been used to assemble a casebook featuring a number of projects of intervention in the historic urban context, such as the development of infrastructure, housing and retailing, but also heritage conservation and presentation, and all submitted by responsible local authorities in World Heritage cities.[14] Types of intervention and approaches taken are sketched in brief outline, with the full contact details of the responsible urban manager and technical officers for quick reference and

---

2. At the State-Region level, cooperation will be established through study tours, i.e. of Indian city managers to visit French regions and cities, and vice versa, with involvement of the Association of Municipal and Development Authorities of India (AMDA) and the Foundation of Indian Heritage Cities Network;

3. At the city-to-city level, which requires major efforts that are resource-intensive, the following opportunities have been discussed, including already ongoing cooperation: Paris–Delhi (ongoing, on urban planning); Grenoble–Bangalore or Hyderabad (new, probably on research cooperation); Rennes–Bhopal (new, on urban heritage and planning); Strasbourg–Udaipur (new, on urban heritage and development with focus on urban mobility); La Rochelle–Pondicherry (ongoing, on urban heritage and development); Lorient–Cochin (new, on urban heritage conservation and tourism); Region Centre–Chettinad, Tamil Nadu (ongoing, on heritage-based development), among others;

4. In addition, Rajasthan was the first State in India that signed an agreement with a consortium of NGOs and not-for-profit organisations on heritage-based development for the protection and enhancement of natural and built heritage, and on poverty reduction through cultural creativity and cultural industries. This consortium programme is called 'Vikas and Virasat' (Development and Heritage) and was initiated in 2005 with the support of UNESCO in New Delhi for the Jaipur Literary Festival, which has now become one of the leading literary festivals in South Asia.

[13] See: http://urbact.eu/fileadmin/Projects/HERO/outputs_media/HerO_-_Good_Practice_Compilation.pdf

[14] Ongoing reporting available at: http://ovpm.org/parameters/ovpm/files/recueil/re-quito.pdf

easy contact to facilitate direct city-to-city cooperation on issues of mutual concern.[15]

In 2007 the City of Kyoto changed its Urban Landscape Policy in recognition of the importance of historic districts, next to the old palaces, shrines, temples and gardens, as urban landscape elements that harbour traditional lifestyles, including the Gion Matsuri-Yamahoko Festival, which was inscribed onto the Representative List of the Intangible Cultural Heritage of Humanity by UNESCO in 2009. Previously, these historic urban districts with their communities of merchants, craftsmen and artisans had received little attention in terms of streetscape preservation, primarily due to the private ownership of the properties. But under the new policy even the buildings on private properties have to be in harmony with the historic urban landscape through strict regulation of height and design.[16]

In situations where conflicts may arise, Local Strategic Partnerships can offer ways to facilitate cooperation in decision-making processes. A Local Strategic Partnership involves the development of a protocol, or a Memorandum of Understanding, as a general framework for improving management of monuments and sites. Such a framework might include, among others, a definition of the parties involved in the agreement and their specific roles, an identification and brief description of the property under consideration with its significance, range of values and vulnerabilities, and details of the nature of the agreement, including the management approach adopted, definition of works or other changes that can be undertaken, and the establishment of a review mechanism of implementation or performance of the agreement.[17]

As explained by Derek Worthing and Stephen Bond, 'a Conservation Plan is a tool for managing heritage sites based on the key idea that in order to manage effectively it is vital that an understanding of why the site is significant and how the different elements of that site contribute to that significance are set out, explained and justified. . . . A conservation plan, in order to be effective, needs to be accompanied by a Management Plan . . . The final two-stage document [conservation plan and management plan], however, must read as one entity, as neither part has any real value unless both are completed in an integrated manner. . . . The management plan is concerned with determining what is required on the site by focusing on significance, thinking about how the place should and can develop, and determining the key management issues related to this and how they will be addressed. That is, there is a need to move from a vision to general policies to specific guidelines and actions'.[18]

---

[15]This case book was presented at the 11th World Congress of the Organization of World Heritage Cities, which took place in Sintra, Portugal, in October 2011.
[16]Kyoto Urban Landscape Policy in 6 languages: http://www.city.kyoto.lg.jp/tokei/page/0000061889.html
[17]Worthing and Bond, 2008: 203.
[18]Ibid.:105, 141.

Box 5.2 New Tool to Protect Heritage Values of Liverpool

The City Council of Liverpool, after mounting civil-society protests against large-scale regeneration works executed in the heart of the city which came under subsequent scrutiny by the World Heritage Committee, prepared a Supplementary Planning Document (SPD) for Liverpool–Maritime Mercantile City World Heritage Site to supplement planning policies contained within the Liverpool Unitary Development Plan (adopted in 2002) and the North West Regional Spatial Strategy (adopted in 2008). The overarching aim of this SPD was to provide a framework for protecting and enhancing the outstanding universal value of Liverpool World Heritage site, while encouraging investment and development that secures a healthy economy and supports regeneration. It was sent out for consultation in the spring of 2009 and adopted by the Liverpool City Council on 9 October 2009. The SPD sets out the relationship with the Planning Policy Framework, the historic context of the site and its buffer zones, general guidance for development in the World Heritage site, as well as specific guidance for the overall site and its six character areas, and, finally, modalities for implementation and monitoring.

Source: http://www.liverpoolworldheritage.com

While these are primarily technical tools, upon endorsement by municipal or national government entities, they can become part of the regulatory framework under which urban heritage is managed. It is essential therefore that such a plan, agreed by all key stakeholders, be formally adopted by Government. IUCN states that *'a management plan therefore can be thought of as representing a 'public contract' between the management organisation and the stakeholders of a World Heritage property. It is also a tool for improving communication, and monitoring and evaluating management activities. Most of all, a well-produced and comprehensive management plan helps reduce and even overcome conflict, by enabling local people to understand and become more involved in the management of World Heritage areas'.*[19]

Over the last three decades there has been an almost continuous flow of ideas and practices emanating from ecology, environmental protection and nature preservation towards the conservation and management of cultural properties (not much the other way around, though). The concepts of environmental capital and environmental capacity have been applied to the built environment, and this has reinforced the importance of incorporating cultural significance and vulnerability into management strategies (Worthing and Bond, 2008). Another innovation from the field of nature preservation, which could prove highly useful to urban heritage management, is to combine the Management Plan with a Business Plan for protected areas. An example of this was the 'Enhancing our Heritage – Skills Sharing Pilot Project', implemented by the World Heritage Centre and the Shell Foundation over the period October 2004 to August 2008 in Uganda. Its aim was to strengthen the capacity of not-for-profit organisations charged with the responsibility for the protection and management of natural World Heritage sites that were under threat. The project was designed to test the relevance and impact of transferring core business skills to site managers.[20] After the training exercise, the Uganda Wildlife Authority proposed a merger of management and business plans for Mount Elgon National Park (MENP), for which currently a 'General Management and Financial Plan' is under development. Alongside traditional chapters, such as Planning Process, Park Description and Management, and Conservation Programmes, innovative items developed after the Shell exercise include a section on Park Benefits and Services (outlining the economic contribution and impact of the park), a Park Resource Requirement Analysis (with investment costs and financial gap analyses), Financial Strategies for Protected Area Revenue Generation, and a Marketing Plan. Once completed, and contingent on feedback from its Board and site managers, a decision will follow on whether this type of plan would become standard for all National Parks in Uganda.

Community Engagement Tools

Community engagement tools include a variety of instruments which inform, mobilise and engage. They draw knowledge and skills from local communities and other groups in society. The tools can perform an advisory function, such as various types of plans, viewscape mapping,

---

[19]IUCN, 2008:2–3; see also: Kerr, 2000; and Ringbeck, 2008.
[20]For full programme outline and final reporting, see: http://whc.unesco.org/en/series/23/

documentation of character-defining features and processes as a baseline process, cognitive mapping by participant groups, anthropology and cultural geography insights, and documentation by locals of oral traditions and customs.

An accurate definition of communities in places like Cairo or Mumbai is problematic; nevertheless, their engagement as primary stakeholders is important, as they are likely to be affected, positively or negatively, by the management of urban heritage.

Stakeholder Analysis and Mapping (SAM) identifies and analyses stakeholders to inform decisions on who to involve in addressing particular issues. It can be used when key stakeholders need to be identified. Annex 1 of *Integrated Assessment: Mainstreaming sustainability into policymaking – A guidance manual*[21] outlines four basic steps, as well as the pros and cons of using this tool.[22]

City Development Strategies (CDS), as promoted by The Cities Alliance, are action plans for equitable and sustainable growth in cities, developed and implemented through the participation of local stakeholders, to

Community workshop in the Solomon Islands

To ensure an effective preservation practice, heritage values need to be expressed by the local community.

[21] UNEP, 2009c: 41–42.
[22] See also: http://www.nssd.net/pdf/resource_book/SDStrat-05.pdf

improve the quality of life for all citizens.[23] The goals of a City Development Strategy include a collective city vision and action plan aimed at improving urban governance and management, increasing investment to expand employment and services, and systematic and sustained reductions in urban poverty. Each city identifies its problems and opportunities, and sets priorities for action. For historic cities the preservation of cultural-historic significance and management of urban heritage should feature as key considerations. A CDS can be prepared rapidly and amended quickly, usually within 12 to 15 months. The CDS methodology typically has four key building blocks:

- Analysis – state of the city and its region, using rapid data assessment and SWOT;
- Vision – futuristic and realistic, long-term, understandable building awareness;
- Strategy – with focus on results, setting priorities, and addressing responsibility;
- Implementation – addresses what, when, how much, whose resources by year, with monitoring and evaluation of impacts.

The Cities Alliance was launched in 1999 with support from the World Bank and UN-Habitat, the political heads of the four leading global associations of local authorities, joined together into I.C.L.E.I. (Local Governments for Sustainability), and ten governments (Canada, France, Germany, Italy, Japan, the Netherlands, Norway, Sweden, the UK and the USA). The Asian Development Bank joined this consortium in 2002.

A recent study by the Cities Alliance (UNEP, 2007) highlights interactions between the city and the environment, and describes how to integrate the environment into urban planning strategies, providing examples and details of instruments that can be used to improve the integration process. The document focuses on the urban challenge and is very relevant to historic cities' management as it adds culture and heritage to environmental considerations.

The report notes (page 24) that in the development of a CDS, a Visioning Conference could be conducted, bringing all stakeholders together to produce a common vision of the future city, and that in the process these individuals with diverse backgrounds and interests will recognise that they share common concerns, forging a strong sense of ownership. Additional benefits include awareness-raising as the public is motivated to become involved; a sense of identity is fostered; everyone's view is heard; and partnerships are formed, which can assist in the implementation. Last but not least, this process provides a basis for conflict resolution.

The report refers to other tools that could support the participatory approach to drawing up action priorities for urban heritage management. One of these is Environmental Profiles, a specialised urban planning tool, which focuses on the environment to provide a common understanding of

---

[23] http://www.citiesalliance.org/ca/cds

how the city's economic sectors interact with the environment in terms of resources and hazards. Such a profile is normally quickly assembled from existing information and data, not through time-consuming research, and can be considered as a form of rapid urban environmental assessment – this could be established for the city's cultural and heritage resources as well. Other tools include a SWOT analysis (Strengths, Weaknesses, Opportunities, Threats), which is useful in that it adds a note of realism to strategic thinking; and Strategic Environmental Assessment (SEA), which will be dealt with in the next section on Technical Tools.

Finally, the *Liveable Cities* study refers to a management system, ecoBUDGET©, that is focused on the management of natural resources and environmental quality by cities. It was developed and patented by I.C.L.E.I. and could be useful for considering cities that are endowed with a rich cultural heritage. In parallel to the financial budgeting system on an annual basis, '*ecoBUDGET routinely integrates environmental target-setting, monitoring and reporting into municipal planning, decision-making and management. Every year a budget for natural resources and environmental quality is developed and approved by the city council. . . . The budget uses physical units, not monetary terms*'.[24] It is a cross-cutting instrument, which offers a way of weaving cultural and heritage aspects into municipal policy-making across departments, making municipal leaders true resource managers, responsible both for finances and cultural assets.

In 2004, as part of the City of Montreal's Master Plan review, the Plateau Mont-Royal Borough organised an extensive public-consultation process to stimulate a collective reflection on planning and heritage conservation issues affecting the area in order to define a vision for the protection and future development of its urban landscape. The most important outcome was that its citizens were more interested in preserving the heritage character of the urban landscape of their neighbourhood as a whole than in conserving a limited series of isolated monuments defined as 'heritage' by experts (Laurin et al., 2007).

In April 2002 the Melbourne Principles for Sustainable Cities were developed as part of an initiative spearheaded by UNEP. The ten Melbourne Principles, as endorsed by the participants of the working group, are intended to guide thinking and help build a vision of environmentally healthy and sustainable cities. For our purposes, the third stated principle is of particular relevance: 'recognise and build on the characteristics of cities including their human, cultural, historic and natural systems'.[25]

The Kyoto Center for Community Collaboration (KCCC),[26] in recognition of the important contribution of traditional wooden houses to the city's historic streetscape, which was the key to a change in Kyoto's urban landscape policy (see paragraph 6.2), has since 1997 initiated the following programmes:

[24] UNEP, 2007: 39.
[25] See: http://www.unep.or.jp/ietc/Publications/Insight/Jun-02/3.asp; for more direct linkages between sustainability and heritage management, see: English Heritage, 2008.
[26] http://www.kyoto-machisen.jp/fund/

1. Studies on the typology and local distribution of traditional wooden houses called Machiya;
2. Research into the needs of homeowners and residents of Machiya;
3. Workshops to promote public recognition and support of the preservation of Machiya;
4. Consultation and management support services for the preservation, renovation and adaptive reuse of Machiya, which includes the establishment of a support fund;
5. Development of new technologies which utilise traditional wooden construction techniques, including technologies for fire and earthquake safety, and new construction methods designed to lower the carbon footprint.

The most important aspect of KCCC's programmes is this extended network of collaboration, which links owners, residents, other community members, professionals in various related fields, NGOs, students and faculty of colleges and universities, and public-administration officials.[27]

Box 5.3 Regensburg's Development Proposals' Assessment

In 2006 the Old Town of Regensburg with Stadtamhof was inscribed onto the World Heritage List. The historic city centre has approximately 17,000 residents (census 2006) and is 183 hectares in size. At its inscription, the establishment of an Independent Steering Committee was announced, constituting an innovative measure for streamlining communication among UNESCO, the World Heritage Committee and the City of Regensburg World Heritage site, which, owing to the federal structure, is especially protracted in Germany. Ensuing time delays can, in certain instances, paralyse processes of development and decision-making in World Heritage cities. The independent committee meets twice a year to monitor the process of construction in the core and buffer zones of the World Heritage city of Regensburg. It will be kept informed on the results of relevant competitions, urban planning and proposed traffic projects and any other plans for development by the City of Regensburg; in those instances where such plans may come into conflict with the preservation of the city's outstanding universal value, it will assume an advisory role.

The steering committee was established in 2008 and consists of six members: two independent consultants from ICOMOS; a representative of the Standing Conference of the Ministers of Education and Cultural Affairs of the *Länder* in the Federal Republic of Germany (KMK); a representative of the Bavarian State Ministry of Science, Research and the Arts as the highest authority for monuments protection; a representative of the Bavarian State Office for the Preservation of Monuments; and the Mayor of Regensburg. In addition to conflict resolution, the steering committee also seeks to raise the level of awareness of the city's World Heritage status among all those involved in building and shaping the city.

In this respect, it functions as a pilot project that could serve as a model for other World Heritage cities. Over the course of the first three meetings, several investigations were conducted involving proposed development plans in various parts of the city. So far, the steering committee has reported that the experience has been decidedly positive, owing to the manageable size of the committee and the non-public nature of the meetings, which has allowed the establishment of a basis of trust in order to examine construction projects at a very early stage.

Source: Communication by Matthias Ripp, site manager of Regensburg, 2010

---

[27] From: *The League of Historical Cities Bulletin*, No. 54, March 2010, Kyoto, Japan.

In March 2009 the City of Helsinki sent out an invitation to tender for design evaluation of the Katajanokka hotel by Herzog & De Meuron architects. The Katajanokka hotel project was started as a separate venture by the city and a real-estate investor, with whom the City of Helsinki had negotiated the reservation of the plot, and formed part of the development of the Eteläsatama area (historical old town with old harbour). The goal of this development was to strengthen the appeal of the city centre and incorporate the area and the passenger port better into the city structure, public seaside city spaces, and pedestrian routes in the city centre. The area is a nationally valuable cultural environment that is part of the historical empire-style centre of Helsinki and a comprehensive plan was created for the area. The design solution for the Katajanokka hotel had aroused considerable public discussion and exceptional opposition both from experts and from citizens, primarily due to the design's unsuitability for the cultural-historic cityscape in terms of its shape, size, direction and façade materials – seen as too much of a contrast with the building's surroundings. The expert officials of the government and the National Board of Antiquities had determined the evaluations of the effects as inconclusive; therefore, foreign city planning and city history experts were asked to provide extended evaluations.[28]

Technical Tools

There are a number of impact-assessment tools that can be classified as community-engagement tools, as they form part of participatory planning processes, yet at the same time can be viewed as technical tools, because most of them involve highly technical procedures and require advanced knowledge and skills.

The Training and Professional Development Committee of the International Association of Impact Assessment (IAIA) states that *'Impact Assessment (IA) is recognized as an essential input to development decisions. IA is a process and method to predict the effects of development on the ecological and human environment, so as to allow adjustments to be made before human, financial and natural resources are committed and options foreclosed. IA is a participatory process, and is often the primary means by which stakeholders have a voice in development decisions. Done right, IA is more than a study and report – it is an enlightened and transparent component of development planning to increase returns, reduce risks, safeguard assets, and promote public confidence. As such, IA is a cornerstone of good business and good governance'.[29]* Several types of impact assessment relevant to urban heritage management will be discussed here.

[28] A comprehensive overview of guidance publications available to the general public on practically every aspect of heritage conservation is provided by the UK's Heritage Lottery Fund at: www.hlf.org.uk/aboutus/Pages/allourpublications.aspx
[29] IAIA, 2007: 1.

Environmental Impact Assessment (EIA) is a process applied mainly at the project level to improve decision-making and to ensure that development options under consideration are environmentally and socially sound and sustainable. The EIA process has generated a new subset of tools, including social-impact assessment, cumulative-effects assessment, environmental-health-impact assessment, risk assessment, biodiversity-impact assessment, heritage-impact assessment and strategic environmental assessment (SEA).[30] *'Environmental assessment is a procedure that ensures that the environmental implications of decisions are taken into account before the decisions are made. Environmental assessment can be undertaken for individual projects, such as a dam, motorway, airport or factory, on the basis of Directive 85/337/EEC, as amended (known as 'Environmental Impact Assessment' – EIA Directive) or for public plans or programmes on the basis of Directive 2001/42/EC (known as 'Strategic Environmental Assessment' – SEA Directive). The common principle of both Directives is to ensure that plans, programmes and projects likely to have significant effects on the environment are made subject to an environmental assessment, prior to their approval or authorisation. Consultation with the public is a key feature of environmental assessment procedures'.*[31]

In November 2002 the Swedish International Development Co-operation Agency (Sida) published its *Sustainable Development? Guidelines for the Review of Environmental Impact Assessments*. The report contains three parts:

1) Review – projects, which constitutes the guidelines for the review of EIAs and includes lists of questions to be taken into consideration in EIA reviews.
2) Review – sectors and regional programmes, which describes how environmental issues in development cooperation are handled at the strategic level.
3) EIAs – regulation and tools, which contains six sections that focus on knowledge about, and the background to, EIAs, including indicators for sustainable development; economic consequences of environmental impacts reviewing how environmental economic analyses can contribute to improving the EIA process and the Environment Impact Statement; and good practices for environmental-impact assessments describing international practices in respect of EIAs.

There is general agreement that environmental-impact assessments are equally useful for inclusion of material assets and cultural heritage into this process, as is stipulated in Sida's requirements for performance and content of an EIA,[32] and the checklists in Appendix 1 refer to the *Cultural Environment* where a project may have impacts.

---

[30] UNEP, 2009b: 63.
[31] http://ec.europa.eu/environment/eia/home.htm
[32] Sida, 2002: 16.

Monaco

Bangkok

Failure to recognise the values of the landscape lead to disorderly development and loss of uniqueness of the territory, identity and quality of the built environment.

The World Bank has produced a *Physical Cultural Resources Safeguard Policy Guidebook* in March 2009, which relates to the Bank's Operational Policy (OP 4.11) and Bank Procedures (BP 4.11) with regard to physical cultural resources. It contains chapters on 1) the Physical Cultural Resources Safeguard Policy; 2) guidance for the World Bank Task Team; 3) guidance for the borrower; 4) guidance for the Environmental Assessment Team (with section 4.4 Conducting the Impact Assessment); and 5) guidance for Environmental Assessment Reviewers.

In addition, the International Finance Corporation (IFC), part of the World Bank Group, has issued Performance Standard 8 on Cultural Heritage, supplemented by Guidance Note 8 on Cultural Heritage, which 'recognises the importance of cultural heritage for current and future generations. Consistent with the *Convention concerning the Protection of the World Cultural and Natural Heritage*, this Performance Standard aims to protect irreplaceable cultural heritage and to guide clients on protecting cultural heritage in the course of their business operations. In addition, the requirements of this Performance Standard on a project's use of cultural heritage are based in part on standards set by the *Convention on Biological Diversity*'.[33]

Strategic Environmental Assessment (SEA) is a tool that is being promoted by the World Bank, European Union and the Organization for Economic Co-operation and Development's Development Assistance Committee (OECD-DAC), among others. It entails a process to ensure that significant environmental effects arising from policies, plans and programmes are identified, assessed, mitigated, communicated to decision-makers and monitored, and that opportunities for public involvement are provided. As EIAs are conducted for projects, SEAs should be initiated early on in the planning process. *'Typically, the initial step involves identifying potential environmental impacts. An assessment then determines which impacts are most significant. Mitigative actions are then proposed, along with monitoring frameworks. Public consultation typically takes place to help identify potential impacts'.*[34] As such, SEA has become an important instrument to help achieve sustainable development in public planning and policy-making. SEA is a generic tool with several approaches, which can be used in a variety of situations, and its importance is widely recognised.[35] Particular benefits include:

- improvement of the evidence base for strategic decisions;
- facilitating and responding to consultation with stakeholders;

---

[33]IFC, 2006. http://www.ifc.org/ifcext/sustainability.nsf/AttachmentsByTitle/pol_ PerformanceStandards2006_PS8/$FILE/PS_8_CulturalHeritage.pdf ; World Bank, 2006. http://web.worldbank.org/WBSITE/EXTERNAL/PROJECTS/EXTPOLICIES/EXTOPMANUAL /0,,contentMDK:20970737~menuPK:64701637~pagePK:64709096~piPK:64709108~theSit ePK:502184,00.html; World Bank, 2009a.
[34]Ahmed and Sánchez-Triana, 2008: 4.
[35]Some references: Dalal-Clayton and Sadler, 1998; OECD, 2006; Fischer, 2007; Partidário, 2007.

- streamlining other processes such as Environmental Impact Assessments of individual development projects;
- European Union Directive 2001/42/EC requires national, regional and local authorities in Member States to carry out strategic environmental assessment on certain plans and programmes that they promote.[36]

The Cities Alliance's *Liveable Cities* (UNEP, 2007) mentions that SEA is a planning instrument that involves extensive, ongoing research and analysis, and is therefore financially intensive, human-resources intensive and time-consuming. It may include a 'cascading process', which means that local councils within the city must prepare statutory area-based plans that take full account of the City Development Strategy and other city-wide strategies. The city authority is responsible for approving area-based plans and monitoring.

In the case of historic cities and World Heritage sites, this tool can be extremely helpful in assessing the potential impact of development programmes upstream before specific project proposals are prepared and considered. 'SEA is an instrument to assume a socio-political role in decision-making, from a results-driven to an action-driven process. With reference to section 20 in the Vienna Memorandum,[37] introducing SEA in public policies can create the incentive to use and enhance value of historic urban landscapes, in particular the resilience of the spirit of place'.[38]

One approach that lies within the scope of SEA, which is promoted by UNEP, is Integrated Assessment (IA). 'Integrated Assessment (IA) is defined as a participatory process of combining, interpreting and communicating knowledge from various disciplines in such a way that a cause–effect chain – involving environmental, social, and economic (ESE) factors – associated with a proposed public policy, plan or programme can be assessed to supply adequate information to decision-makers'. Being cross-sectorial by definition, it aims to integrate environmental, social, and economic issues, proactively and as early as possible, at strategic levels into the

---

[36]Within the context of the European SEA Directive, the learning dimension of SEA, particularly transformative learning as an established feature of environmental planning and management, is explored; see: Jha-Thakur et al., 2009: 133–144.

[37]*'An essential factor in the planning process is a timely recognition and formulation of opportunities and risks, in order to guarantee a well-balanced development and design process. The basis for all structural interventions is a comprehensive survey and analysis of the historic urban landscape as a way of expressing values and significance. Investigating the long-term effects and sustainability of the planned interventions is an integral part of the planning process and aims at protecting the historic fabric, building stock and context'.*

[38]Maria Partidário, Professor at the Technical University of Lisbon, Portugal, and former President of the International Association of Impact Assessment (IAIA), at the HUL Expert Planning Meeting at UNESCO Headquarters, 13 November 2008.

Uçhisar in Cappadocia in Turkey

Mt. Emei in the Sechuan Province of China

Mt. Athos in Greece

Understanding the spirit of the place is a condition for harmonious development of new functions in a historical context.

policy-making process in order to create policy options 'to enhance sustainability rather than proposing options for mitigation and compensation'.[39] UNEP's Guidance Manual (2009) is addressed to two types of users: firstly, the practitioners and planners who are interested in a more integrated, proactive and flexible use of Integrated Assessment to improve policy-making and planning processes; secondly, the policy-makers and decision-makers who wish to seek guidance on how to make public policies contribute to sustainable development. It proposes a 'building block' approach to the conduct of IA to make assessment less procedural and more flexible, tailored to different assessment contexts and policy processes. The Guidance Manual is supplemented by a Reference Manual for *Integrated Policymaking for Sustainable Development* (UNEP, 2009b), with a view to embedding sustainability within policy-making processes.

Sustainability Frameworks present indicators and benchmarks to enable the measurement of sustainability performance and the assessment of impacts of projects and policies against a reference framework. There are many different types of sustainability frameworks, but all share a systematic structure in which general sustainability principles must be translated into concrete indicators that are measurable. The Integrated Assessment process can identify existing sustainability frameworks, assist in their

[39]UNEP, 2009c: 8–9.

development, evaluate options and assess subsequent trade-offs against established frameworks.[40]

Overall, the cultural heritage sector in the environmental assessment process has focused almost exclusively on determining whether there has been a negative impact on the authenticity and integrity of the physical structures and sites themselves, hardly ever on the well-being of the communities associated with the heritage resources. Therefore, slowly but increasingly, subsets of impact assessments have emerged that pay particular attention to the socio-cultural impacts of development proposals on local communities.[41] Anthropology and cultural geography insights, including documentation by locals of oral traditions and customs, are part and parcel of indigenous people's Cultural Impact Assessments. Under New Zealand's Resource Management Act of 1991 and its Historic Places Act of 1993 provisions are included for the preparation of Maori cultural impact assessments (although there is no national policy statement for cultural heritage). They are used as a tool to inform and influence 'resource consent decision making' and 'to communicate a Maori world view and articulate concerns regarding the alienation of ancestral lands and resources'.[42] The methodology used includes regular aspects such as literature reviews, consultation and identification of issues and opportunities, an assessment of effects, and recommendations, but is supplemented by an overview of tradition and historic occupation and use, including sites of significance. Under this heading particular issues are addressed, such as the association of the place with indigenous-descent groups; or a connection with a specific ancestor or traditional event; or relationships between the place and astrological, natural or metaphysical phenomena; any significant activities, uses or practices that are taking place at the site.

The conference 'Cultural Impact Assessment: Beyond the Biophysical' was held by the International Association of Impact Assessment's Western and Northern Canada Affiliate (IAIA-WNC) in Yellowknife, Canada, in February 2008.[43] Subjects included:

- Identifying and mitigating cultural impacts;
- Using indigenous knowledge in impact assessment;
- Understanding cultural landscapes;
- Assessing impacts on intangible cultural resources;
- Overcoming common hurdles in cultural impact assessment.

In May 2010 ICOMOS published a Draft 'Guidance on Heritage Impact Assessments for Cultural World Heritage Properties', which was drawn up following an international workshop in Paris in September 2009. The aim

---

[40] Annex 1 of *Integrated Assessment: Mainstreaming sustainability into policymaking – A guidance manual* outlines three steps, as well as the pros and cons of using this tool (UNEP, 2009c: 46–47).

[41] On 25 May 2005 ICOMOS-UK held a workshop at Greenwich to discuss setting-up a research project related to the 'Impact of World Heritage Status on World Heritage Site Communities in the UK', which due to a lack of funding did not materialise.

[42] Nelson Coffin, 2008.

[43] Conference proceedings at: http://www.iaiawnc.org/CulturalConf08.html

of the draft document was to provide guidance on the process of commissioning a Heritage Impact Assessment (HIA) for World Heritage properties in order to effectively evaluate the impact of potential developments on the property's Outstanding Universal Value. The rationale for ICOMOS issuing these guidelines was their view that the procedure of Environmental Impact Assessment (EIA) was not immediately useful without certain adaptations. As EIA assesses impacts on, for instance, protected buildings, archaeological sites or specified viewpoints separately, this 'often produces disappointing results when applied to cultural World Heritage properties as the assessment of impacts is not clearly and directly tied to the attributes' that carry the Outstanding Universal Value, while cumulative impacts and incremental adverse changes may also pass undetected more easily.

Box 5.4 Tower of London (UK)

In 2003 two high-rise building projects were under development in the vicinity of the Tower of London, a World Heritage property since 1988. These buildings would have affected the Tower's setting and key views within the overall cityscape, also threatening its integrity as an example of Norman military architecture and a symbol of royalty. The fact that local authorities approved this project suggested that policies to protect the city's World Heritage sites were not being applied effectively, and the site risked being inscribed onto the List of World Heritage in Danger. In response to this situation, local authorities carried out the necessary studies to assess the visual impacts of contemporary building projects. A draft of this Visual Impact Study was published in 2009. The management plan for the site, however, which has been under development since 2001, has not yet been approved; as a consequence there is also no adequate or commonly agreed buffer zone. While a coherent local approach is still under discussion, new high-rise projects have emerged that could alter the site's visual relationship, in volume and scale, with the city.

Source: World Heritage Committee State of Conservation Report 30 COM 7B.74

With regard to technical tools for planning and design activity related to contemporary interventions and infill in historic areas, several have been developed over the last decade alone. In 2001 English Heritage and the Commission for Architecture and the Built Environment (CABE) published *Building in Context – New development in historic areas*, 'to stimulate a high standard of design when development takes place in historically sensitive areas.' It contains 15 examples that are distinctly contemporary, but which have used intelligent and imaginative approaches to understand and respect history and context, and it derives lessons on both design and the development and planning process. In 2003 English Heritage and CABE published *Guidance on Tall Buildings*, which was based on a consultation document of 2001 and a Parliamentary Committee report on tall buildings of 2002. This 'good practice note' could be of value to local planning authorities in drawing up their planning policies, as it sets out how both organisations will evaluate proposals for tall buildings based on a set of nine criteria, which include the relationship to context, including natural topography, scale, height, urban grain, streetscape and built form, and the effect on the skyline.

In June 2005 the New South Wales Heritage Office and the Royal Australian Institute of Architects published *Design in Context – Guidelines for Infill Development in the Historic Environment*, a handsomely illustrated booklet containing case studies and their implications. It also spells out six design criteria, which are character, scale, form, siting, materials and colour, and detailing, which can be used to guide new development in a conservation area, heritage precinct or land adjacent to a heritage item with a view to maintain and enhance the area's distinctive identity and sense of place.

The question of how to determine compatibility for new structures in a relatively (visually) consistent historic district is addressed through the FRESH approach: Footprint and Foundation; Roof shape; Envelope; Skin; and Holes (doors, windows, attic vents, etc.). A note is provided to explain that '*this mnemonic trick helps make buildings fit in; it does not help them be great architecture*'.[44]

In addition to the above-mentioned publications, which can serve as technical tools for planning and design activity, particular mention should be made of Paolo Marconi's 'Manuale del recupero' (rehabilitation manuals) of Rome, then developed for several other Italian cities. What started in 1983, as an attempt to introduce new conservation guidelines and standards for the technical specifications of Rome's master plan, resulted in the completion of manuals for Rome in 1989 and 1993 and the establishment of a new practice dedicated to acquiring knowledge about the pre-modern art of building, including the vernacular. Its basic character, a practical-oriented one, provides a new dimension to the care and conservation of the built environment.

The rehabilitation manuals are inventories of building elements consisting of detailed drawings and technical files, which combine three complementary kinds of information: an explanation of the materials and building

[44]Gorski, 2009: 8.

elements that need to be respected; the establishment of what materials to use by the conservation plan; and the suggestion of intervention criteria through actual examples. It is important to note that the *manuali* view historic city centres as being the result of a centuries-old practice of pre-modern building, which requires a provision of guidelines for a general plan of maintenance based upon the review of pre-modern materials and techniques.

In the quest for sustainable or 'green' planning and design, municipal governments and communities are utilising smart growth strategies to create mixed-use, pedestrian-friendly and transit-oriented developments, to revitalise downtowns, to encourage infill (over greenfield developments) and to institute 'green (or smart) building' policies.[45] A 'green (or smart) building' is synonymous with a high-performance building,[46] which is the result of a holistic approach to design and construction seeking sustainability through the efficient use of land and energy, improved indoor air quality, and water and resource conservation, primarily by using regional and recycled materials.[47]

In June 2008 the Climate Group published the report *SMART 2020: Enabling the Low Carbon Economy in the Information Age*, which looked at ways to optimise city systems for efficiency, in particular through the use of Information and Communications Technologies (ICT).[48] 'Smart cities' are the ones that focus on making city operation activities more efficient through the use of a smart grid (a set of hardware and software tools that enable electricity generators to route power more efficiently through a two-way, real-time information exchange with customers on their real demand, thus reducing the need for excess capacity), smart buildings (see above), smart transport, smart industrial systems, and logistics optimisation – for example, through improvements in the design of transport networks, mixing centralised distribution networks with management systems for flexible home-delivery services, as well as eco-driving, route optimisation

---

[45] On 20 October 2009 a total of 114 cities from 19 Asia-Pacific Rim countries, through its Executive Bureau of United Cities and Local Governments (UCLG), adopted the 'Changwon Declaration on Green Growth' to recognise the usefulness and importance of green growth strategies; at: http://www.uclg-aspac.org/forkami/temp/file/sing_docs/Changwon_Declaration_on_Green_Growth.pdf

[46] The United States Green Building Council (USGBC) LEED *Reference Guide for New Construction & Major Renovation* (Version 2.1, 2003) states that 'Green Building design strives to balance environmental responsibility, resource efficiency, with occupant comfort, well-being, and community sensitivity. The Green Building design includes all players in an integrated development process, from the design team (building owners, architects, engineers, and consultants), the construction team (material manufacturers, contractors, and waste haulers), maintenance staff, and building occupants. The Green Building process results in a high quality product that maximizes the owner's returns on investment.'

[47] With regard to Energy and the Built Environment, for instance, information is proliferating by the month, with themes and titles ranging from 'Photovoltaic in the Urban Environment' to 'Wind Power and Biofuels for Transport' and 'Solar Domestic Water Use', all available at www.earthscanpublishing.com

[48] See: http://www.theclimategroup.org/publications/2008/6/19/smart2020-enabling-the-low-carbon-economy-in-the-information-age/

and inventory reduction. It distinguishes five key areas that make a smart city into a sustainable city:

1. Monitoring and managing the footprint of the city;
2. Connected mobility solutions and electric vehicles;
3. Distributed and community energy solutions;
4. Smarter buildings that are transparent about energy consumption, use and generation;
5. Smart energy, water and waste management.

In contrast to all these smart and sophisticated technologies (sometimes labeled as 'eco-bling'), there is also a wide spectrum of low-key, common-sense practices for sustainability in architectural design – in other words: stick to the simple and local. The optimisation of natural light, shade and ventilation, the use of renewable sources of natural energy, an elimination of waste and pollution, and the reduction of the amount of energy embodied in the construction material itself are some examples put forward by Peter Buchanan.[49] The author further stresses that every building should be closely integrated into its context, by paying as much attention to factors such as micro-climate, topography and vegetation, as to the regular functional and formal programmes that are addressed in standard architectural practice.

Given that in the developed world the built environment accounts for 40 to 50 per cent of total energy consumption, much of which is used in the form of electricity for artificial lighting, air conditioning and digital equipment, and given that a large part of the average municipal waste stream comes from building sites, it is essential that the building industry takes a closer look at ways to cut energy consumption.

In this spirit, the Living Building Concept was launched in 2006 with a radical vision of a complete overhaul of the building industry.[50] It was based on the idea that the building industry becomes part of the everyday world of consumers, where demand can be met by specialists who have products available, pre-designed, tested and tried, for the client to choose from. Instead of first employing an architect, followed by a construction engineer, then technicians for installations and equipment, after which a builder has to put the building together, during which the wheel is continuously reinvented with no one responsible for the end product, it should instead be possible to buy a house as you would buy a computer. The Living Building Concept advocates that construction firms maintain extensive catalogues offering an infinite number of variations for every need and wish. Along the lines predicted by Toffler (1984), this is made possible by the digital age: future building components will all be industrially produced, in every variation possible, with standardised connections in order to ensure a tight fit whatever the dimensions or form – every building, residential or

---

[49] Buchanan, 2005.
[50] The Living Building Concept was put forward by Professor Hennes de Ridder, Chair of Methodological and Integral Design at the Faculty of Civil Engineering of Delft University of Technology, the Netherlands.

utilitarian, will become a building package. All components can be assembled, but also disassembled and reused, while variation will increase instead of leading to more uniformity (which seems hard to imagine given today's uniform contemporary built environment). Such a radical overhaul, De Ridder argues,[51] would bring substantial cost savings (10 billion euros a year, for a total industry worth in excess of 70 billion euros in the Netherlands alone), a significant reduction in building waste (currently buildings are designed with an economic lifespan of 35 years, while a well-produced concrete pillar lasts for 300 years and a brick for 3,000 years), a reduction of up to 30 per cent in road transport (the building industry accounts for one quarter of road transport in the Netherlands), a phenomenal increase in the speed of the actual building process and delivery of products, which can all be guaranteed by the producer (contrary to current practices), and are flexible in design and adaptation. Countering critics who complain that it would be difficult or impossible to change the building industry, De Ridder argues that such radical overhauls have already happened in the shipbuilding and car-manufacturing industries, with corresponding improvements in design, quality, price and performance.

Financial Tools

Economic analysis is playing an increasing role in urban management, specifically in the decision-making process, the development of government policies and in the quest for private investment for the conservation of the historic environment. Some might argue that what cannot be measured, cannot be managed. However, the tools for economic analysis as they relate to urban heritage conservation are limited and difficult to apply (Dupuis, 1989; Klamer and Zuidhof, 1998; Serageldin, 1999; Lawler et al., 2008). However, in recent years, researchers have begun focusing on the economic impact of heritage preservation, measuring, for instance, the impact of the rehabilitation process on jobs and household income, the role of heritage buildings as incubators of small business enterprises, the incremental impact of heritage tourism, the contribution of heritage conservation in the revitalisation of historic city centres, and the impact of historic districts on property values, among others.[52] To date no comprehensive study has been conducted to look at the overall role of World Heritage from a sustainable-development perspective, however, several investigations have been undertaken – some commissioned by the World Heritage Centre,[53] some independently by others –[54] on different aspects of socio-economic development.

[51] http://www.livingbuildingconcept.nl/
[52] Some of the findings of this research from both the USA and abroad were presented at The World Bank, Washington, DC, on 22 April 2009 by Donovan Rypkema, President of Heritage Strategies International (Rypkema,1994).
[53] Such as: Prud'homme, 2008; Wilson, 2009.
[54] For example: Buckley, 2004; Williams, 2004; PricewaterhouseCoopers LLP, 2007; Rebanks Consulting Ltd, 2009.

Box 5.5 The Historic Urban Landscape Approach: An Action Plan

Istanbul

Cordoba

Through the passage of time, monuments and cities acquire layers of significance from different cultures and civilisations. These layers constitute a richness and need to be recognised and enhanced in the preservation strategies.

While stressing the need to take into account the singularity of the context of each historic city, which will result in a different approach to its management, nevertheless, six critical steps should be identified when implementing the Historic Urban Landscape approach. They would include the following:

1) Undertake comprehensive surveys and mapping of the city's natural, cultural and human resources (such as water catchment areas, green spaces, monuments and sites, viewsheds, local communities with their living cultural traditions);

2) Reach consensus using participatory planning and stakeholder consultations on what values to protect and to transmit to future generations and to determine the attributes that carry these values;

3) Assess vulnerability of these attributes to socio-economic stresses, as well as to impacts of climate change;

4) With these in hand, and only then, develop a city development strategy (CDS) to integrate urban heritage values and their vulnerability status into a wider framework of city development, the overlay of which will indicate A) strictly no-go areas; B) sensitive areas that require careful attention to planning, design and implementation; and C) opportunities for development (among which are high-rise constructions);

5) Prioritise actions for conservation and development;

6) Establish the appropriate partnerships and local management frameworks for each of the identified projects for conservation and development in the CDS, as well as develop mechanisms for the coordination of the various activities between different actors, both public and private.

Source: UNESCO Culture Sector internal discussion document, 2010

Between 2009 and 2010, the Inter-American Development Bank (IDB) in Washington, DC carried out research into *The Sustainability of Urban Heritage Preservation: Interventions to Support Economic and Residential Investments in Urban Heritage Areas of Latin America and the Caribbean.* The IDB actively supports Latin American and Caribbean governments in their efforts to preserve and develop urban heritage areas. To ensure the success of these efforts the IDB encourages public leadership for the preservation process with the involvement of all interested social actors to ensure support and bring in more resources. Private investment in urban heritage areas is considered essential to enhance the long-term sustainability of the preservation process. The objective of the research into the Sustainability of Urban Heritage Preservation was to increase available knowledge on factors contributing to the long-term sustainability of urban heritage preservation efforts. In particular, the IDB sought to broaden understanding of the economic aspects of sustainable preservation that are complementary to the social, environmental and institutional aspects of heritage preservation. Several dossiers were assessed using the case-study methodology, looking at successful, and less successful, urban heritage preservation efforts in the two different contexts.[55]

---

[55] For the various case studies, see: http://www.iadb.org/publications/search.cfm?topic=citi& countryID=&lang=en.

One critical element highlighted by the above-mentioned studies is that when urban heritage conservation is addressed through development programmes, funding strategies are required to support conservation management. This often necessitates operational partnerships, while institutional capacity building becomes essential if urban heritage management is to be integrated into local development strategies. In his very comprehensive work, Robert Pickard (2009) builds on previous recommendations, resolutions and conventions of the Council of Europe that have sought to raise awareness of appropriate forms of funding and fiscal measures to be utilised in relation to architectural heritage. It contains a wealth of information ranging from Council of Europe advice on funding and fiscal measures, alternative revenue-raising methods such as charitable trusts, heritage foundations in various European countries, revolving funds, and limited-liability companies, endowment funds and tax relief, grant-aided subsidies, loan and credit facilities, as well as fiscal measures to benefit heritage conservation.[56]

One example of a limited-liability company that merits special attention because of its enormous success is *Stadsherstel Amsterdam NV*, or the Amsterdam Restoration Company Inc. (Tung, 2001; Pickard, 2009). In spite of its Inc.-structure, Stadsherstel is not a profit-seeking company. In accordance with regulations, any profits are reinvested in maintaining Amsterdam's monuments. Among the shareholders are large Dutch banks and insurance companies, who are willing to accept lower-than-usual profits in return for a socio-cultural programme that provides visibility and improves their image, while the City of Amsterdam is a major shareholder as well. The invested capital enables Stadsherstel to buy properties, usually listed monuments that are in dire need of restoration. Restoration activities are also financed by the company's own capital, supplemented by government subsidies, and the property is rehabilitated through adaptive reuse to accommodate housing or small enterprises, after which the building is put into operation. Rental revenue covers maintenance, acquisition of new properties, and restoration and upgrading interventions. Since its foundation 55 years ago (in 1956), Stadsherstel has undertaken 500 projects of urban rehabilitation, investing on average 10 million euros per year in restoration and upgrading, of which 3 million euros are from subsidies (30 per cent), either through state or municipal funding. As at 2006, it owned 921 residential buildings in the inner city of Amsterdam, all rented out on the market. The total value of company assets was in excess of 178 million euros, with possibility of incremental sale of assets.[57] The model of Stadsherstel Amsterdam has been copied in many historic cities in the Netherlands, and also in the Netherlands Antilles (Willemstad, Curaçao), while currently an effort is being made to introduce this model to Paramaribo, Suriname.

---

[56] Available at: http://book.coe.int/ftp/3255.pdf
[57] Source: http://www.stadsherstel.nl/

6. The Historic Urban Landscape: Preserving Heritage in an Urban Century

The clearest advantage we have today is the experience of yesterday.

Richard Buckminster Fuller

The Historic City Meets Globalisation

Historic urban conservation has, for more than a century, been a major focus of planning, architectural debate and public policy. For the last fifty years the issue of urban heritage conservation has occupied the centre stage of urban policies with important positive results, and equally important failures. Thanks to efforts by specialists, preservationists and citizens' groups in every part of the world, there is now a consensus that urban heritage conservation is an important part of social and community values essential to define identity, nurture culture, inform education and promote economic development. These concerted efforts have, however, been able to save only part of the world's urban heritage: major losses have been registered, and are ongoing, due to geo-political conflict, speculative urban development, decay and a lack of interest from public authorities. And yet, what has been preserved has an enormous value for the world, as evinced by the predominance of this heritage category in the World Heritage List. Today, this heritage represents a resource of great cultural and economic value, whose complex nature has not always been properly reflected in national and local development policies.

Contemporary thinking on urban heritage conservation points to a need to reassess the historical divide between 'conservation' and 'development' in the theory and practice of urban planning. This is indeed what the Historic Urban Landscape approach aims to accomplish in the coming decades. Historic urban areas are certainly a small part of the urbanised

The Historic Urban Landscape: Managing Heritage in an Urban Century, First Edition. Francesco Bandarin, Ron van Oers.

world, and yet, they play a very important role in the formation of national and local identity, as places of memory and social value, and as magnets for economic and creative activity.

The function of the historic city has undergone dramatic changes in the past century. The historic city of the nineteenth and early-twentieth century was in many cases a place of social marginality and dereliction, with a decaying physical fabric incorporating the great monuments of the past that had to be extracted from their context to be preserved. The historic city was therefore treated with two very different approaches: conservation for its monumental part; and removal or transformation for the supporting, ordinary fabric. In the second half of the twentieth century we witnessed the birth of a completely new attitude, with attention shifting to an 'integrated' conservation and restoration of the historic city, albeit as a 'special district' that was separated from the rest of the city from a functional, as well as from a normative, viewpoint. Parallel to this was the enlargement of the urban conservation community as the original core of enlightened visionaries of the cultural elite was extended to citizens' groups, national and international institutions, and to a large community of experts from various disciplines.

Today there is a growing consensus that the historic city should be viewed not only as a unity of architectural monuments and supporting fabric, but also as a complex layering of meanings, connected both to its natural environment and to its geological structure,[1] as well as to its metropolitan hinterland (Ascher, 2010). Here, values residing in tangible and intangible heritage contribute to the creation of a spirit of place, which is both singular and irreplaceable, and where important functions linked to civic identity, and to the economy of the arts, creative industries and to tourism find their privileged location. In fact, it is this very success that poses threats to the preservation of the values and spirit of place (Ashworth and Turnbridge, 1990). Hence, the key factor for the conservation of the historic city is the establishment of a balanced, integrated and sustainable management process. This requires a clear vision and innovative policies from the main public actors, based on a reflection of the values that need to be protected with strong integration into the regular planning and development processes at the city and metropolitan scales. Sustainability, a goal that was largely ignored in the past century, needs to become the rule of the game should the historic city continue to be the main legacy of our heritage in the era of globalisation.[2]

Urban heritage nowadays is subject to powerful processes of change. Ironically, the same 'iconic' status that prompted its conservation is today driving the main forces of change which affect its social structure, functional use and physical shape. The central role historically played by urban

---

[1] For innovative interpretations of these relationships, see: Heiken, Funiciello and De Rita, 2005; Sanderson, 2009.
[2] Keene, John, 2001. 'The Links Between Historic Preservation and Sustainability: an Urbanist's Perspective'. Teutonico, Jeanne Marie; Matero, Frank, 2003: 11–19.

Naples

Cusco

Urban archaeology is a valuable tool to understand the layering of values in the city through the exposure and interpretation of the physical remains of past cultures and societies.

heritage in the formation of collective memory and identity attracts new functions, new social groups and new uses, of which tourism is one of the more powerful. These factors become agents of change of the uniqueness and authenticity of the social and physical fabric. In the face of these processes many of the existing tools and chartered principles reveal their weaknesses. In addition, what constitutes heritage is not fixed: we have learned that it evolves with society and reflects its changing values over time. It is therefore incumbent upon contemporary societies to redefine the role, meaning and purpose of heritage (Australia ICOMOS Charter for Places of Cultural Significance, the Burra Charter of 1999).[3] Modern life is geographically mobile and made up of a plurality of experiences, lived in different ways and at different times, by a variety of social and generational groups, local and non-local. It is virtually impossible to define a single dimension of the different parts of an urban complex, more so for the most layered, meaningful and dynamic parts, such as the historic areas. Inherited conceptual frameworks must be revisited to develop an approach that not just integrates heritage into changing social values, but also informs the entire urban socio-cultural sphere with the added value of the richness of that heritage. Even if this process is likely to be based less on planning and public control, and more on the dynamics of the market, it remains important to establish close links between the conservation of urban heritage with its historic layers and the careful management of development, as this can sustain the production of quality space and ensure the sustainability of large-scale urban processes.

Mostar Bridge

[3] ICOMOS, 2001:38.

Kiev Lavra Monastery

Red Square in Moscow

Places of significance maintain their value even after traumatic destructions and reconstruction. The memory value of the place can be preserved through collective efforts and rituals.

These and other considerations were at the origin of an innovative cultural operation, which has been under way for the past eight years, from 2003 to 2011, aimed at defining a new approach to the conservation of historic cities.

As shown by cases discussed by the World Heritage Committee in recent years, several of which have been presented here in boxes, we have seen that several forces of change have generated conflict and challenges to the cultural significance and values of historic cities. In a way this is nothing new, as this was observed by Lewis Mumford as long as 70 years ago: '*In the city, remote forces and influences intermingle with the local: their conflicts are no less significant than their harmonies*'.[4]

However, a more careful and detailed reading of the phenomena will reveal different contributions per sector at different levels of operation, such as that of the economy: '*a focus on cities . . . decomposes the nation state into a variety of sub-national components . . . and it signals the declining significance of the national economy as a unitary category in the global economy*'.[5]

Contemporary urban conservation practice has seldom looked into these dimensions and has therefore never been able to properly address the issue of management of change on an adequate scale. The concept of sustainable change in historic urban areas, which is a priori a management process, seeks to ensure a continuity of qualities that are defined in relation to relevant parameters, such as a definition of the historicity of the urban fabric and layering of time, next to a characterisation of the living community with its needs and wishes.

While the majority of experts and practitioners agree on the fact that there is a risk of disintegration of communities, eroding the capacities to regenerate values (Jokilehto, 1999a), there is to date no comprehensive theory of urban or territorial conservation capable of providing a conceptual basis applicable to the guidance of the transformation of historic settlements; instead, there have been a variety of sector initiatives and practical attempts, which need to be re-conceptualised and integrated into a flexible, operational framework.

---

[4] Mumford, 1938: 4.

[5] Sassen: 'Whose City is it?'. Foo and Yuen, 1999:145. Sassen continues to explain (p.149) that '*It is precisely because of the territorial dispersal facilitated by telecommunication advances that agglomeration of centralising activities has expanded immensely. This is not a mere continuation of old patterns of agglomeration but, one could posit, a new logic for agglomeration. Many of the leading sectors in the economy operate globally, in uncertain markets, under conditions of rapid change in other countries (e.g., deregulation and privatisation), and are subject to enormous speculative pressures. What glues these conditions together into a new logic for spatial agglomeration is the added pressure of speed. . . . There are indeed major new actors making claims on these cities, notably foreign firms who have been increasingly entitled to do business through progressive deregulation of national economies, and the large increase over the last decade in international businesspeople. These are among the new city users. They have profoundly marked the urban landscape. Their claim to the city is not contested, even though the costs and benefits to cities have barely been examined.*'

Avila, Spain

Recife, Brazil

Inappropriate modern development in planning and design diminishes the tangible and intangible values of historic places. Visual impacts of new constructions should be measured and assessed in the early stage of the design process.

The Contemporary Reflection on the City

The contemporary reflection on the city opens up new avenues for the management of the historic city and for the proper integration of the concepts and practice of heritage conservation into a broader urban and territorial planning framework. This comes, perhaps, as a reaction to the 'postmodern paradigm' (Jencks, 2002), which has dominated the debate in architecture and urbanism in the last decades of the twentieth century, especially the surge of the 'iconic' in design practice, with its strong position of disregard for the context and the historic continuity of the built environment.[6] Perhaps the tipping point of this reaction was an essay published by Rem Koolhaas, entitled *Junkspace* (Koolhaas, 2000). Although Koolhaas himself is the author of large-scale, iconic buildings, his analysis looks at the global processes generated by the acceleration of development. This icastic text draws attention to the vastness and chaotic state of the 'debris' left by mankind on the planet as a reflection of the conflicting and contradictory cultural state of modern society, represented in its circulation and consumption spaces. While the text makes no direct reference to the city, it presents a portrait of the modern built environment as repetitive and depressive. Jameson (2003) interprets this text as a call for a return to 'history', out of the pseudo-world of postmodernism, to look for the material and cultural conditions that make possible the real world. This position is supported by the subsequent research interests of Koolhaas, recently formalised in his position on historic preservation at the Venice Biennale (Koolhaas, 2010).

In reality, as seen previously, reactions to postmodernism had already appeared in the early 1980s (Frampton, 1983). The approach of *Critical Regionalism* was an attempt to resist the standardisation of the built environment, brought about by modern industrial construction techniques and by a prevalence of the 'scenographic and visual' aspects of design over the 'tectonic and tactile', and to reaffirm the need to link architecture to an understanding of the site and the materiality of building. The objective of architecture then becomes the search for a synthesis between nature and technique. The term Critical Regionalism had in fact been coined by Alexander Tzonis and Liane Lefaivre,[7] acknowledging their debt to the ideas of Lewis Mumford (Tzonis and Lefaivre, 1990), who was also concerned with the standardisation of the built environment generated by the principles of the International Style. They affirm that the concept is grounded in a

---

[6]Koolhaas' *'Fuck the context'* expression refers to the 'death of urbanism'. In this view, the city development process is not manageable any more, and follows independent fluxes and mutations; see: Koolhaas, Rem, 'Bigness or the problem of Large', Koolhaas, 1995: 494–516.

[7]Alexander Tzonis (1937–) is a Greek architect, researcher and author. His contributions to architectural theory and history are aimed at bringing together scientific and humanistic approaches. Since 1975 he has collaborated on most projects with his wife, the architectural historian Liane Lefaivre.

concern for regional elements and place in design, derived from historic layers, as a reaction to the industrialised models proposed by modern architecture.

The debate kindled in the past decades by these positions has been of particular importance in orienting architects and policy-makers towards a new consideration of tradition, values and meaning of place as a basis for the management and development of the built environment. While in the original formulations of Critical Regionalism attention was primarily on the aesthetics of architecture, gradually the attention of the critics has shifted towards issues related to environmental and ecological processes (Canizaro, 2007).

Of particular interest for our analysis is the 'manifesto' proposed by Steven Moore[8] on his formulation of *Regenerative Regionalism*.[9] By adding the political variable to the aesthetic, Moore defines a set of principles[10] for future reflection on the management of the built environment, based on the participation of 'regenerative' architecture in the tectonic history of a place, and on the construction of integrated cultural and ecological processes. Technological choices should reject spectacular and aesthetic design and be linked to the needs of the citizens. Finally, architecture should focus on the creation of critical and historically instructive places, able to inform citizens of possible alternative development processes to the ones proposed by industry. These critical orientations are matched by an important reorientation in the professional world of urban planning and architecture towards a more ecologically sensitive design practice. This reorientation is of particular importance for urban conservation, as it is based on a renewed approach to urban management, where the opposition between historic

---

[8]Steven Moore (1940–) is an American architect, Professor of Architecture and Planning at The University of Texas at Austin and Director of the Design With Climate Program. He has practised as the design principal of Moore/Weinrich Architects in Maine and has received numerous regional and national awards for design distinction. His main focus of research is the link between energy efficiency, sustainable development and social/cultural values. In 2001, he co-founded the Centre for Sustainable Development at the University of Texas.

[9]Moore, Steven A., 2007. 'Technology, Place and Non-modern Regionalism'. Canizaro, Vincent (ed.), 2007: 432–442.

[10]Excerpts from Moore's 'Eight Points for Regenerative Regionalism: A Non-modern Manifesto' (full text can be found at: http://regenit.wordpress.com/2009/03/11/steven-moore-eight-points-for-regenerative-architecture/):

'1) A regenerative architecture will construct social settings that can be lived differently.

2) So as to participate in local constellations of ideas, a regenerative architecture will participate in the tectonic history of a place.

3) Rather than construct objects, the producers of regenerative architecture will participate in the construction of integrated cultural and ecological processes.

4) A regenerative architecture will resist the centers of calculation by magnifying local labor and ecological variables.

5) Rather than participate in the aestheticized politics implicit in technological displays, regenerative architecture will construct the technologies of everyday life through democratic means.

6) The technological interventions of regenerative architecture will contribute to the normalization of critical practices.

7) The practice of regenerative architecture will enable places by fostering convergent human agreements.

8) A regenerative architecture will prefer the development of life-enhancing practices to the creation of critical and historically instructive places.'

built environment and new development is set aside in favour of an integration of design and management factors based on long-term values, renewable energy flows, and respect for the relationship between spiritual and material consciousness. An example of this approach is given by the work of architect William McDonough,[11] who defined the *Hannover Principles*[12] on the occasion of the Hannover World Fair in 2000.

Chandigarh

[11]William McDonough is an American designer and teacher involved in reforming design approaches to address issues of sustainable development. He has been associated with the University of Virginia and Stanford University and is an active consultant both in the USA and internationally.

[12]The Hannover Principles, by William McDonough and Michael Braungart, 1992.

  '1. *Insist on rights of humanity and nature to co-exist in a healthy, supportive, diverse and sustainable condition.*

  2. *Recognize interdependence. The elements of human design interact with and depend upon the natural world, with broad and diverse implications at every scale. Expand design considerations to recognizing even distant effects.*

  3. *Respect relationships between spirit and matter. Consider all aspects of human settlement including community, dwelling, industry and trade in terms of existing and evolving connections between spiritual and material consciousness.*

  4. *Accept responsibility for the consequences of design decisions upon human well-being, the viability of natural systems and their right to co-exist.*

  5. *Create safe objects of long-term value. Do not burden future generations with requirements for maintenance or vigilant administration of potential danger due to the careless creation of products, processes or standards.*

  6. *Eliminate the concept of waste. Evaluate and optimize the full life-cycle of products and processes, to approach the state of natural systems, in which there is no waste.*

  7. *Rely on natural energy flows. Human designs should, like the living world, derive their creative forces from perpetual solar income. Incorporate this energy efficiently and safely for responsible use.*

Brasilia

Berlin

Modern urban design can help to define cultural significance and the spirit of place by expressing meanings that meet the aspirations and value systems of society.

Integrating Heritage Conservation and Urban Development

The growing awareness of the need to ensure sustainability of the design and management processes of the built environment (Register, 2006; Thomas, 2003) appears to be the main focus of new approaches that have gained ground at the beginning of the twenty-first century. Without attempting to embrace the complexity of the global drive towards the revision of the practice of urban management, it is useful to focus on two approaches that are today setting the tone of the discussion on the future of the city, including that of the historic city. The first approach is based on the tradition of planning and management of the city as a built form of material culture, along the lines of nineteenth-century theories (Sitte) through twentieth-century experiences (Giovannoni) and modern approaches (De Carlo, Benevolo, Rowe). The second approach is rooted in the 'organic' views of Geddes and of the regional planners, and is inspired by research on the meaning of place (Norberg-Schulz) and by 'territorial' approaches in architecture (Gregotti), in regional planning (Lynch), and in ecological management (McHarg).

All these approaches have in common the search for a new integration of tradition and modernity, of the built and the non-built environment, an attitude that has allowed important developments in the theory and practice of urban design and management, and indeed in the nature of planning itself. This new approach to urban design is exemplified by the work of urban planner Joan Busquets,[13] based on the rejection of one-dimensional views of the city and an acceptance of the multiplicity of forms and dimensions of the urban scene.[14] The rapid growth of cities and their increasing global importance is erasing the traditional dichotomies of city versus countryside, of built versus natural, and is prompting new urban paradigms. The new approach is grounded in respect for urban forms inherited from

8. *Understand the limitations of design. No human creation lasts forever and design does not solve all problems. Those who create and plan should practice humility in the face of nature. Treat nature as a model and mentor, not as an inconvenience to be evaded or controlled.*

9. *Seek constant improvement by the sharing of knowledge. Encourage direct and open communication between colleagues, patrons, manufacturers and users to link long term sustainable considerations with ethical responsibility, and re-establish the integral relationship between natural processes and human activity.*

   The Hannover Principles should be seen as a living document committed to the transformation and growth in the understanding of our interdependence with nature, so that they may adapt as our knowledge of the world evolves.'

[13] Joan Busquets (1938–) is a Spanish architect and Professor of Urbanism at the Barcelona School of Architecture (ETSAB). In 2002 he became the Martin Bucksbaum Professor at the GSD of Harvard University. Since 1990 he has been responsible for urban planning and architecture projects in various Spanish and European cities. He has contributed to the definition of urban strategies for Rotterdam, Toledo, The Hague, Trento, Lisbon, Sao Paulo and Singapore. He was awarded the National Urbanism Prize in 1981 and 1983, and the European Gubbio Prize in 2000.

[14] Busquets, Joan, 2006. 'Urban Composition: City Design in the 21st Century'. Graafland, Arie; Kavanaugh, Leslie J. (eds.), 2006: 495–504.

the past, places where society has found, and still finds, expression of its traditions, values and belief systems, constituting a reference for the design of new interventions in the urban scene. Busquets acknowledges the complexity of the urban form and its fragmented state, and the toolkit he proposes is designed to address the most important issues of today, namely, the recomposition of the different parts of the city; the creation of flexible spaces for multiple functions; the connection with the territorial scale; and the retrofitting of the historic fabric.

Urbanism is not a theory or doctrine any more, but rather a set of principles that accompany the creation of possible alternative scenarios for the evolution of the city. A similar approach can be found in the work of certain contemporary architects who are open to integrating design processes with the management of the built environment. Steven Holl (2009) in the USA,[15] for instance, contends that the objective of design is the creation of quality spaces and the fusion of landscape, urbanism and architecture. The need to ensure an effective 'connectivity' between the different elements of city design and city management is at the origin of an ambitious initiative taken in 2003 by the European Council of Town Planners[16] to draft a new *Charter of Athens*.[17] This document addresses the future of the city in its social, economic and environmental dimensions, calling for enhanced connectivity between the different parts of the city (against segregation) and between the city and its environment. Connectivity also has a time dimension and concerns the relationship between the city's past and future.

Another approach, termed by some authors *Landscape Urbanism* (Waldheim, 2005) or *Ecological Urbanism* (Mostafavi and Doherty, 2010), is an attempt to define urban development on a large territorial scale, where all factors are taken into consideration, unlike traditional urban planning, which is normally limited to the spatial aspects. This new interdisciplinary approach sees the city as part of a broader context, made up of its natural features, its processes of depositing layers of significance and its resources, and aims to define ways in which conservation and development of physical spaces can be planned according to sustainability principles. However, Landscape Urbanism is seen not only as a method, but also as a way to reassert the public's right to a balanced environment against the excesses brought about by the predominance of private interests in the city development process. It acknowledges urbanisation as a long-term process, which is fluid and non-linear. In opposition to the formalistic approach of

---

[15] Steven Holl (1947–) is an American architect and urban designer, author of several important projects in the USA and Europe, and Professor of Architecture at Columbia University in New York. His research is centred on a phenomenological approach to architecture, based on the writings of the French philosopher Merleau-Ponty and of the Finnish architect and theoretician Juhani Pallasmaa.

[16] The ECTP Athens Charter was adopted for the first time in 1998.

[17] Vogelij, Jan, 2006. 'The New Charter of Athens 2003: the ECTP's vision on the European City of the 21st Century'. Graafland and Kavanaugh, 2006: 47–59.

New Urbanism[18] (Katz, 1994), Landscape Urbanism looks at the territory, and not at the city, as the new dimension of design and planning. In this respect, Landscape or Ecological Urbanism tries to overcome the classic duality between city and nature by defining an integrated vision.[19]

These trends towards an integration of approaches to the design and management of the built environment are of great interest for urban conservation, as they could allow, for the first time since the fracture of modernism, an integration of heritage conservation and urban development in a unitary concept and practice. Policies and toolkits still need to be defined, and results need to be demonstrated, but across the world examples exist and experiments are taking place. This new attitude is indeed reflected in the Historic Urban Landscape approach, aimed at addressing the issue of integrated planning of the urban development and heritage conservation process.[20]

Historic Urban Landscape: a Tool for the Management of Change

We live today in a world dominated by global exchanges and information. This condition has accelerated all the social and economic processes affecting urban life, with outcomes that we still do not fully grasp. Urban life is, and will continue to be, the dominating condition of mankind for this century. The city, therefore, is going to be – even more than in the past – at the centre of social and spatial policies, and of projects related to economic and physical structure. In this context, the historic city can play an extremely important role, as the expression of history and place of memory, as an example of spatial quality, as the core of sustainable development processes and as an engine of economic development.

To play this role, however, the historic city needs to be integrated into the overall dynamics of urban development. At present, the historic city is

---

[18]New Urbanism is a movement developed in the USA to promote the creation and restoration of mixed-use communities with diverse, walkable, compact and vibrant components. The principles of New Urbanism are the following:

1. Walkability
2. Connectivity
3. Mixed-Use and Diversity
4. Mixed Housing
5. Quality Architecture and Urban Design
6. Traditional Neighborhood Structure
7. Increased Density
8. Smart Transportation
9. Sustainability
10. Quality of Life

[19]Shannin, Kelly, 2006. 'Concluding with Landscape Urbanism Strategies'. Graafland and Kavanaugh, 2006: 569–591.
[20]Gabrielli, Bruno, 2010. 'Urban Planning Challenged by Historic Urban Landscape', in: Van Oers (ed.), 2010: 19–25.

Rome

Beijing

Iconic buildings attract public attention and are promoted by architects and politicians. However, they rarely meet social needs and sustainability requirements, nor ensure the continuity of urban form.

still a 'special district', a separate area for city planners and policy-makers. Being a separate object in the urban management process has perhaps been beneficial in several instances, as it has allowed the establishment of special zoning and density regulations, made possible the transfer of public resources, and the use of fiscal and financial incentives to the private sector. However, in many cases it has also accelerated the substitution of the original population and the development of specialised functions, in the form of tourism.

The contemporary debate on urban conservation now aspires to go beyond this established practice for the following reasons.

Firstly, the concept and definition of the historic city have evolved. While in traditional practice the historic city coincided essentially with the pre-industrial city, today other parts stemming from the nineteenth and twentieth centuries are also considered to be heritage, such as Andrassy Avenue in Budapest, or the White City of Tel Aviv for instance, as well as some completely modern cities, like Brasilia or Chandigarh, or some urban areas, such as the Shanghai Bund or the Siedlungen in Berlin. In fact, the partition between what is 'historic' and what is not is increasingly seen as an artificial one, as every city is densely layered as a series of 'episodes', where heritage is viewed as the flow and mix of these events rather than as an arbitrary selection of some urban parts defined as 'historic'.

Secondly, cities change, sometimes in ways that are faster or more unpredictable than the planners expect or can manage. How to manage change has long been a key concern among conservators, whether it relates to monuments, archaeological areas or historic cities. No theory or doctrine has been clearly defined in this arena, and probably cannot be defined as in this case professional judgement will prevail over formalised principles. However, while in the field of monuments conservation as a long and accumulated practice is somehow guiding professional choices, this is not the case for urban conservation. Historic cities are complex organisms, made up not only of their architectural structures, but also of their social structures, activities, rituals, uses and so on. Throughout history this has always been subject to change, and it continues to change today, at an accelerated rate. Venice (Italy), Lijiang (China) and Salvador de Bahia (Brazil) are well preserved as historical urban areas, but both their social structure and functions have changed dramatically. Should they still be considered as urban heritage? Varanasi in India has, instead, maintained *in toto* its social and spiritual values, but its physical fabric is severely compromised; Warsaw in Poland – as well as parts of many other urban areas destroyed by war or natural disaster – has been completely reconstructed: do these still qualify as urban heritage? It is clear that an important theoretical and practical revision of the current paradigms on urban heritage is necessary.[21]

---

[21] Icomos has opened this discussion at the international level and it featured at the VI Annual Meeting of the ICOMOS ISC Theory and Philosophy of Conservation and Restoration, '*Paradigm Shift in Heritage Protection: Tolerance for Changes, Limits for Changes*' – Florence (Italy), 4–6 March 2011.

Thirdly, long-term economic sustainability of heritage conservation is becoming a key issue in urban management. Urban conservation has always had to address the problem of additional financial resources needed to subsidise part of the intervention costs. This cost differential has tended to be supported by public finance, either through direct financial transfers or via fiscal incentives, as part of social investment or of conservation programmes. However, these models are not sustainable in the long term in a world where public finance is under increasing stress, and innovative resource-generating models need to be identified. Furthermore, in a largely urbanised world, environmental sustainability is based on effective urban management models. The built environment needs therefore a large-scale process of 'retrofitting', which needs to be included in conservation paradigms.

And lastly, the decline – if not the demise – of planning as the main tool of urban policy-making demands a serious reflection on the relationship between the public interest and the market in urban conservation, a discussion that so far has not been given the importance it deserves.[22]

The Historic Urban Landscape approach is an attempt – perhaps not the only and certainly not the last – to address the issue of urban conservation in ways that reflect the great diversity of cultural traditions in different societies, in order to 'break the walls' of separation between conservation and development.

The Historic Urban Landscape approach is intended to support new practices and updated tools, rather than provide definitive answers, such as the existing 'prescriptive' charters. It is in fact a new type of instrument, flexible and evolving.

As change is part of the cycle of life of any built and natural environment, an appropriate way to cope with it is to define management systems aimed at preserving values within sustainable processes. The historic city has a lot to offer in support of this challenge. It is in fact one of humanity's most precious resources for the future.

Epilogue

The first decade of the twenty-first century has been a time of reckoning for urban conservators to assess the successes and failures of over half a century of policy formulation and programme development, and to look at the challenges ahead. In a world where the main factors of change are linked to global economic and cultural phenomena, the apparatus developed by urban planners and architects to manage historic cities seems only partially – and locally – adequate to understand and drive market processes and to ensure continuity of heritage values as they were defined in the course of a long intellectual and operational history. The current discussion

---

[22] Koolhaas, Rem. 'Whatever happened to urbanism?'. Koolhaas, Rem and Mau, Bruce, 1995: 958–971.

Cusco

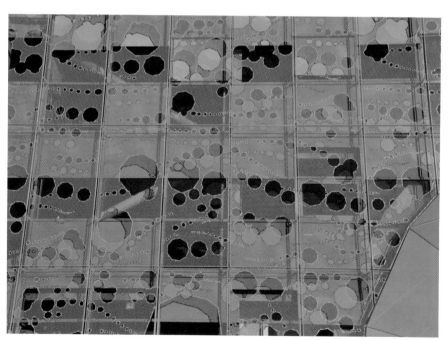

Lyon

Human creativity, a timeless tension of our species, has generated along the millennia endless varieties of forms and meanings. Historic cities are the places where the complexity of cultural expressions through time can be experienced, enjoyed and understood. This awareness is an indispensable resource to meet the challenge of the urban century.

on the transition from the classical paradigm of 'conservation' to the one of 'managing change' confirms that a major effort is being undertaken to identify new paradigms and new processes. This discussion is currently developing along several, sometimes intersecting, lines, which include:

1) The research into the 'limits of acceptable change', which is still inscribed in the tradition of the urban conservation doctrine and the search for a more articulated reading of the relationship between values to be preserved and the conservation of their physical supports.

2) The study of urban conservation as an environmentally sustainable process, in order to highlight the value of the inherited urban fabric as a component of urban sustainable management.

3) The research into new interpretations of heritage, which include modern and contemporary creativity, as well as intangible dimensions of heritage.

4) The research into integrating the management processes for historic and modern areas and the inclusion of natural heritage components in the planning process.

5) The reinforcement and the empowerment of local communities in identifying and taking part in the preservation of heritage values within an open and democratic process.

All these lines of research are opening up important new ground for urban conservation, in ways that could bring forth in the coming years a new concept of urban conservation. It will certainly still be based on the principle of transmission of values to future generations, but also encompass other goals and ambitions.

The scope of this reflection goes beyond the limited 'precinct' of the traditional historic city, and embraces issues that are fundamental to the urban future, such as sustainability, mobility and migration, quality of life, meaning of place, social balance and equity, cultural creativity, technological innovation and economic opportunity.

In a way, the challenge launched by this reflection and by the Historic Urban Landscape initiative touches on the very nature of urban conservation. Should this survive as a specialised discipline or should it become part and parcel of the way in which we identify, plan, design, implement and monitor our actions on this planet?

Annex 1. Note on the Development of the Historic Urban Landscape Approach

Origins of the Historic Urban Landscape Approach

Chapter 1 traced the origins of the notion of the historic urban landscape in urban conservation doctrine, as it was developed roughly over the past century. Although this doctrine was never clearly and comprehensively articulated, there has been a progressive expansion of theory and practice that can be tracked in the development of Charters and Conventions related to cultural heritage conservation and urban management.

This legacy formed the basis of discussion during the debates on the Historic Urban Landscape that took place from the issuing of the Vienna Memorandum in 2005 onwards. During a series of expert meetings, held in various parts of the world and at UNESCO Headquarters from 2005 to 2010, the discussion essentially focused on two primary issues: first, the definition of Historic Urban Landscape (HUL), and second, the elaboration of new or updated strategies and tools to tackle the significant changes and challenges that have come about since 1976 with the adoption of the last UNESCO Recommendation related to heritage preservation.[1]

---

[1] Cities and urban issues have been dealt with by UNESCO through its various sectors, primarily the Natural Sciences Sector, the Social and Human Sciences Sector, and the Culture Sector. The Natural Sciences Sector addresses cities and urban issues through its Man and the Biosphere Programme (MAB), which explores the application of the biosphere concept to urban areas – see Chapter 3. The Social and Human Sciences Sector implements the Management of Social Transformations Programme (MOST), which networks on urban research, urban management and civil society participation. Within the Culture Sector the Creative Cities Network and the World Heritage Cities Programme are the most prominent activities related to urban issues. Reforms are currently under way to better link and harmonise the various cities' activities into a major UNESCO-wide Urban Programme.

The Historic Urban Landscape: Managing Heritage in an Urban Century, First Edition. Francesco Bandarin, Ron van Oers.
© 2012 Francesco Bandarin and Ron van Oers. Published 2012 by Blackwell Publishing Ltd.

The definition of Historic Urban Landscape first appeared in the Vienna Memorandum, in paragraph 7, referring to *'ensembles of any group of buildings, structures and open spaces, in their natural and ecological context, including archaeological and palaeontological sites, constituting human settlements in an urban environment over a relevant period of time, the cohesion and value of which are recognized from the archaeological, architectural, prehistoric, historic, scientific, aesthetic, socio-cultural or ecological point of view. This landscape has shaped modern society and has great value for our understanding of how we live today'.*[2]

After it was issued in Vienna, Austria, in May 2005, it rapidly became one of the most hotly debated and contested conservation documents of the time. Professional entities, conservation groups and research institutes began to examine and discuss its merits and flaws, and their feedback was instrumental in the further development and refinement of the definition and approach.

One of the first fruitful discussions in this regard took place at the Round Table on Heritage and the Conservation of Historic Urban Landscapes organised at the Faculty of Environmental Design of the University of Montreal, under the direction of Dr Christina Cameron. Several heritage conservation and policy experts, among others, scrutinised the Vienna Memorandum and remarked that it was best seen as a transitional document that supports the gradual shift away from a preoccupation with the historic city as visual object to an interest in the historic environment as a space for ritual and human experience; that it could be regarded as a consolidation of professional thinking, but not (yet) as an international recommendation; and that it was a good beginning, but that it contained gaps that would lead to conflicting interpretations.

In her conclusions, the Chair reflected that there was no consensus as regards the term 'historic urban landscape', as the definition differed from traditional terminology in use by specialists in urban studies, and that confusion existed over the relationship of the term 'historic urban landscape' to other World Heritage definitions, such as 'cultural landscape', 'urban ensemble' and 'heritage landscape'. *'The Vienna Memorandum is a transitional document. It hints at a vision of human ecology, although for the most part it remains rooted in the world of buildings and fixed objects that are observed and measured scientifically. It signals a change towards sustainable development and a broader concept of urban space. The way forward appears to be through the concept of "landscape", not so much the designed and evolved landscapes that are familiar to most conservation specialists, but rather associative landscapes or, as Julian Smith calls them, "landscapes of the imagination"'.*[3]

---

[2] *The Vienna Memorandum on World Heritage and Contemporary Architecture – Managing the Historic Urban Landscape*, UNESCO World Heritage Centre and City of Vienna, 2005, at: http://whc.unesco.org/uploads/activities/documents/activity-47-2.pdf
[3] Proceedings of the Round Table on 'Heritage and the Conservation of Historic Urban Landscapes', organised by the Canada Research Chair on Built Heritage, Montreal, 9 March 2006, p. 83; see: http://whc.unesco.org/uploads/activities/documents/activity-47-4.pdf

In 2007 the United States National Committee of the International Council on Monuments and Sites (US-ICOMOS) initiated and moderated a global ICOMOS discussion on historic urban landscapes over the Internet.[4]

Important observations in this discussion included the sense that the landscape terminology, when applied to historic cities and towns, could assist in moving beyond the architecture of cities and towards a more holistic sense of landscape scale; that Historic-Urban-Landscape was referred to as a neologism combining three accepted terms with, albeit complex, histories and associations. Essential in this construct, it was emphasised, is that, for many, 'landscape' has become the lens through which the contemporary city is represented and the medium through which it is constructed, so HUL immediately suggests the necessity for interdisciplinary action; and that there was acceptance that conceptualising the city as a cultural landscape would help in clarifying other sets of tangible elements, which have not yet been properly identified, let alone documented.[5]

In November 2007 the World Heritage Centre organised a third regional Expert Meeting, in Olinda, Brazil, where several papers were delivered that further built upon a slowly emerging consensus.

The meeting elaborated that the notion of 'historic urban landscape' in itself was not necessarily new, as the sight of an urban landscape has often been used to describe a settlement that has been built following the forms of the territory and thus becoming itself a landscape.

Nevertheless, one of the limitations in existing doctrinal texts is that they primarily focus on architecture, even when related to historic urban areas. Indeed, the 1975 Council of Europe Charter, which introduced the concept of integrated conservation, was focusing on architectural heritage (hence its title, i.e. the European Charter of Architectural Heritage), while the 1976 UNESCO Recommendation also defined the notion in relation to 'historic and architectural areas', which is taken to mean 'any groups of buildings, structures and open spaces'.

Missing, it was suggested, were the notions that would make an urban area *urban* beyond architecture – 'the same as taking a landscape beyond the trees, rocks and waterways, and trying to understand its dynamics as a "landscape"'.[6] Furthermore, whereas most experts in the discussion groups were comfortable with the terms of 'landscape' and 'urban landscape', some questioned the need and necessity of including the word 'historic' in the definition. Jokilehto further reflected that the term 'history',

---

[4]In this HUL Forum, 64 professionals from the USA, Canada, Italy and Mexico, among others, participated and it had observers from the National ICOMOS Committees of Argentina, Australia, Austria, Canada, Cuba, Czech Republic, Israel, Greece, Malta, Mexico, the Netherlands, South Africa, Spain, Sweden and the UK.

[5]Araoz, G. and O'Donnell, P.M.,'US-ICOMOS Final Summary of the Discussion on Historic Urban Landscapes', web-based report, September 2007.

[6]Jokilehto, J., 'Reflection on HUL as a Tool for Urban Conservation', in: Van Oers and Haraguchi, 2010, p. 52.

in the English language, has been defined in two senses: the first as the temporal progression of large-scale human events and actions; and the second as the discipline or inquiry in which knowledge of the human past is acquired or sought. *'Historic could thus be understood not just as something being old, but rather as something that is significant as a source for the discipline of history, i.e. something that can be associated with a particular meaning and eventually value. When dealing with cultural heritage, the term historic would thus become a qualifier as heritage'*.[7]

While discussions at the international level continued, in which the World Heritage Centre fully participated, planning started for the development of a new international standard-setting instrument on the conservation of historic urban landscapes that would further elaborate on the principles put forward in the Vienna Memorandum, as per the original request of the World Heritage Committee (2005).

At UNESCO Headquarters in Paris a group of experts convened on 13 and 14 November 2008 to discuss the format and structure of the new Recommendation, and which technical issues would need to be addressed in the document to underline the changing conditions under which urban development projects are nowadays implemented, which are impacting upon the safeguarding of urban heritage values – the six issues described in Chapter 3 of this book.

It also updated the definition of Historic Urban Landscape by significantly downsizing on the material aspects and introducing intangible notions that were deemed essential in the understanding and experience of the urban condition: *'Historic urban landscape is a mindset, an understanding of the city, or parts of the city, as an outcome of natural, cultural and socio-economic processes that construct it spatially, temporally, and experientially. It is as much about buildings and spaces, as about rituals and values that people bring into the city. This concept encompasses layers of symbolic significance, intangible heritage, perception of values, and interconnections between the composite elements of the historic urban landscape, as well as local knowledge including building practices and management of natural resources. Its usefulness resides in the notion that it incorporates a capacity for change'*.

While this definition is more encompassing and highly inclusive, arguably the key that makes all the difference is to be found in the tail-end: the acceptance of *change* as an inherent part of the urban condition.

And this has perhaps been the biggest hurdle on the path to progress in the urban conservation discipline over the last decade, as in particular the conservation community found this difficult to accept vis-à-vis their core ideology to preserve monuments and sites as unchanged as possible, or otherwise was not able to reach a consensus on *how much* change would be permissible.[8]

---

[7] Ibid., p. 54.
[8] Van Oers, 2010, 'Managing Cities and the Historic Urban Landscape Initiative – An Introduction', in: Van Oers and Haraguchi, 2010, p. 14.

In a position paper issued to the ICOMOS Executive Council meeting in Malta, in October 2009, the current President of ICOMOS, Gustavo Araoz, argued that over the past 10 years a *'paradigm shift for heritage places'* had occurred, due to *'the evolution of the role that heritage plays in society, the appropriation of heritage by communities and the growing acceptance of heritage as a public commodity with economic value from which profit can be derived [which] have brought about deep changes in the way that the government and the public sector perceive and use their heritage resources'.*[9]

In order to address this paradigm shift, he has called for ICOMOS to engage in a global exercise to discuss and define the 'tolerance for change' of monuments and sites. The purpose is to collect ideas and proposals that would seek a more systematic and objective approach to dealing with the dynamic nature of heritage places, their setting and context, and the constant evolution of the values that they carry.

His proposal, however, met with strong opposition, in particular from the members of the Scientific Committee for the Theory and the Philosophy of Conservation and Restoration at their meeting organised in Prague, Czech Republic, from 5 to 9 May 2010.

Its members argued that it was against the core ideology of the organisation, which is 'preserving, not altering and destroying' monuments and sites, as expressed by the organisation's former President.[10]

Further refinement of the definition and approach took place at two more expert meetings, one in Stone Town, Zanzibar (from 30 November to 3 December 2009), and the other in Rio de Janeiro, Brazil (from 7 to 9 December 2009).[11]

The meeting in Zanzibar[12] was important as regards the views and expressions of more traditional societies (in comparison to heavily urbanised Europe, North America and South America in particular) towards the relationships between the urban heritage of settlements and their natural and rural surroundings.

---

[9] Araoz, G., 'Protecting Heritage Places under the New Heritage Paradigm & Defining its Tolerance for Change – A Leadership Challenge for ICOMOS', unpublished position paper for the ICOMOS Executive Council, October 2009.

[10] Taken from: 'Policy Guidelines set down by the President', by Michael Petzet, Final version, Paris, 10 March 2008, and later published in: Michael Petzet, *International Principles of Preservation*, Monuments and Sites XX, ICOMOS 2009, p. 7. On 26 May 2010 a disclaimer was put on the ICOMOS website stating that 'the "Principles" represent a personal view of the preservation world, and as such should be published by the author in his own name and without direct ICOMOS involvement, or the ICOMOS name or logo in the title or represented in any way as an endorsement of the publication.' – see: http://www.international.icomos.org/Disclaimer_Website-Mon-&-Sites-XX.pdf.

[11] One of the reasons why Brazil hosted two HUL meetings (November 2007 in Olinda, and December 2009 in Rio) was related to the huge importance attached by this Member State to the debate and its outcomes, since it is running urban conservation programmes in approximately 170 historic cities throughout its territory.

[12] Forty experts from ten countries, among which representatives of six (of a total of eight) World Heritage-designated cities in the African region, participated in Zanzibar.

Among others, it was emphasised that urban conservation should not be limited to building preservation, but become part of environmental policies, and that the multi-layered mosaic of African landscapes highlight the need for an inclusive approach, which should be based on a recognition of the continuity of local value systems and the dynamics of informal, community-driven processes.[13] At the meeting in Rio de Janeiro, which was called for by the World Heritage Committee (in 2009) to examine the inclusion of the concept of Historic Urban Landscape into the *Operational Guidelines for the Implementation of the World Heritage Convention*, it was agreed that the HUL approach should not become another box to put heritage into, but become part of an attitude as to how cities develop, to address the contemporary city with a conservation attitude: a new model of urban development in which heritage values provide guidance and direction.

As such, not only World Heritage cities should be managed as HUL, but also their buffer zones, as they form part of the *genius loci* of the site. HUL goes beyond traditional boundaries and limits of protected areas, and depends on the site's Outstanding Universal Value (OUV). In addition, it was argued that alongside cities, the HUL approach would also be applicable to the management of all the other heritage categories, being monuments, groups of buildings, sites and cultural landscapes.

The OUV, then, is what has been recognised by the World Heritage Committee and the international community to be of value, and hence what needs to be protected (through identification of attributes and their relationships – also those that are at the surface and not obviously linked – and the Statement of OUV could be considered as 'just-in-time information'), while HUL is how you manage the site: by retaining values in a changing environment.

Last but not least, an updated definition of HUL was agreed upon, which was fine-tuned in February 2010 at a planning meeting in Paris for the drafting of a first text of the new Recommendation on Historic Urban Landscape.

'*The Historic Urban Landscape is the urban settlement understood as a historic layering of cultural and natural values, extending beyond the notion of "historic centre" or "ensemble" to include the broader urban context and its geographical setting. This wider context includes the site's topography, geomorphology and natural features; its built environment, both historic and contemporary; its infrastructures above and below ground; its open spaces and gardens; its land use patterns and spatial organization; its visual relationships; and all other elements of the urban structure. It also includes social and cultural practices and values, economic processes, and the intangible dimensions of heritage as related to diversity and identity.*'[14]

---

[13]*Zanzibar Recommendations on the Application of the Concept of the Historic Urban Landscape in the African Context*, available at: http://whc.unesco.org/en/events/613

[14]Definition as put forward in the First Draft text of the Recommendation on the Historic Urban Landscape, UNESCO Paris, 27 June 2010, which was sent out to all of UNESCO's 193 Member States on 25 August 2010 for review and comments.

This definition found its way into the First Draft text of the Recommendation on the Historic Urban Landscape as it will provide the basis for a comprehensive approach for the identification, conservation and management of historic urban landscapes within an overall sustainability framework.

It is integrative, inclusive, holistic and participatory in its views towards the role of urban heritage in the development of the city, similar to the European Commission's directive that *an integrated ecosystem approach has to be adopted and the relationships and exchanges between the urban area and the surrounding landscape must be fully integrated in the . . . approach*.[15]

The General Assembly of ICOMOS in Colombo, Sri Lanka, in 1993, concluded by criticising the dominance of Western philosophical thinking in conservation and called for the creation of regional conservation Charters to balance the pluralistic and sometimes divergent viewpoints emanating from the sheer diversity of cultures.

In this vein, particular attention has been given, during the process of re-evaluation of existing policies and practices and the re-formulation of an updated approach, to documents that would reflect other than European–North American concepts of urban heritage management.

From 25 to 27 May 2011 an Inter-Governmental Meeting of Experts (category II) on the Historic Urban Landscape took place at UNESCO headquarters, in pursuance of General Conference Resolution 35C/42 (16 October 2009). According to the *Rules of Procedure concerning Recommendations to Member States and International Conventions*, the Member States were requested to submit their comments on the First Draft text to UNESCO by 25 December 2010 and these comments, incorporated in a Revised Draft text, were presented and discussed at the meeting with Representatives of Member States of UNESCO. On 27 May a final Draft text of a new UNESCO Recommendation on the Historic Urban Landscape was finalised and adopted by the Expert Meeting. This final Draft text was submitted to the 36th session of UNESCO's General Conference and was adopted on 10 November 2011 by consensus. The text of the new UNESCO Recommendation on the Historic Urban Landscape is included in Annex 3.

---

[15] European Commission directive C (2008) 4598 of 28 August 2008.

Annex 2. The 2005 Vienna Memorandum

 United Nations Educational, Scientific and Cultural Organization
Organisation des Nations Unies pour l'éducation, la science et la culture

Centre du patrimoine mondial
World Heritage Centre

VIENNA MEMORANDUM on

'World Heritage and Contemporary Architecture –
Managing the Historic Urban Landscape'

PREAMBLE

1. Recalling that the Vienna Memorandum is the result of an international conference on the subject of 'World Heritage and Contemporary Architecture', which was requested by the World Heritage Committee at its 27th session (Paris, 30 June-5 July 2003, Decision 27COM 7B.108) and held from 12 to 14 May 2005 in Vienna, Austria, under the patronage of UNESCO and attended by more than 600 experts and professionals from 55 countries;

2. Bearing in mind the scope of UNESCO's *Convention concerning the Protection of the World Cultural and Natural Heritage* (World Heritage Convention, 1972), and recalling its Articles 4 and 5, striving for global collaboration and the need for global discussions on the subject of the strong economic dynamic and recent structural changes in cities inscribed on UNESCO's World Heritage List;

3. Further recalling that sites are inscribed on the World Heritage List on the basis of the Statement of Outstanding Universal Value and that the preservation of this value should be at the centre of any conservation policy and management strategy;

The Historic Urban Landscape: Managing Heritage in an Urban Century, First Edition. Francesco Bandarin, Ron van Oers.
© 2012 Francesco Bandarin and Ron van Oers. Published 2012 by Blackwell Publishing Ltd.

4. Considering in particular the 1964 "International Charter for the Conservation and Restoration of Monuments and Sites" (Venice Charter), the 1968 "UNESCO Recommendation concerning the Preservation of Cultural Property endangered by Public or Private works", the 1976 "UNESCO Recommendation concerning the Safeguarding and Contemporary Role of Historic Areas", the 1982 ICOMOS-IFLA "International Charter for Historic Gardens" (Florence Charter), the 1987 ICOMOS "Charter for the Conservation of Historic Towns and Urban Areas" (Washington Charter), the 1994 Nara Document on Authenticity, as well as the HABITAT II Conference and Agenda 21, which was ratified by Member States in Istanbul (Turkey) in June 1996;

5. Desiring that the *Vienna Memorandum* be seen, within the continuum of these aforementioned documents and the current debate on the sustainable conservation of monuments and sites, as a key statement for an integrated approach linking contemporary architecture, sustainable urban development and landscape integrity based on existing historic patterns, building stock and context.

DEFINITIONS

6. The present Memorandum refers to historic cities already inscribed or proposed for inscription on the UNESCO World Heritage List, as well as to larger cities that have World Heritage monuments and sites within their urban territories.

7. The historic urban landscape, building on the 1976 "UNESCO Recommendation concerning the Safeguarding and Contemporary Role of Historic Areas", refers to ensembles of any group of buildings, structures and open spaces, in their natural and ecological context, including archaeological and palaeontological sites, constituting human settlements in an urban environment over a relevant period of time, the cohesion and value of which are recognized from the archaeological, architectural, prehistoric, historic, scientific, aesthetic, socio-cultural or ecological point of view. This landscape has shaped modern society and has great value for our understanding of how we live today.

8. The historic urban landscape is embedded with current and past social expressions and developments that are place-based. It is composed of character-defining elements that include land uses and patterns, spatial organization, visual relationships, topography and soils, vegetation, and all elements of the technical infrastructure, including small scale objects and details of construction (curbs, paving, drain gutters, lights, etc.).

9. Contemporary architecture in the given context is understood to refer to all significant planned and designed interventions in the built historic environment, including open spaces, new constructions, additions to or extensions of historic buildings and sites, and conversions.

10. The expanding notion of cultural heritage in particular over the last decade, which includes a broader interpretation leading to recognition of human coexistence with the land and human beings in society, requires new approaches to and

methodologies for urban conservation and development in a territorial context. The international charters and recommendations have not yet fully integrated this evolution.

11. The *Vienna Memorandum* focuses on the impact of contemporary development on the overall urban landscape of heritage significance, whereby the notion of historic urban landscape goes beyond traditional terms of "historic centres", "ensembles" or "surroundings", often used in charters and protection laws, to include the broader territorial and landscape context.

12. The historic urban landscape acquires its exceptional and universal significance from a gradual evolutionary, as well as planned territorial development over a relevant period of time through processes of urbanization, incorporating environmental and topographic conditions and expressing economic and socio-cultural values pertaining to societies. As such, protection and conservation of the historic urban landscape comprises the individual monuments to be found in protection registers, as well as ensembles and their significant connections, physical, functional and visual, material and associative, with the historic typologies and morphologies.

PRINCIPLES and AIMS

13. Continuous changes in functional use, social structure, political context and economic development that manifest themselves in the form of structural interventions in the inherited historic urban landscape may be acknowledged as part of the city's tradition, and require a vision on the city as a whole with forward-looking action on the part of decisionmakers, and a dialogue with the other actors and stakeholders involved.

14. The central challenge of contemporary architecture in the historic urban landscape is to respond to development dynamics in order to facilitate socio-economic changes and growth on the one hand, while simultaneously respecting the inherited townscape and its landscape setting on the other. Living historic cities, especially World Heritage cities, require a policy of city planning and management that takes conservation as one key point for conservation. In this process, the historic city's authenticity and integrity, which are determined by various factors, must not be compromised.

15. The future of our historic urban landscape calls for mutual understanding between policy makers, urban planners, city developers, architects, conservationists, property owners, investors and concerned citizens, working together to preserve the urban heritage while considering the modernization and development of society in a culturally and historic sensitive manner, strengthening identity and social cohesion.

16. Taking into account the emotional connection between human beings and their environment, their sense of place, it is fundamental to guarantee an urban environmental quality of living to contribute to the economic success of a city and to its social and cultural vitality.

17. A central concern of physical and functional interventions is to enhance quality of life and production efficiency by improving living, working and recreational conditions and adapting uses without compromising existing values derived from the character and significance of the historic urban fabric and form. This means not only improving technical standards, but also a rehabilitation and contemporary development of the historic environment based upon a proper inventory and assessment of its values, as well as adding high-quality cultural expressions.

GUIDELINES for CONSERVATION MANAGEMENT

18. Decision-making for interventions and contemporary architecture in a historic urban landscape demand careful consideration, a culturally and historic sensitive approach, stakeholder consultations and expert know-how. Such a process allows for adequate and proper action for individual cases, examining the spatial context between old and new, while respecting the authenticity and integrity of historic fabric and building stock.

19. A deep understanding of the history, culture and architecture of *place*, as opposed to object buildings only, is crucial to the development of a conservation framework and single architectural commissions should be informed by urbanism and its tools for analyses of typologies and morphologies.

20. An essential factor in the planning process is a timely recognition and formulation of opportunities and risks, in order to guarantee a well-balanced development and design process. The basis for all structural interventions is a comprehensive survey and analysis of the historic urban landscape as a way of expressing values and significance. Investigating the long-term effects and sustainability of the planned interventions is an integral part of the planning process and aims at protecting the historic fabric, building stock and context.

21. Taking into account the basic definition (according to Article 7 of this *Memorandum*), urban planning, contemporary architecture and preservation of the historic urban landscape should avoid all forms of pseudo-historical design, as they constitute a denial of both the historical and the contemporary alike. One historical view should not supplant others, as history must remain readable, while continuity of culture through quality interventions is the ultimate goal.

GUIDELINES for URBAN DEVELOPMENT

22. Ethic standards and a demand for high-quality design and execution, sensitive to the cultural-historic context, are prerequisites for the planning process. Architecture of quality in historic areas should give proper consideration to the given scales, particularly with reference to building volumes and heights. It is important for new development to minimize direct impacts on important historic elements, such as significant structures or archaeological deposits.

23. Spatial structures in and around historic cities are to be enhanced through urban design and art as they are key elements of the renaissance of historic cities: urban design and art express their specific historical, social and economic components and transmit them to forthcoming generations.

24. Preservation of World Heritage sites also involves the design of public space: particular attention is to be paid to functionality, scale, materials, lighting, street furniture, advertising, and vegetation, to name a few. Urban planning infrastructure in heritage zones must include all measures to respect the historic fabric, building stock and context, and to mitigate the negative effects of traffic circulation and parking.

25. Townscapes, roofscapes, main visual axes, building plots and types are integral parts of the identity of the historic urban landscape. With regard to renewal, the historic roofscape and the original building plots serve as the basis for planning and design.

26. As a general principle, proportion and design must fit into the particular type of historic pattern and architecture, while removing the core of building stock worthy of protection ("façadism") does not constitute an appropriate means of structural intervention. Special care should be taken to ensure that the development of contemporary architecture in World Heritage cities is complementary to values of the historic urban landscape and remains within limits in order not to compromise the historic nature of the city.

WAYS and MEANS

27. Management of the dynamic changes and developments in World Heritage historic urban landscapes encompasses precise knowledge of the territory and its elements of heritage significance identified through scientific methods of inventory, the relevant laws, regulations, tools and procedures, which are formalized in a Management Plan, according to the *Operational Guidelines for the Implementation of the World Heritage Convention*.

28. The development and implementation of a Management Plan for historic urban landscapes requires the participation of an interdisciplinary team of experts and professionals, as well as timely initiation of comprehensive public consultation.

29. Quality management of the historic urban landscape aims at permanent preservation and improvement of spatial, functional and design-related values. In this respect, special emphasis is to be placed on the contextualization of contemporary architecture in the historic urban landscape and Cultural or Visual Impact Assessment studies should accompany proposals for contemporary interventions.

30. Economic aspects of urban development should be bound to the goals of long-term heritage preservation.

31. Historic buildings, open spaces and contemporary architecture contribute significantly to the value of the city by branding the city's character. Contemporary architecture can be a strong competitive tool for cities as it attracts residents, tourists, and capital. Historic and contemporary architecture constitute an asset to local communities, which should serve educational purposes, leisure, tourism, and secure market value of properties.

RECOMMENDATIONS

The following considerations are directed to the World Heritage Committee and UNESCO:

A) With regard to historic urban areas already inscribed on the World Heritage List, the concept of the historic urban landscape and the recommendations expressed in this Memorandum need to be taken into account when reviewing any potential or ascertained impact on the integrity of a World Heritage property. These principles should be enhanced by plans which delineate the specific measures to be taken for the protection of the historic urban landscape.

B) When considering the inscription of new properties and sites of historic urban areas on the World Heritage List, it is recommended that the concept of the historic urban landscape be included in the nomination and evaluation process.

C) UNESCO is invited to study the possibility for formulating a new recommendation to complement and update the existing ones on the subject of historic urban landscapes, with special reference to the contextualization of contemporary architecture which should be submitted, at a future date, to the General Conference of UNESCO.

(20 May 2005)

Annex 3. The UNESCO Recommendation on the Historic Urban Landscape

United Nations
Educational, Scientific and
Cultural Organization

Organisation
des Nations Unies
pour l'éducation,
la science et la culture

RECOMMENDATION ON THE HISTORIC URBAN LANDSCAPE

PREAMBLE

Considering that historic urban areas are among the most abundant and diverse manifestations of our common cultural heritage, shaped by generations and constituting a key testimony to humankind's endeavours and aspirations through space and time,

Further considering that urban heritage is for humanity a social, cultural and economic asset, defined by an historic layering of values that have been produced by successive and existing cultures and an accumulation of traditions and experiences, recognized as such in their diversity,

Also considering that urbanization is proceeding at an unprecedented scale in the history of humankind and that throughout the world this is driving socio-economic change and growth, which should be harnessed at the local, national, regional and international levels,

Recognising, the dynamic nature of living cities,

The Historic Urban Landscape: Managing Heritage in an Urban Century, First Edition. Francesco Bandarin, Ron van Oers.
© 2012 Francesco Bandarin and Ron van Oers. Published 2012 by Blackwell Publishing Ltd.

Noting, however, that rapid and frequently uncontrolled development is transforming urban areas and their settings, which may cause fragmentation and deterioration to urban heritage with deep impacts on community values, throughout the world,

Considering, therefore, that in order to support the protection of natural and cultural heritage, emphasis needs to be put on the integration of historic urban area conservation, management and planning strategies into local development processes and urban planning, such as, contemporary architecture and infrastructure development, for which the application of a landscape approach would help maintain urban identity,

Considering that the principle of sustainable development provides for the preservation of existing resources, the active protection of urban heritage and its sustainable management is a condition *sine qua non* of development,

Recalling that a corpus of standard-setting documents, including conventions, recommendations and charters, exists on the subject of the conservation of historic areas[1], all of which remain valid,

Noting, however, that under processes of demographic shifts, global market liberalization and decentralization, as well as mass tourism, market exploitation of heritage, and climate change, conditions have changed and cities are subject to development pressures and challenges not present at the time of adoption of the last UNESCO recommendation on historic areas in 1976 (i.e. the Recommendation concerning the Safeguarding and Contemporary Role of Historic Areas),

Further noting the evolution of the concepts of culture and heritage and of the approaches to their management, through the combined action of local initiatives and international meetings[2], which have been useful in guiding policies and practices worldwide,

---

[1]In particular the 1972 UNESCO Convention concerning the Protection of the World Cultural and Natural Heritage, the 2005 UNESCO Convention on the Protection and Promotion of the Diversity of Cultural Expressions, the 1962 UNESCO Recommendation concerning the Safeguarding of the Beauty and Character of Landscapes and Sites, the 1968 UNESCO Recommendation concerning the Preservation of Cultural Property Endangered by Public or Private Works, the 1972 UNESCO Recommendation concerning the Protection, at National Level, of the Cultural and Natural Heritage, the 1976 UNESCO Recommendation concerning the Safeguarding and Contemporary Role of Historic Areas; the 1964 ICOMOS International Charter for the Conservation and Restoration of Monuments and Sites (Venice Charter), the 1982 ICOMOS International Charter for Historic Gardens (Florence Charter), and the 1987 ICOMOS Charter for the Conservation of Historic Towns and Urban Areas (Washington Charter), the 2005 ICOMOS Xi'an Declaration, as well as the 2005 Vienna Memorandum.

[2]In particular the 1982 *World Conference on Cultural Policies* in Mexico City, the 1994 *Nara Meeting on Authenticity*, the 1995 summit of the *World Commission on Culture and Development*, the 1996 *HABITAT II Conference* in Istanbul with ratification of Agenda 21, the 1998 UNESCO *Intergovernmental Conference on Cultural Policies for Development* in Stockholm, the 1998 joint World Bank-UNESCO *Conference on Culture in Sustainable Development–Investing in Cultural and Natural Endowments*, the 2005 *International Conference on World Heritage and Contemporary Architecture in Vienna*, the 2005 ICOMOS *General Assembly on the Setting of Monuments and Sites* in Xi'an, and the 2008 ICOMOS *General Assembly on the Spirit of Place* in Québec.

Desiring to supplement and extend the application of the standards and principles laid down in existing international instruments,

Having before it proposals concerning the historic urban landscape as an approach to urban heritage conservation, which appear on the session's agenda as item 8.1,

Having decided at its thirty-fifth session that this issue should be addressed through a Recommendation to Member States,

Adopts the present Recommendation. The General Conference recommends that Member States adopt the appropriate legislative institutional framework and measures, with a view to apply the principles and norms set out in this Recommendation in the territories under their jurisdiction.

The General Conference recommends that Member States bring this Recommendation to the attention of the local, national and regional authorities and of institutions, services or bodies and associations concerned with the safeguarding, conservation and management of historic urban areas and their wider geographical settings.

INTRODUCTION

1. Our time is witness to the largest human migration in history. Now, more than half of the world's population lives in urban areas. Urban areas are increasingly important as engines of growth and as centres of innovation and creativity; they provide opportunities for employment and education and respond to people's evolving needs and aspirations.

2. Rapid and uncontrolled urbanization, however, may frequently result in social and spatial fragmentation and in a drastic deterioration of the quality of the urban environment and of the surrounding rural areas. Notably, this may be due to excessive building density, standardized and monotonous buildings, loss of public space and amenities, inadequate infrastructure, debilitating poverty, social isolation, and an increasing risk of climate-related disasters.

3. Urban heritage, including its tangible and intangible components, constitutes a key resource in enhancing the liveability of urban areas and fosters economic development and social cohesion in a changing global environment. As the future of humanity hinges on the effective planning and management of resources, conservation has become a strategy to achieve a balance between urban growth and quality of life on a sustainable basis.

4. In the course of the past half century, urban heritage conservation has emerged as an important sector of public policy worldwide. It is a response to the need to preserve shared values and to benefit from the legacy of history. However, the shift from an emphasis on architectural monuments primarily towards a broader recognition of the importance of the social, cultural and economic processes in the conservation

of urban values, should be matched by a drive to adapt the existing policies and to create new tools to address this vision.

5. This Recommendation addresses the need to better integrate and frame urban heritage conservation strategies within the larger goals of overall sustainable development, in order to support public and private actions aimed at preserving and enhancing the quality of the human environment. It suggests a landscape approach for identifying, conserving and managing historic areas within their broader urban contexts, by considering the inter-relationships of their physical forms, their spatial organization and connection, their natural features and settings, and their social, cultural and economic values.

6. This approach addresses the policy, governance and management concerns involving a variety of stakeholders, including local, national, regional, international, public and private actors in the urban development process.

7. This Recommendation builds upon the four previous UNESCO Recommendations related to heritage preservation, recognizing the importance and the validity of their concepts and principles in the history and practice of conservation. In addition, modern conservation conventions and charters address the many dimensions of cultural and natural heritage and constitute the foundations for this Recommendation.

I. DEFINITION

8. The historic urban landscape is the urban area understood as the result of a historic layering of cultural and natural values and attributes, extending beyond the notion of "historic centre" or "ensemble" to include the broader urban context and its geographical setting.

9. This wider context includes notably the site's topography, geomorphology, hydrology and natural features; its built environment, both historic and contemporary; its infrastructures above and below ground; its open spaces and gardens, its land use patterns and spatial organization; perceptions and visual relationships; as well as all other elements of the urban structure. It also includes social and cultural practices and values, economic processes and the intangible dimensions of heritage as related to diversity and identity.

10. This definition provides the basis for a comprehensive and integrated approach for the identification, assessment, conservation and management of historic urban landscapes within an overall sustainable development framework.

11. The historic urban landscape approach aims at preserving the quality of the human environment, enhancing the productive and sustainable use of urban spaces while recognizing their dynamic character, and promoting social and functional diversity. It integrates the goals of urban heritage conservation and those of social and economic development. It is rooted in a balanced and sustainable relationship between the urban and natural environment, between the needs of present and future generations and the legacy from the past.

12. The historic urban landscape approach considers cultural diversity and creativity as key assets for human, social and economic development and provides tools to manage physical and social transformations and to ensure that contemporary interventions are harmoniously integrated with heritage in a historic setting and take into account regional contexts.

13. The historic urban landscape approach learns from the traditions and perceptions of local communities while respecting the values of the national and international communities.

II. CHALLENGES AND OPPORTUNITIES FOR THE HISTORIC URBAN LANDSCAPE

14. The existing UNESCO Recommendations recognize the important role of historic areas in modern societies. They also identify a number of specific threats to the conservation of historic areas and provide general principles, policies and guidelines to meet such challenges.

15. The historic urban landscape approach reflects the fact that the discipline and practice of urban heritage conservation have evolved significantly in recent decades, enabling policy-makers and managers to deal more effectively with new challenges and opportunities. The historic urban landscape approach supports communities in their quest for development and adaptation, while retaining the characteristics and values linked to their history, collective memory, and to the environment.

16. In the past decades, due to the sharp increase in the world's urban population, the scale and speed of development and the changing economy, urban settlements and their historic areas have become centres and drivers of economic growth in many regions of the world, and have taken on a new role in cultural and social life. As a result, they have also come under a large array of new pressures, including:

Urbanization and Globalization

17. Urban growth is transforming the essence of many historic urban areas. Global processes have a deep impact on the values attributed by communities to urban areas and their settings, and on the perceptions and realities of inhabitants and users. On the one hand, urbanization provides economic, social and cultural opportunities that can enhance the quality of life and traditional character of urban areas; on the other hand, the unmanaged changes in urban density and growth can undermine the sense of place, integrity of the urban fabric, and the identity of communities. Some historic urban areas are losing their functionality, traditional role and populations. The historic urban landscape approach may assist in managing and mitigating such impacts.

Development

18. Many economic processes offer ways and means to alleviate urban poverty and to promote social and human development. The greater availability of innovations, such as

information technology and sustainable planning, design and building practices, can improve urban areas, thus enhancing the quality of life. When properly managed through the historic urban landscape approach, new functions such as services and tourism, are important economic initiatives that can contribute to the well-being of the communities and to the conservation of historic urban areas and their cultural heritage while ensuring economic and social diversity and the residential function. Failing to capture these opportunities leads to unsustainable and unviable cities, just as implementing them in an inadequate and inappropriate manner results in the destruction of heritage assets and irreplaceable losses for future generations.

Environment

19. Human settlements have constantly adapted to climatic and environmental changes including those resulting from disasters. However, the intensity and speed of present changes are challenging our complex urban environments. Concern for the environment, in particular for water and energy consumption, calls for approaches and new models for urban living, based on ecologically sensitive policies and practices aiming at strengthening sustainability and the quality of urban life. Many of these initiatives, however, should integrate natural and cultural heritage as resources for sustainable development.

20. Changes to historic urban areas can also result from sudden disasters and armed conflicts. These may be short lived but can have lasting effects. The historic urban landscape approach may assist in managing and mitigating such impacts.

III. POLICIES

21. Modern urban conservation policies, as reflected in existing international recommendations and charters, have set the stage for the preservation of historic urban areas. However, present and future challenges require the definition and implementation of a new generation of public policies identifying and protecting the historic layering and balance of cultural and natural values in urban environments.

22. Conservation of the urban heritage should be integrated in general policy planning and practices and those related to the broader urban context. Policies should provide mechanisms for balancing conservation and sustainability in the short- and long-term. Special emphasis should be placed on the harmonious integration between the historic urban fabric and contemporary interventions. In particular, the responsibilities of the different stakeholders are the following:

a) Member States should integrate urban heritage conservation strategies into national development policies and agendas according to the historic urban landscape approach. Within this framework, local authorities should prepare urban development plans taking into account the area's values, including landscape and other heritage values, and their associated features.

b) Public and private stakeholders should cooperate *inter alia* through partnerships to ensure the successful application of the historic urban landscape approach.

c) International organizations dealing with sustainable development processes should integrate the historic urban landscape approach into their strategies, plans and operations.

d) National and international non-governmental organizations should participate in developing and disseminating tools and best practices for the implementation of the historic urban landscape approach.

23. All levels of government – local, national/federal, regional – aware of their responsibility, should contribute to the definition, elaboration, implementation and assessment of urban heritage conservation policies. These policies should be based on a participatory approach of all stakeholders and coordinated from both an institutional and sectorial viewpoint.

IV. TOOLS

24. The approach based on the historic urban landscape implies the application of a range of traditional and innovative tools adapted to local contexts. Some of these tools, which need to be developed as part of the process involving the different stakeholders, might include:

a) **Civic engagement tools** should involve a diverse cross-section of stakeholders and empower them to identify key values in their urban areas, develop visions that reflect their diversity, set goals, and agree on actions to safeguard their heritage and promote sustainable development. These tools, which constitute an integral part of urban governance dynamics, should facilitate intercultural dialogue by learning from communities about their histories, traditions, values, needs, and aspirations and by facilitating the mediation and negotiation between conflicting interests and groups.

b) **Knowledge and planning tools** should help protect the integrity and authenticity of the attributes of urban heritage. They should also allow for the recognition of cultural significance and diversity, and provide for the monitoring and management of change to improve the quality of life and of urban space. These tools would include documentation and mapping of cultural and natural characteristics. Heritage, social and environmental impact assessments should be used to support and facilitate decision-making processes within a framework of sustainable development.

c) **Regulatory systems** should reflect local conditions and may include legislative and regulatory measures aiming at the conservation and management of the tangible and intangible attributes of the urban heritage, including their social, environmental and cultural values. Traditional and customary systems should be recognized and reinforced as necessary.

d) **Financial tools** should aim to build capacities and support innovative income-generating development, rooted in tradition. In addition to government and global funds from international agencies, financial tools should be effectively employed to foster private investments at the local level. Micro credit and other flexible financing to support local enterprise, as well as a variety of models of partnerships, are also central to making the historic urban landscape approach financially sustainable.

V. CAPACITY-BUILDING, RESEARCH, INFORMATION AND COMMUNICATION

25. Capacity-building should involve the main stakeholders: communities, decision-makers, and professionals and managers, in order to foster understanding of the historic urban landscape approach and its implementation. Effective capacity-building hinges on an active collaboration of these main stakeholders, aimed to adapt the implementation of this Recommendation to regional contexts to define and refine the local strategies and objectives, action frameworks and resource mobilization schemes.

26. Research should target the complex layering of urban settlements, in order to identify values, understand their meaning for the communities and present them to visitors in a comprehensive manner. Academic and university institutions and other centres of research should be encouraged to develop scientific research on aspects of the historic urban landscape approach and cooperate at the local, national, regional and international level. It is essential to document the state of urban areas and their evolution, to facilitate the evaluation of proposals for change and to improve protective and managerial skills and procedures.

27. Encourage the use of information and communication technology to document, understand and present the complex layering of urban areas and their constituent components. The collection and analysis of this data is an essential part of the knowledge of urban areas. To communicate with all sectors of society, it is particularly important to reach out to youth and all under-represented groups in order to encourage their participation.

VI. INTERNATIONAL COOPERATION

28. Member States and international governmental and non-governmental organizations should facilitate public understanding and involvement in the implementation of the historic urban landscape approach, by disseminating best practices and lessons learned from different parts of the world, in order to strengthen the network of knowledge-sharing and capacity-building.

29. Member States should promote multinational cooperation between local authorities.

30. International development and cooperation agencies of Member States, non-governmental organisations and foundations, should be encouraged to develop methodologies which take into account the historic urban landscape approach and to harmonise them with their assistance programmes and projects pertaining to urban areas.

Bibliography

Adams, W.M., 2006. 'The Future of Sustainability: Re-Thinking Environment and Development in the Twenty-First Century'. Report of the IUCN Renowned Thinkers Meeting, 29–31 January 2006. Gland: IUCN.

Aga Khan Trust for Culture, 1989. *The Hassan Fathy Collection. A Catalogue of Visual Documents at the Aga Khan Award for Architecture*. Bern: Aga Khan Trust for Culture.

Agnew, Neville; Demas, Martha, 2002. *Principles for the Conservation of Heritage Sites in China*. Los Angeles: The Getty Conservation Institute.

Ahmed, Kulsum; Sánchez-Triana, Ernesto, (eds.), 2008. *Strategic Environmental Assessment for Policies – An Instrument for Good Governance Overview*. Washington DC: The World Bank.

Appleyard, Donald (ed.), 1979. *The Conservation of European Cities*. Cambridge, Massachusetts: MIT Press.

Araoz, Gustavo, 2011. 'Preserving Heritage Places under a New Paradigm'. *Journal of Cultural Heritage Management and Sustainable Development*. Vol. 1, Issue 1.

Argan, Giulio Carlo, 1963. 'On the Typology of Architecture'. *Architectural Design* N. 33: 564–565.

Ascher, François, 2010. *Les nouveaux principes de l'urbanisme*. La Tour d'Aigues: Edition de l'Aube.

Ashworth, Gregory; Turnbridge, John, 1990. *The Tourist-Historic City*. London: Belhaven.

Avrami, Erica; Mason, Randall; De la Torre, Marta, 2000. *Values and Heritage Conservation*. Research Report. Los Angeles: The Getty Conservation Institute.

Aymonino, Carlo, 2000. *Il Significato delle Città*. Venezia: Marsilio. (Originally published in 1975.)

Bandarin, Francesco, 2006. 'Towards a new standard-setting instrument for Managing the Historic Urban Landscape'. *Conservation in changing societies*. Leuven: Raymond Lemaire Centre.

Bandarin, Francesco, 2007. 'Looking Ahead: the World Heritage Convention in the 21st Century'. *World Heritage: Challenges for the Millennium*. Paris: UNESCO World Heritage Centre.

Bandarin, Francesco, 2011a. 'From Paradox to Paradigm? Historic Urban Landscape as an urban conservation approach'. Taylor, K. and Lennon, J. 2012. *Managing Cultural Landscapes*. London and New York: Routledge. Chapter 11.

Bandarin, Francesco, 2011b. 'A new international instrument: the proposed UNESCO Recommendation for the Conservation of Historic Urban Landscape'. Heft, 3/4: 179–182. Bonn: Bundesinstitut für Bau-, Stadt und Raumforschung.

Bandarin, Francesco, 2011c. 'Utopien und ihre Rekonstruktion'. Demand, Thomas; Kittelman, Udo, 2011. *Nationalgalerie. 'How German is it?'* Berlin: Suhrkamp. 333–350.

Bandarin, Francesco; Hosagrahar, Jyoti; Albernaz, Frances, 2011. 'Why Development needs Culture'. *Journal of Cultural Heritage Management and Sustainable Development*, Vol.1, N.1: 15–25.

Benevolo, Leonardo, 1993. *La città nella storia d'Europa*. Bari: Laterza.

Berghauser Pont, Meta; Haupt, Per, 2010. *Space Matrix – Space, Density and Urban Form*. Rotterdam: NAi Publishers.

Bertaud, Alain, 2003. 'Metropolis: The Spatial Organization of Seven Large Cities'. Watson, Donald; Plattus, Alan; Shibley, Robert G. (eds.), 2003. *Time-Saver Standards for Urban Design*. New York: McGraw Hill.

Bianca, Stefano, 2000. *Urban Form in the Arab World. Past and Present*. Zurich: vdf.

Bianca, Stefano; Jodidio, Philip (eds.), 2004. *Cairo – Revitalising a Historic Metropolis*. Turin: Umberto Allemandi Editore for the Aga Khan Trust for Culture.

Bidou-Zachariasen, Catherine (ed.), 2003. *Retours en ville – des processus de "gentrification" urbaine aux politiques de "revitalisation" des centres*. Paris: Descartes et Cie, collection 'Les urbanités'.

Bigio, Antony Gad, 2010. '*The Sustainability of Urban Heritage Preservation: The Case of Marrakesh*'. Washington, DC: IDB Discussion Paper.

Bohl, Charles C.; Lejeune, Jean-François, 2009. *Sitte, Hegemann and the Metropolis*. London: Routledge.

Boito, Camillo, 1893: *Questioni pratiche di belle arti*. Milano: Hoepli.

Bruns, Diedrich, 2007. *Integration of Landscapes in National Policies: Urban, Peri-Urban and Sub-Urban Landscape*. Meeting of the Council of Europe on the European Landscape Convention. Strasbourg: Council of Europe, 22–23 March 2007.

Buchanan, Peter, 2005. *Ten Shades of Green Architecture and the Natural World*. New York: The Architectural League of New York.

Buckley, Ralf, 2004. 'The Effects of World Heritage Listing on Tourism to Australian National Parks'. *Journal of Sustainable Tourism*, Vol. 12, No. 1: 70–84.

Burke, Gerald, 1976. *Townscapes*. Harmondsworth, Middlesex: Penguin Books Ltd.

Burns, Carol; Kahn, Andrea, 2005. *Site Matters. Design Concepts, Histories and Strategies*. New York, Routledge.

Calabi, Donatella, 1979. *Il 'male' città: diagnosi e terapia: didattica e istituzioni nell' urbanistica inglese del primo '900*. Rome: Officina Edizioni.

Campbell, Tim E., 2003. 'Unknown Cities: Metropolis, Identity and Governance in a Global World'. *Development Outreach*, Volume 5, number 3. Washington DC: The World Bank Institute.

Caniggia, Gianfranco; Maffei, Gian Luigi, 2001. *Interpreting Basic Building*. Firenze: Alinea.

Canizaro, Vincent (ed.), 2007. *Architectural Regionalism: Collected Writings on Place, Identity, Modernity and Tradition*. New York: Princeton Architectural Press.

Cassar, May, 2005. *Climate Change and the Historic Environment*. London: Centre for Sustainable Heritage, University College London.

Choay, Françoise, 1992. *L'allégorie du patrimoine*. Paris: Seuil.

Choay, Françoise (ed.), 2002. *La Conférence d'Athènes sur la conservation artistique et historique des monuments (1931)*. Paris: Les Editions de l'Imprimeur.

Choay, Françoise, 2006. *Pour une anthropologie de l'espace*. Paris: Seuil.

Choay, Françoise, 2009. *Le patrimoine en questions. Anthologie pour un combat*. Paris: Seuil.

City of Cape Town, 2005. *Integrated Metropolitan Environmental Policy (IMEP). Cultural heritage strategy for the City of Cape Town*. Cape Town: Environmental Management Branch, Heritage Resources Section.

Cohen, Nahum, 1999. *Urban conservation*. Cambridge, Massachusetts: MIT Press.

Collins, George R.; Crasemann Collins, Christiane, 1986. *Camillo Sitte: the Birth of Modern Town Planning*. Mineola, New York: Dover.

Considérant, Victor, 2009. *Le socialisme devant le vieux monde ou le vivant devant les morts*. Paris: Librairie Phalanstérienne. (Originally published in 1848.)

Conzen, M.R.G., 2004. *Thinking about Urban Form. Papers on Urban Morphology, 1932–1998*. Bern: Peter Lang.

Corboz, André, 2009. *De la ville au patrimoine urbain. Histoire de forme et de sens.* Québec: Presse de l'Université du Québec.

Council of Europe, 2000. *European Landscape Convention.* European Treaty Series No. 176. Florence: Council of Europe.

Crasemann Collins, Christiane, 2005. *Werner Hegemann and the search for universal urbanism.* New York: Norton.

Cullen, Gordon, 1961. *Townscape.* London: The Architectural Press.

Culot, Maurice; Barey, André; Culot Lefèbvre, Philippe, 1982. *La déclaration de Bruxelles.* Bruxelles: Editions AAM.

Curtis, William J.R., 1986. *Le Corbusier. Ideas and Forms.* London: Phaidon Press.

Curtis, William J.R., 1996. *Modern Architecture since 1900.* London: Phaidon Press.

Dalal-Clayton, Barry; Sadler, Barry, 1998. *Strategic Environmental Assessment and Developing Countries.* London: IIED.

Dear, Michael J., 2000. *The Postmodern Urban Condition.* Oxford: Blackwell Publishers.

De Carlo, Giancarlo, 1972. *An Architecture of Participation.* The Melbourne Architectural Papers. Melbourne: The Royal Australian Institute of Architects.

De Mulder, Eduardo F.J.; Kraas, Frank, 2008. 'Megacities of tomorrow'. *A World of Science*, Natural Sciences Quarterly Newsletter, UNESCO. 6 (4): 2–10.

Descamps, Françoise (ed.), 2009. *Proceedings of the World Congress of the Organisation of World Heritage Cities, Quito 2009.* Los Angeles: The Getty Conservation Institute.

Di Biagi, Paola (ed.), 1998. *La Carta di Atene. Manifesto e frammento dell'urbanistica moderna.* Roma: Officina Edizioni.

Dufieux, Philippe, 2009. *Tony Garnier: la Cité industrielle et l'Europe.* Lyon: CAUE du Rhône.

Dupuis, Xavier, 1989. *La prise en compte de la dimension culturelle du développement: un bilan méthodologique.* Paris: UNESCO.

Durrell, Lawrence, 1969. *Spirit of Place: Letters and Essays on Travel.* London: Faber & Faber.

Eisenman, Peter, 1984. 'The End of the Classical. The End of the Beginning, the End of the End'. *Perspecta: The Yale Architectural Journal* 21: 154–172.

Elias, Derek, 2005. 'Spared by the Sea'. *The New Courier*, May. Paris: UNESCO.

Engels, Friedrich, 1993. *The Condition of the Working Class in England.* Oxford: Oxford University Press. (Originally published in German in 1845.)

English Heritage, 1997. *Sustaining the Historic Environment.* London: English Heritage.

English Heritage, 2000. *Power of Place: A Future for the Historic Environment.* London: English Heritage.

English Heritage, 2008. *Conservation Principles. Policies and Guidance for the Sustainable Management of the Historic Environment.* London: English Heritage.

Erder, Cevat, 1987. *Our Architectural Heritage: From Consciousness to Conservation.* Paris: UNESCO.

Ernstson, Henrik; Van der Leeuw, Sander E.; Redman, Charles L.; Meffert, Douglas J.; Davis, George; Alfsen, Christine; Elmqvist, Thomas, 2010. 'Urban Transitions: On Urban Resilience and Human-Dominated Ecosystems'. *AMBIO: A Journal of the Human Environment.* 39 (8): 531–545.

European Science Foundation, 2010. *Landscape in a Changing World. Bridging Divides, Integrating Disciplines, Serving Society.* Science Policy Briefing, October 2010.

European Union, 2000. *European Spatial Development Perspectives.* Potsdam: European Union.

Fahr-Becker, Gabriele, 2008. *Wiener Werkstätte 1903–1932.* Paris: Taschen France.

Falser, Michael; Lipp, Wilfred; Tomaszewski, Andrzej, 2010. *Conservation and Preservation. Proceedings of the International Conference of the ICOMOS International Scientific Committee for the Theory and Philosophy of Conservation and Restoration, 23–27 April 2008, Vienna.*

Farr, Douglas, 2008. *Sustainable Urbanism.* Hoboken, New Jersey: Wiley.

Fathi, Hassan, 1973. *Architecture for the Poor. An experiment in rural Egypt.* Chicago: the University of Chicago Press.

Feilden, B.; Jokilehto, J.,1998. *Management Guidelines for World Cultural Heritage Sites.* Rome: ICCROM.

Firestone, Michal, 2007. 'Historic Urban Landscape initiative. Draft Summary'. Unpublished Report, ICOMOS Scientific Council.

Fischer, Thomas, 2007. *The Theory and Practice of Strategic Environmental Assessment – Towards a More Systematic Approach.* London: Earthscan.

Fishman, Robert, 1977. *Urban Utopias in the XXth Century.* Cambridge, Massachusetts: MIT Press.

Florida, Richard, 2002. *The Rise of the Creative Class. And How It's Transforming Work, Leisure, Community and Everyday Life.* New York: Perseus Book Group.

Foo, Ah Fong; Yuen, Belinda (eds.), 1999. *Sustainable Cities in the 21st Century.* Singapore: University of Singapore Press.

Frampton, Kenneth, 1983. 'Towards a Critical Regionalism: Six Points for an Architecture of Resistance', in: Foster, Hal (ed.): *The Anti-Aesthetic: Essays on Postmodern Culture.* Port Townsend, Washington: Bay Press. 16–30.

Frampton, Kenneth, 2007. *Modern Architecture: A Critical History.* London: Thames and Hudson.

Freestone, Robert, 2000. *Urban Planning in a Changing World. The Twentieth century Experience.* London: Spon Press.

Fritsch, Theodor, 1896. *Die Stadt des Zukunft.* Leipzig: Hammer. (2nd edition 1912.)

Garnier, Tony, 1917. *Une Cité industrielle. Etude pour la construction des villes.* Paris: Massin.

Geddes, Patrick, 2010. *Cities in evolution: Evolution: an Introduction to the Town Planning Movement and to the Study of Civics.* Nabu Press. (Originally published in 1915.)

Gorski, Esser, 2009. *Regulating New Construction in Historic Districts.* Washington, DC: The National Trust for Historic Preservation.

Graafland, Arie; Kavanaugh, Leslie J. (eds.), 2006. *Crossover: Architecture, Urbanism, Technology.* Rotterdam: 010 Publishers.

Guccione, Margherita; Vittorini, Alessandra, 2005. *Giancarlo De Carlo. Le ragioni dell'Architettura.* Roma: MIBAC/MAXXI.

Gugic, Goran, 2009. *Managing Sustainability in Conditions of Change and Unpredictability.* Krapje, Croatia: Lonjsko Polje Nature Park Public Service.

Giambruno, Mariacristina (ed.), 2007. *Per una storia del restauro urbano.* Novara: De Agostini, Città Studi Edizioni.

Giovannoni, Gustavo, 1931. *Vecchie città ed edilizia nuova.* Torino: UTET.

Gregotti, Vittorio, 1966. *Il territorio dell'architettura.* Milano: Feltrinelli.

Gregotti, Vittorio, 1985. 'Territory and Architecture', in: *Architectural Design Profile* 59, no. 5–6: 28–34.

Guo, Y.; Zan, Luca; Liu, S., 2008. *The Management of Cultural Heritage in China.* Milano: EGEA S.p.A.

Habraken, John, 2000. *The Structure of the Ordinary: Form and Control in the Built Environment,* ed. by Jonathan Teicher. Cambridge, Massachusetts: MIT Press.

Hall, Peter, 1988. *Cities of Tomorrow: an Intellectual History of Urban Planning in the XXth Century.* Oxford: Blackwell Publishers.

Hankey, Donald (ed.), 1998. *Case Study: Lahore, Pakistan. Conservation of the Walled City.* Washington, DC: The World Bank.

Hayden, Dolores, 1995. *The Power of Place. Urban Landscape as Public History.* Cambridge, Massachusetts: MIT Press.

Hays, Michael K., 2000. *Architecture Theory since 1968*. Cambridge, Massachusetts: MIT Press.

Healey, Patsy, 2005. *Collaborative Planning: Shaping Places in Fragmented Societies*. Houndsmill, Basingstoke, Hampshire: Palgrave Macmillan.

Healey, Patsy, 2010. *Making Better Places. The Planning Project in the Twenty-First Century*. Houndsmill, Basingstoke, Hampshire: Palgrave Macmillan.

Hegemann, Werner; Peets, Elbert, 1988. *The American Vitruvius: an Architect's Handbook of Civic Art*. New York: Princeton Architectural Press.

Heiken, Grant; Funiciello, Renato; De Rita, Donatella, 2005. *The Seven Hills of Rome*. Princeton: Princeton University Press.

Henket, Hubert-Jan; Heyned, Hilde (eds.), 2002. *Back from Utopia. The Challenge of the Modern Movement*. Rotterdam: 010 Publishers.

Hobsbawm, Eric, 1983. 'Mass-producing traditions: Europe, 1870–1914', in: Hobsbawm, Eric; Ranger, Terence, *The Invention of Tradition*. Cambridge: Cambridge University Press: 263–307.

Holl, Steven, 2009. *Urbanisms: Working with Doubt*. New York: Princeton Architectural Press.

Hosagrahar, Jyoti, 2005. *Indigenous Modernities. Negotiating Architecture and Urbanism*. London: Routledge.

Howard, Ebenezer (1902). *Garden Cities of To-morrow*. London: S.Sonnenschein & Co. Ltd.

IAIA, 2007. *The Big Picture*. International Association of Impact Assessment, Annual Report.

Iamandi, Cristina, 1997. 'Charters of Athens of 1931 and 1933: Coincidence, controversy and convergence'. *Conservation and Management of Archaeological Sites* 2(1): 17–28.

ICOMOS, 2001. *International Charters for Conservation and Restoration*. Paris: ICOMOS.

ICOMOS, 2008. *The World Heritage List. What is OUV? Defining the Outstanding Universal Value of Cultural World Heritage Properties*. Paris: ICOMOS.

IFC, 2006. *Performance Standard 8 – Cultural Heritage*. Washington, DC: International Finance Corporation.

Innes, Judith; Booher, David, 2010. *Planning with Complexity. An Introduction to Collaborative Rationality for Public Policy*. New York: Routledge.

International Architecture Biennale Rotterdam, 2007. *Visionary Power. Producing the Contemporary City*. Rotterdam: NAi Publishers.

IUCN, 1980. *The World Conservation Strategy*. Geneva: International Union for the Conservation of Nature; United Nations Environment Programme; World Wildlife Fund.

IUCN, 2008. *Management Planning for Natural World Heritage Properties – A Resource Manual for Practitioners*. IUCN World Heritage Studies, N. 5. Gland: International Union for the Conservation of Nature.

Jacobs, Jane, 1993. *The Death and Life of Great American Cities*. New York: The Modern Library. (Originally published in 1961.)

Jameson, Fredric, 2003. *Future City*. New Left Review 21, May–June 2003: 65–79.

Jencks, Charles, 1988. *The Prince, the Architects and the New Wave Monarchy*. London: Academy Editions.

Jencks, Charles, 2002. *The New Paradigm in Architecture. The Language of Post-Modernism*. New Haven: Yale University Press.

Jencks, Charles, 2005. *Iconic Building*. New York: Rizzoli.

Jencks, Charles; Kropf, Karl, 2006. *Theories and Manifestoes of Contemporary Architecture*. London: Wiley.

Jenks, Michael; Burton, Elisabeth; Williams, Cathy, 1996. *The Compact City. A Sustainable Urban Form?* London: Spon Press.

Jha-Thakur, U.; Gazzola, P.; Peel, D.; Fischer, T.B.; Kidd, S., 2009. 'Effectiveness of strategic environmental assessment – the significance of learning', *Impact Assessment and Project Appraisal*, 27(2).

Jokilehto, Jukka, 1999a. 'Management of Sustainable Change in Historic Urban Areas'. Zancheti, Silvio (ed.). *Conservation and Urban Sustainable Development – A Theoretical Framework*. Recife: CECI.

Jokilehto, Jukka, 1999b. *A History of Architectural Conservation*. Oxford: Butterworth-Heinemann.

Jokilehto, Jukka, 2010b. 'Notes on the Definition and Safeguarding of HUL'. *City & Time* 4 (3): 4.

Judd, Dennis R.; Fainstein, Susan S., 1999. *The Tourist City*. New Haven, Yale University Press.

Kaplan, Robert D., 2000. *The Coming Anarchy*. New York: Vintage Books, New York.

Kaplan, Wendy; Crawford, Alan, 2005. *The Arts & Crafts Movement in Europe and America: Design for the Modern World 1880 1920*. London: Thames & Hudson.

Katz, Peter, 1994. *The New Urbanism: Toward an Architecture of Community*. New York: McGraw-Hill Professional.

Kerr, James Semple, 2000. *The Conservation Plan*. 6th Edition. Canberra: The National Trust of Australia.

Klamer, Arjo; Zuidhof, Peter-Wim, 1998. *The Role of the Third Sphere in the World of the Arts*. Paper presented at the XX Conference of the Association of Cultural Economics International, Barcelona.

Koolhaas, Rem, 1978. *Delirious New York: a retroactive manifesto for Manhattan*. New York: Oxford University Press.

Koolhaas, Rem, 2000. 'Junkspace'. *A+U Special Issue: OMA@Work*, May: 16–24.

Koolhaas, Rem, 2010. *CRONOCAOS*. OMA*AMO Exhibition. Venice: Biennale.

Koolhaas, Rem; Mau, Bruce, 1995. *S,M,L,XL*. New York: Monacelli Press.

Kostof, Spiro, 1991. *The City Shaped*. London: Thames and Hudson.

Kostof, Spiro, 1992. *The City Assembled*. London: Thames and Hudson.

Krier, Leon, 1978. *Rational Architecture Rationelle: the Reconstruction of the European City*. Bruxelles: Archives d'Architecture Moderne.

Krier, Leon, 2009. *The Architecture of Community*. Washington: Island Press.

Krier, Leon; Culot, Maurice, 1980. *Contreprojets, Controprogetti, Counterprojects*. Bruxelles: Editions AAM.

Landry, Charles, 2000. *The Creative City: A Toolkit for Urban Innovators*. London: Earthscan.

Lanzafame, Francesco; Quartesan, Alessandra (eds.), 2009. *Downtown Poverty – Methods of Analysis and Interventions*. Washington, DC: Inter-American Development Bank.

Larkham, Peter J., 1996. *Conservation and the City*. Routledge: New York.

Laurin, Claude; Laterreur, Isabelle; Schwartz, Marlène; Bronson, Susan, 2007. 'Montreal's Plateau Mont-Royal Borough: An innovative approach to conserving and enhancing an historic urban neighborhood'. Paper presented at the 5th International Seminar on *Changing Role and Relevance of Urban Conservation Charters*. Recife: CECI.

Lawler, Eilìs; Neitzert, Eva; Nicholls, Jeremy, 2008. *Measuring Value: a guide to Social Return on Investment (SROI)*. London: New Economics Foundation.

Leal, Eusebio, 2006. *A Singular Experience – Appraisals of the Integral Management Model of Old Havana, World Heritage Site*. Havana: Office of the City Historian.

Le Corbusier, 1935. *La ville radieuse*. Paris: Éditions de l'Architecture d'Aujourd'hui.

Le Corbusier, 1957. *La Charte d'Athènes*. Paris: Editions de Minuit. Ld. (Originally published in 1941.)

Le Corbusier, 1977. *Vers une Architecture*. Paris: Edition Arthaud. (Originally published in 1923.)

Lefebvre, Henri, (2000). *La production de l'espace*. Paris: Economica. (Originally published in 1974.)

Lichfield, Nathaniel, 1988. *Economics in Urban Conservation*. Cambridge, Cambridge University Press.

Logan, William S. (ed.), 2002. *The Disappearing 'Asian' City: Protecting Asia's Urban Heritage in a Globalizing World*. Oxford: Oxford University Press.

Lynch, Kevin, 1960. *The image of the city*. Cambridge, Massachusetts: MIT Press.

Lynch, Kevin, 1972. *What Time is This Place?* Cambridge, Massachusetts: MIT Press.

Lynch, Kevin, 1976. *Managing the Sense of a Region*. Cambridge, Massachusetts: MIT Press.

Lynch, Kevin, 1981. *Good City Form*. Cambridge, Massachusetts: MIT Press.

Lynch, Kevin, 1984. 'Reconsidering the Image of the City', in: Rodwin, Lloyd; Hollister, Robert M., 1984. *Cities of the Mind*. New York: Plenum Press.

McDonough, William, 1992. *The Hannover Principles: Design for Sustainability*. New York: William McDonough Architects.

McDonough, William, 2003. 'From Principles to Practice: Creating Sustaining Architecture for the Twenty-First Century'. Green@work, May/June. Republished in: Sykes, Krista A. (ed.), 2010. *Constructing a New agenda. Architectural Theory 1993–2009*. New York: Princeton University Press: 218–225.

McGranahan, Gordon; Balk, Deborah; Anderson, Bridget, 2007. 'The rising tide: assessing the risks of climate change and human settlements in low elevation coastal zones'. *Environment and Urbanization* (19) (1): 17–37.

McHarg, Ian, 1969. *Design with Nature*. Philadelphia: The Falcon Press.

McHarg, Ian, 1981. 'Human Ecological planning at Pennsylvania'. *Landscape Planning* 8: 109–120.

McKean, John, 2003. 'Il Magistero: De Carlo's dialogue with historical forms'. *Places*, Vol. 16, No. 1: 54–63.

Meadows, Donella H.; Meadows, Dennis L.; Randers, Jorgen; Behrens, William W. III, 1972. *The Limits of Growth. A Report for the Club of Rome's Project on the Predicament of Mankind*. New York: Universe Books.

Meadows, Donella H.; Randers, Jorgen; Meadows, Dennis L., 2004. *Limits to Growth: The 30-Year Update*. White River Junction, VT: Chelsea Green Publishing Company.

Mongin, Olivier, 2005. *La condition urbaine. La ville à l'heure de la mondialisation*. Paris: Seuil.

Morris, William, 1878. 'The restoration of ancient buildings'. *The Builder*, December.

Mostafavi, Mohsen; Doherty, Gareth (eds.), 2010. *Ecological Urbanism*. Baden: Lars Müller Publishers.

Mumford, Eric, 2000. *The CIAM discourse on Urbanism*. Cambridge, Massachusetts: MIT Press.

Mumford, Lewis, 1938. *The Culture of Cities*. London: Secker and Warburg.

Muñoz, Vinas Salvador, 2005. *Contemporary Theory of Conservation*. Oxford: Elsevier.

Muratori, Saverio, 1960. *Studi per una operante storia urbana di Venezia. Quadro generale dalle origini agli sviluppi attuali*. Roma: Istituto Poligrafico dello Stato.

Muratori, Saverio, 1967. *Civiltà e territorio*, Roma: Centro Studi di Storia Urbanistica.

Nelson Coffin, A., 2008. 'Maori Cultural Impact Assessment and Mapping', Paper presented at the International Association of Impact Assessment Conference in Perth, Australia, 4–10 May 2008.

Nesbitt, Kate (ed.), 1996. *Theorizing a New Agenda for Architecture. An Anthology of Architectural Theory. 1965–1995*. New York: Princeton University Press.

Netherlands State Government, 1999. *The Belvedere Memorandum: a Policy Document Examining the Relationship Between Cultural History and Spatial Planning*. The Hague.

Ng, Edward (ed.), 2009. *Designing High-Density Cities For Social and Environmental Sustainability*. London: Earthscan.

Norberg-Schulz, Christian, 1976. 'The Phenomenon of Place', in: *Architectural Association Quartely* 8, No. 4: 3–10.

Norberg-Schulz, Christian, 1980. *Genius Loci: Towards a Phenomenology of Architecture*. New York: Rizzoli.

Norberg-Schulz, Christian, 2000. *Architecture: Presence, Language, Place*. Milan: Skira.

Nurse, Keith, 2007. 'Culture as the Fourth Pillar of Sustainable Development'. *INSULA – International Journal of Island Affairs*, Year 16, No. 1. Paris: UNESCO.

OECD, 2006. *Applying Strategic Environmental Assessment*. DAC Guidelines and References Series. Paris: Organisation for Economic Co-operation and Development.

OECD, 2010. *Territorial Reviews: Venice, Italy*. Paris: Organisation for Economic Co-operation and Development.

Ost, Christian G., 2009. *A Guide for Heritage Economics in Historic Cities – Values, Indicators, Maps, and Policies*. Brussels: ICHEC Brussels School of Management.

Parsons, Kermit Carlyle, 1998. *The Writings of Clarence S. Stein: Architect of the Planned Community*. Baltimore: The Johns Hopkins University Press.

Partidário, Maria do Rosario, 2007. *Strategic Environmental Assessment – Good Practices Guide*, Amadora: Portuguese Environmental Agency.

Pedersen, Poul Baek (ed.), 2009. *Sustainable Compact City*. Århus: Arkitektskolens Forlag. 2nd Edition.

Petruccioli, Attilio, 2007. *After Amnesia. Learning from the Islamic Mediterranean Urban Fabric*. Bari: ICAR.

Pevsner, Nikolaus, 2005. *Pioneers of Modern Design*. New Haven: Yale University Press.

Pickard, Robert, 2009. *Funding the architectural heritage: a guide to policies and examples*. Strasbourg: Council of Europe.

Pinder, David, 2005. *Visions of Cities. Utopianism, Power and Politics in Twentieth-Century Urbanism*. Edinburgh: Edinburgh University Press.

Pinon, Pierre, 2002. *Atlas du Paris Haussmannien. La ville en héritage du Second Empire à nos jours*. Paris: Editions Parigramme.

Poëte, Marcel, 2000. *Introduction à l'urbanisme*. Paris: Sens &Tonka. (Originally published in 1929.)

Poulot, Dominique, 2006. *Une Histoire du patrimoine en Occident*. Paris: PUF.

PricewaterhouseCoopers LLP, 2007. *The Costs and Benefits of UK World Heritage Status. A literature review for the Department for Culture, Media and Sport*. London: DCMS.

Prud'homme, Rémy, 2008. *Les impacts socio-économiques de l'inscription d'un site sur la Liste de Patrimoine Mondial: Trois études*. Paris: UNESCO.

Purchla, Jacek, 2005. *Heritage and Transformation*. Kraków, International Cultural Centre.

Ragon, Michel, 1986. *Histoire de l'architecture et de l'urbanisme modernes*. Paris: Casterman.

Rebanks Consulting Ltd, 2009. *World Heritage Status – Is there opportunity for economic gain?* UK: Lake District World Heritage Project.

Register, Richard, 2006. *EcoCities: Rebuilding Cities in Balance with Nature*. Gabriola Island, British Columbia: New Society Publishers.

Reiner, Thomas, 1963. *The place of the ideal community in urban planning*. Philadelphia: University of Pennsylvania Press.

Relph, Edward, 1987. *The Modern Urban Landscape*. Baltimore: The Johns Hopkins University Press.

Riegl, Alois, 1903. *Der moderne Denkmalkultus, sein Wesen und seine Entstehung*. Vienna. (English translation: Forster and Ghirardo, 'The Modern Cult of Monuments: Its Character and Its Origins', in: *Oppositions*, number 25, Fall 1982, pp. 21–51.)

Ringbeck, Birgitta, 2008. *Management Plans for World Heritage Sites – A practical guide*. Berlin: The German Commission for UNESCO.

Roberts, Peter; Sykes, Hughes (eds.), 2000. *Urban Regeneration: a Handbook*. London: Sage.

Robinson, Mike; Picard, David, 2006. *Tourism, Culture and Sustainable Development*. Paris: UNESCO.

Rodwell, Dennis, 2007. *Conservation and Sustainability in Historic Cities*. Oxford: Blackwell Publishing Ltd.

Rodwin, Lloyd; Hollister, Robert M., 1984. *Cities of the Mind*. New York: Plenum Press.

Rojas, Eduardo, 2002. *Urban Heritage Conservation in Latin America and the Caribbean. A Task for All Social Actors*. Sustainable Development Department Technical Papers Series Publication SOC-125. Washington, D.C.: Inter-American Development Bank.

Roncayolo, Marcel; Paquot, Thierry (eds.), 2001. *Villes et civilisation urbaine, XVIII-XX siècle*. Paris: Larousse.

Rosan, Christina; Ruble, Blair A.; Tulchin, Joseph. S. (eds.), 1999. *Urbanization, Population, Environment and Security – A Report of the Comparative Urban Studies Project*. Washington, DC: Woodrow Wilson Center.

Rossi, Aldo, (1978). *L'Architettura della Città*. Milano: CittàStudiedizioni.

Rowe, Colin; Koetter, Fred, 1978. *Collage City*. Cambridge, Massachusetts: MIT Press.

Ruskin, John, (1960). *The Stones of Venice*. New York: Hill and Wang. (Originally published in 1853.)

Ruskin, John, (1989). *The Seven Lamps of Architecture*. London: Dent and Sons. (Originally published in 1849.)

Rykwert, Joseph, 1989. *The Idea of a Town*. Cambridge, Massachusetts: MIT Press.

Rypkema, Donovan, 1994. *The Economics of Historic Preservation: A Community Leader's Guide*. Washington, DC: The National Trust for Historic Preservation.

Sachs, Jeffrey, 2003. 'The New Urban Planning'. *Development Outreach*, Volume 5, Number 3. Washington, DC: The World Bank Institute.

Safranski, Rüdiger, 2007. 'Hoeveel globalisering verdraagt een mens?' *Opinio*, Opinio Media BV, 19–25 oktober.

Sanderson, Eric W., 2009. *Mannahatta. A Natural History of New York City*. New York: Abrams.

Sanson, Parcal, 2007. *Le Paysage Urbain. Représentations, Significations, Communication*. Paris: Harmattan.

Sassen, Saskia, 2001. *The Global City*. Princeton: Princeton University Press.

Satterthwaite, David, 2008. 'Adapting to Climate Change'. Id 21 Insights, N. 71.

Savir, Uri, 2003. 'Glocalization – A New Balance of Power'. *Development Outreach*, Volume 5, Number 3. Washington, DC: The World Bank Institute.

Savourey, Cathy, 2005. *Ten years of decentralized cooperation between the cities of Chinon and Luang Prabang sponsored by UNESCO*. Paris: UNESCO.

Schumacher, Thomas L., 1971. 'Contextualism: Urban Ideals and Deformations'. *Casabella* N. 359–360: 79–86.

Schuyler, David, 1986. *The New Urban Landscape. The Redefinition of City Form in Nineteenth-Century America*. Baltimore: The Johns Hopkins University Press.

Schwartz, Frederic J., 1996. *The Werkbund: Design Theory and Mass Culture before the First World War*. New Haven: Yale University Press.

Secchi, Bernardo, 2005. *La città del ventesimo secolo*. Roma: Laterza.

Semes, Steven W., 2009. *The Future of the Past. A conservation Ethic for Architecture, Urbanism and Historic Preservation*. New York: Norton.

Serageldin, Ismail, 1999. *Very Special Places: The Architecture and Economics of Intervening in Historic Cities*. Washington, DC: The World Bank.

Serageldin, Ismail; Shluger, Ephim; Martin-Brown, Joan (eds.), 2001. *Historic Cities and Sacred Sites. Cultural Roots for Urban Futures*. Washington, DC: The World Bank.

Sida, 2002. *Sustainable Development? Guidelines for the Review of Environmental Impact Assessments*. Stockholm: Swedish International Development Cooperation Agency.

Simonis, Udo; Hahn, Eckhart, 1990. *Ecological Urban Restructuring*. Paris: Organization for Economic Co-operation and Development.

Sitarz, Daniel (ed.), 1994. *Agenda 21: The Earth Summit Strategy to save Our Planet*. Boulder, Colorado: Earth Press.

Sitte, Camillo, 1965. *City Planning According to Artistic Principles*. London: Collins. (Originally published in German as *Der Städtebau nach seinen künstlerischen Grundsätzen* in 1889.)

Smets, Marcel, 1995. *Charles Buls. Les principes de l'Art Urbain*. Liège: Pierre Mardaga.

Stein, Clarence, 1951. *Toward New Towns for America*. Cambridge, Massachusetts: MIT Press.

Stubbs, John H., 2009. *Time Honoured. A Global View of Architectural Conservation*. Hoboken, New Jersey: Wiley.

Sykes, Krista A. (ed.), 2010. *Constructing a New Agenda. Architectural Theory 1993-2009*. New York: Princeton University Press.

Tatom, Jacqueline; Stauber, Jennifer (eds.), 2009. *Making the Metropolitan Landscape*. New York: Routledge.

Teutonico, Jeanne Marie; Matero, Frank, 2003. *Managing Change: Sustainable Approaches to the Conservation of the Built Environment*. Los Angeles: The Getty Conservation Institute.

Thomas, Randall (ed.), 2003. *Sustainable Urban Design. An Environmental Approach*. New York: Spon Press.

Tiesdell, Steven; Oc, Taner; Heath, Tim, 1996. *Revitalising Historic Urban Quarters*. Oxford: Architectural Press.

Toffler, Alvin, 1984. *The Third Wave*. New York: Bantam Books.

Tomaszewski, Andrej, 2010. 'Conservation between "tolerance for change" and "management of change"'. Paper presented at the 5th Conference of the ICOMOS International Scientific Committee for the Theory and Philosophy of Conservation, Prague, 5–9 May 2010.

Tung, Anthony M., 2001. *Preserving the World's Great Cities*. New York: Random House.

Turgeon, Laurier (ed.), 2009. *Spirit of Place: between Tangible and Intangible Heritage*. Québec: Les Presses de l'Université Laval.

Turner, John, 1976. *Housing by People: Towards Autonomy in Building Environments, Ideas in progress*. London: Marion Boyars.

Tzonis, Alexander; Lefaivre, Liane, 1990. 'Why Critical Regionalism Today?' *Architecture and Urbanism* 236: 22–33.

UCLG, 2007. *Decentralization and Local Democracy in the World, First Global Report*. Barcelona: United Cities and Local Governments.

UNCTAD, 2008. *Creative Economy Report 2008*. New York: United Nations.

UNECE, 2007. *Guidebook on Promoting Good Governance in Public–Private Partnerships*. New York and Geneva: United Nations Economic Commission for Europe.

UNEP, 2005. *Making Tourism More Sustainable – A Guide for Policy Makers*. Nairobi: UNEP and UNWTO.

UNEP, 2007. *Liveable Cities: The Benefits of Urban Environmental Planning*. Nairobi: UNEP; Cities Alliance; ICLEI.

UNEP, 2008. *Global Green New Deal – Environmentally Focused Investment Historic Opportunity for 21st Century Prosperity and Job Generation*. Nairobi: United Nations Environment Programme.

UNEP, 2009a. *Global Green New Deal Policy Brief*. Nairobi, Kenya: United Nations Environment Programme.

UNEP, 2009b. *Integrated policy-making for sustainable development*. Nairobi: United Nations Environment Programme.

UNEP, 2009c. *Integrated Assessment: Mainstreaming sustainability into policymaking – A guidance manual*. Nairobi: United Nations Environment Programme.

UNESCO, 1996. *Our Creative Diversity. Report of the World Commission on Culture and Development*. Paris: UNESCO.

UNESCO, 1998. *Linking Nature and Culture. Global Strategy Natural and Cultural Heritage Expert Meeting*. Amsterdam: Dutch Ministry of Education, Culture and Science.

UNESCO, 2004. *Partnerships for World Heritage Cities: Culture as a Vector for Sustainable Urban Development*. World Heritage Papers No. 9. Paris: UNESCO.

UNESCO, 2009. *Preliminary study on the technical and legal aspects relating to the desirability of a standard-setting instrument on the conservation of the historic Urban Landscape*. 181 Executive Board Session Doc.29. Paris: UNESCO.

UNESCO World Heritage Centre, 2007. *World Heritage. Challenges for the Millennium*. Paris: UNESCO.

UNESCO World Heritage Centre, 2008. *Policy Document on the Impacts of Climate Change on World Heritage Properties*. Paris: UNESCO.

UNESCO World Heritage Centre and City of Vienna, 2005. *Proceedings of the International Conference "World Heritage and Contemporary Architecture – Managing the Historic Urban Landscape"*. Vienna: City of Vienna.

UN-HABITAT, 2003. *The UN-HABITAT Strategic Vision*. Nairobi: The United Nations Human Settlements Programme.

UN-HABITAT, 2008. *State of the World Cities 2010-2011. Bridging the Urban Divide*. London: Earthscan.

UN-HABITAT, 2009. *Planning Sustainable Cities. Global Report on Human Settlements*. London: Earthscan.

United Nations, 1993. *Earth Summit Agenda 21. The UN Programme of Action from Rio*. New York: United Nations.

United Nations World Commission on Environment and Development, 1987. *Our Common Future*. Oxford: Oxford University Press.

Unwin, Raymond, 1909. *Town Planning in practice: an introduction to the Art of Designing Cities and Suburbs*. London: Adelphi Terrace.

Vance, James E., 1990. *The Continuing City. Urban Morphology in Western Civilization*. Baltimore: The Johns Hopkins University Press.

Van Oers, Ron, 2007a. 'Preventing the Goose with the Golden Eggs from catching Bird-Flu', in: *Cities between Integration and Disintegration*. Istanbul: Proceedings of the 42nd Congress of The International Society of City and Regional Planners (ISoCaRP).

Van Oers, Ron, 2007b. 'Safeguarding the Historic Urban Landscape'. *Topos*, 58: 91–99.

Van Oers, Ron, 2008. 'Towards new international guidelines for the conservation of historic urban landscapes'. *City & Time* 3 (3): 43–51.

Van Oers, Ron; Haraguchi, S. (eds.), 2010. *Managing Historic Cities*. World Heritage Papers 27. Paris: UNESCO World Heritage Centre.

Venturi, Robert, 1966. *Complexity and Contradiction in Architecture*. New York: The Museum of Modern Art.

Venturi, Robert, 2004. *Architecture as Signs and Systems*. Cambridge, Massachusetts: The Belknap Press of Harvard University.

Venturi, Robert; Scott Brown, Denise; Izenour, Steven, 1982 (Revised Edition). *Learning from Las Vegas*. Cambridge, Massachusetts: MIT Press.

Vidler, Anthony, 1976. 'The Third Typology'. *Oppositions* 7: 1–4.

Viollet-Le-Duc, Eugène Emmanuel, 1977. *Entretiens sur l'Architecture*. Paris: Mardaga. (Originally published between 1863 and 1872.)

Von Droste, Bernd, 1991. '*From Urban Growth to Sustainable Development*'. Yokohama: National University. Unpublished Paper delivered at the Japanese Institute for Study in Ecology.

Von Droste, Bernd; Plachter, Harald; Rössler, Mechtild, 1995. *Cultural Landscapes of Universal Value: Components of a Global Strategy*. Jena: Gustav Fischer Verlag.

Waldheim, Charles, 2005. *The Landscape Urbanism Reader*. New York: Princeton Architectural Press.

Waller, Philip (ed.), 2000. *The English Urban Landscape*. Oxford: Oxford University Press.

Welter, Volker M., 2002. *Biopolis: Patrick Geddes and the City of Life*. Cambridge, Massachusetts: MIT Press.

Welter, Volker M., 2003. 'From locus genii to heart of city: embracing the spirit of the city'. Whyte, Iain Boyd (ed.), *Modernism and the Spirit of the City*. London: Routledge.

Whitehand, Jeremy W.R., 1992. *The making of the Urban Landscape*. Oxford: Blackwell Publishers.

Wieckzorek, Daniel, 1982. *Camillo Sitte et les débuts de l'urbanisme moderne*. Bruxelles-Liège: Pierre Mardaga.

Williams, Kevin, 2004. 'The Meanings and Effectiveness of World Heritage Designation in the USA'. *Current Issues in Tourism*, Vol. 7, No. 4 & 5: 412–416.

Wilson, Meredith, 2009. *Nominating Chief Roi Mata's Domain (Vanuatu) for World Heritage Listing – An Assessment of Costs and Benefits*. Paris: UNESCO.

World Bank, 2000a. *Culture Counts*. Proceedings of the Conference convened by the World Bank, UNESCO and the Government of Italy, Florence, 4–7 October 1999. Washington, DC: The World Bank.

World Bank, 2000b. *Cities in Transition: A Strategic View of Urban and Local Government Issues*. Washington, DC: The World Bank.

World Bank, 2006. *Operational Policy 4.11 – Physical Cultural Resources*. Washington, DC: The World Bank.

World Bank, 2009a. *World Bank Physical Cultural Resources Safeguard Policy Guidebook*. Washington, DC: The World Bank.

World Bank, 2009b. *Systems of Cities. The World Bank Urban and Local Government Strategy*. Washington, DC: The World Bank.

Worldwatch Institute, 2007. *State of the World 2007: Our Urban Future*. Washington, DC.

Worthing, Derek; Bond, Stephen, 2008. *Managing Built Heritage – The Role of Cultural Significance*. Oxford: Blackwell Publishing.

Yacoob, May; Margo, Kelly, 1999. 'Secondary Cities in West Africa: The Challenge for Environmental Health and Prevention'. Washington, DC: Woodrow Wilson International Center for Scholars. Comparative Urban Studies Occasional Series, 21: 17.

Yusuf, Abdulqafi, 2007. *Standard-setting in UNESCO*. Leiden: Martinus Nijhoff.

Zancheti Mendes, Silvio, 2010. *The Sustainability of Urban Heritage Preservation: The Case of Salvador de Bahia*. Washington, DC: IDB Discussion Paper.

Zucconi, Guido, 1989. *La città contesa. Dagli ingegneri sanitari agli urbanisti (1885-1942)*. Milano: Jaca Book.

Zucconi, Guido, 1997. *Gustavo Giovannoni, dal capitello alla città*. Milano: Jaca Book.

Index

Note: Page numbers in *italics* refer to illustrations; references to footnotes are indicated by an 'n' following the page number, e.g. 64n

The Historic Urban Landscape: Managing Heritage in an Urban Century, First Edition. Francesco Bandarin, Ron van Oers.
© 2012 Francesco Bandarin and Ron van Oers. Published 2012 by Blackwell Publishing Ltd.